The Body of the Goddess

Rachel Pollack was born in Brooklyn, New York,
in 1945. She holds an honours degree in English
from New York University, a Masters in English
from Claremont Graduate School and has taught English
at New York State University. The author of several books,
she is the winner of the Arthur C. Clarke award
for science fiction for *Unquenchable Fire*.

The Body
of the Goddess

Sacred Wisdom in Myth,
Landscape and Culture

RACHEL POLLACK

ELEMENT

Shaftesbury, Dorset • Rockport, Massachusetts • Brisbane, Queensland

© Element Books Limited 1997
Text © Rachel Pollack 1997

First published in Great Britain in 1997 by
Element Books Limited
Shaftesbury, Dorset SP7 8BP

Published in the USA in 1997 by
Element Books, Inc.
PO Box 830, Rockport, MA 01966

Published in Australia in 1997 by
Element Books Limited
for Jacaranda Wiley Limited
33 Park Road, Milton, Brisbane 4064

Cover design by Pinpoint Design
Design by Phil Payter Graphics
Typeset by Phil Payter Graphics
Colour photographs courtesy of Ancient Art and Architecture collection.
Printed and bound in Great Britain by Hartnolls, Bodmin

British Library Cataloguing in Publication
data available

Library of Congress Cataloging in Publication
data available

ISBN 1-85230-871-0

Contents

List of Figures

List of Plate Illustrations

The Body of the Goddess is dedicated to all those
who traveled with me to the sacred places:
Edith Katz, Maryanne-Renee Vrijdaghs, Helle Agathe Beierholm,
Witta Jensen, K. Frank Jensen, Sol Pollack, Tana Dineen, Ann Ogborn,
Susan Coker, Alma Routsong, Leslie Hunt, Fiona Green,
Margaret McWilliams, Marian Green, Eva M, Donna Hutchinson,
Fara Shaw Kelsey, Paul Shaw Malboeuf ...

and especially Maria Fernandez, who offered friendship, a haven,
and a pomegranate seed, all at the right moment.

Acknowledgements

Someone once defined an expert as a person who knows more and more about less and less. During the writing of this book I have often felt that I knew less and less about more and more. In trying to follow the theme of the Goddess's body I have drawn heavily on the work of so many people in so many fields of study and expression – historians, archaeologists, artists, priestesses, scientists, psychologists, diviners, novelists, theologians, classicists, and simply friends who have traveled and done their own research. If I have misrepresented people's ideas or discoveries – and I am sure I have, despite all best intentions – the fault is entirely my own, and I apologize. Where I have leapt off in my own direction from other people's research, I have tried to make this clear. If I have muddied anyone else's work with my own speculations, again I apologize.

This book does not attempt to be a book of history or scholarship, much less theology (or thealogy). The religion of the Goddess is not simply a subject of history but is alive today, in the vast research of people like Marija Gimbutas, and also in poetry and art, and in the rituals people do alone and in groups, in temples and caves, and also in their own backyards and kitchens. I have tried to honor all these levels of the resurgent Goddess religion, and to express my gratitude for all the contributions these people have made, both the scholars and the worshippers, and especially those whose desire to know more has led them into rigorous research, as well as those who have found that scholarship has led them to belief and passionate commitment.

Three scholars deserve special mention. The first is Marija Gimbutas, the archaeologist who matched her vast research with the courage to step outside the official academic ideology and recognize the reality of a wide-ranging complex religion in all the art and excavated ruins of pre-historic Europe. The second writer, less known today, is Gertrude Rachel Levy. When I first began reading the modern Goddess writers I noticed one work mentioned again and again: Levy's *The Gate of Horn*. Writing half a century ago, Levy had the gift not only to assemble and present a staggering amount of information but also to synthesize it and to think in broad original concepts. It was Gertrude Rachel Levy who first observed that the shape of the prehistoric temples of Malta formed the outline of a woman's body. The final figure is Vincent Scully, author of *The Earth, the Temple, and the Gods.* Recently retired, Scully was a revered professor of architectural history at Yale University. When he turned his attention to the Greek temples and the earlier palaces of Crete, he did so with an eye for the truth of the landscape and a passion for the sacred forms alive in the beauty of the Earth.

INTRODUCTION

The Spiraling Journey of Images

The end of the 20th century has witnessed something truly remarkable – the re-emergence of a religion seemingly dead for so many years the world had all but forgotten it ever existed. This religion is the worship of a Great Goddess who can carry many names and images but who always represents the deity as a female presence: life-giving, nurturing, sometimes terrifying, but always tied to nature and to the truth of our own bodies. And not just women's bodies. Men too have discovered spiritual reality in the image of a living all-embracing Goddess who creates the world and all life out of Her body, not just once in the long ago, but continually in the unfolding processes of existence.

In part, this religion sprang into life again through the discoveries of archaeology. As excavations revealed more and more of the human past, they also revealed a great abundance of female images: engravings on the walls of caves; vulva symbols marked on tombs as if to promise rebirth out of the divine body; frescoes of Goddesses fanned by worshippers in a garden of paradise; statues of fierce bare-breasted women holding snakes; 30,000-year-old figurines of women with huge breasts and hips; Goddesses giving birth while sitting serenely on thrones flanked by lions; temples shaped like an idealized outline of a woman. When these images were joined to existent knowledge of Goddesses in India, Ancient Egypt, pre-conquest Mexico, Africa, and elsewhere, people understood, as if in a flash of sacred insight, that all over the world humanity once worshipped the deity in the form of a woman, and continued to do so for thousands, even tens of thousands of years.

To discover that something once existed allows it to exist again. If humanity worshipped Goddesses in the past, why not now? And how would such worship differ from the religion of an all-male Godhead detached from the world? Some people began to write books synthesizing all that information revealed by archaeology. Others sculpted new statues or built temples or traveled to caves or ruins to revive ancient rituals. Still others formed circles of worshippers in their communities to celebrate the seasons and the special moments of their lives. Out of all this something new and wholly modern has emerged, blending knowledge of the past with understanding of who we are now.

At its best, this something does not just substitute Goddess for God. Instead, it explores the possibilities of religion based on the body. For while a God must create the world out of pure thought, a Goddess will do so in the way that women have always done, through giving birth out of Her abundant womb. This simple fact allows a religion to emerge that accepts nature and our own bodies as they really are, not as enemies, or prisons of the soul, or temptations of evil, but as miraculous creations, with all their strengths and weaknesses.

People sometimes criticize contemporary Goddess worshippers for mingling research and fantasy, archaeology and wish fulfillment. It seems to me that such criticism misses the point. The modern Goddess religion is not trying to recreate conditions exactly as they were in the Stone Age, or in ancient Crete, or any other time or place. Instead, we seek to learn from those people as we allow the Goddess to come alive in a way that matches our own experience. For me, the home-made quality of modern Goddess worship, especially the rituals, has always been one of its attractions.

In Carol Christ's book, *The Laughter of Aphrodite*, she describes a ritual she and Alexis Masters did in honor of Aphrodite on the island of Lesbos, home of Aphrodite's great poet, Sappho. As they made their way to the temple they chose the objects and clothes they would use for the ritual from things they encountered in shops and along the paths – a postcard of a woman weaving, a bottle opener of the God Priapus with a giant erection, and a white dress with golden threads. At that moment, the two women realized they must dress in white and gold to ask the Goddess for initiation into Her mysteries. They then went on to a grocery for red wine, golden retsina, golden cookies, milk and honey, and yoghurt, all foods which symbolize the Goddess's body.

By using objects we have found and aspects of our daily lives, we allow our religious instinct to join with our immediate reality. When Maria Fernandez and I went to Eleusis to celebrate the first day of the Mysteries (for 2,000 years the primary religious event of the ancient world), we consulted various books on what the Greeks and Romans brought. But we also brought food, stones found along the way, wild flowers, and objects from our personal belongings. In this way, Eleusis, this place so charged with history, became real to us in our lives.

In writing this book I have drawn upon scholarship, art, speculations, and my personal experiences of the sacred, both at recognized sites, and in other places, including the woods beside my house. I have done my best in the writing to keep a distinction between all these sources, especially between historical information and my own ideas. Nevertheless, all these strands weave together in the telling, just as it seems to me they do in the Goddess religion itself.

Originally I conceived of this book as a series of journeys to sacred places. I would visit the Greek temples, and the prehistoric caves in France, and describe the places and their significance. As I began to research the background and archaeology of those places, the book came alive in a different way. The world of the Goddess became a world of knowledge and ideas, of history and art, a world of images, shining before us with all their meanings and mystery. In my journey through this world the physical travels remained important, for there are things we can discover with our own eyes that we will never find in research. But at the same time, the collective knowledge and speculations of all those who have gone before us can open us to unexpected wonders. And simple thinking becomes vital as well. Religious awareness grows as we ponder the meaning of an image, or the connections between religious belief and daily life, or what it can mean for people to base their understanding of sacred truth on the direct reality of bodies.

No book on the sacred can possibly cover every aspect of how we approach this experience. This becomes especially true in a book based in part on personal journeys. At the start of this work I decided to focus primarily on the places I would actually visit. Because I was living in Europe at the time, the book draws heavily on the ancient traditions of European Goddesses (and to a lesser extent North American Goddesses), leaving out such important sources as India, China, Japan, Central and South America, and the many traditions of Africa and the African Diaspora. While I have gleaned knowledge and ideas and ways of looking from my readings in other traditions, and have cited them wherever it seemed correct, I have kept primarily to my decision to balance the research with the journeys.

This focus on direct experience has meant that I have not attempted to discuss every Goddess within the European traditions. The chapters on Greece say little about Athena, for instance, and less about Hera. I have trusted my intuition to lead me to those Goddesses who spoke most about the body.

The book itself is a journey, traveling from the Stone Age to contemporary science. But even though it moves through time it is not a linear journey. Instead, I would describe it as a spiral, constantly turning back on itself to look at previously seen images in a fresh way. In his great work, *The Earth, the Temple, and the Gods*, Professor Vincent Scully detailed the procession of the initiates who traveled from Athens to Eleusis to celebrate the Greater Mysteries of the Goddesses Demeter and Persephone. Scully describes how landscape images of the Goddess's power (a cone-shaped mountain, a double cleft peak) would appear, disappear, and reappear again at different stages of the journey. In much the same way, different images, themes, ideas, even characters appear in this book, tell us their messages, then vanish – only to reappear later, in more detail or in another context.

The Goddess religion itself is not linear. But neither is it simply a circle, not in the sense of something static that repeats itself over and over without change. Its cycles are those of a spiral procession, moving away and back again. For tens of thousands of years the creative power of the divine female body dominated spiritual awareness. With the rise of warrior Gods and transcendent religion detached from nature and bodies, the Goddess seemed to vanish. In many places, not even a memory remained. And yet, She has suddenly returned to us at this most unlikely of times. Though part of this return involves those discoveries of archaeology and the decoding of ancient texts and images, She is not the same as the Goddess of thousands of years ago. A religion based on the divine body is a religion of change, of that spiral movement turning and opening into new experience. Like an individual body, the Earth itself changes, not only cyclically with the seasons, but also more permanently over long periods of time, as mountains erupt or erode, glaciers rise and fall, and even the atmosphere alters its chemical composition.

Though the book follows the Goddess from the Stone Age to modern science, it begins with a preparation for the journey. The first two chapters form a meditation on the very concept of the Goddess's body. They examine what it means to us to exist as bodies, or to allow our awareness of the sacred to emerge from the joining of nature and imagination. These two chapters move through the entire world of images and ideas surrounding the divine body.

The journey begins properly with Chapter 3, as we descend into the caves of the Old Stone Age in Europe. There we encounter the great paintings of 20,000 years ago as well as the many carvings of the female body, some with mountainous breasts and hips, some faceless or entirely without heads, even some with long phallic necks leading us to ponder the mingling of male and female in the divine body.

Chapters 4 and 5 look at the New Stone Age and the great changes that came with the development of agriculture. Chapter 4 moves among the stone circles, giant passage mounds, and other monuments that remain so mysteriously across the European landscape and elsewhere. Chapter 5 examines the cultural patterns of those times, especially the evidence of societies that lived for thousands of years without violence. The chapter ends with the question of how and why the civilization of the Goddess became lost, not just in Europe and the Middle East but in places as isolated from each other as Japan and Tierra del Fuego.

Chapter 6 takes us to Crete where the European Goddess religion opened to its last and greatest flowering. We learn to look deeply at the body forms alive within the landscape. From "Minoan" Crete we move to the later culture of the Greeks, where the archaic Goddesses managed to survive and take on new meanings despite their transformation into the lesser figures of Classical mythology.

In Chapter 7 we meet the full power of that survival as we journey into the Eleusinian Mysteries. I have tried to look deeply into these rites, seeking the Goddess Persephone, whose name means "She Who Shines in the Dark", as She gleams brightly in the dark fears and wonder of our own lives. After I had written the first draft of this book and was reading it through to revise it, I discovered a main character emerging, like the heroine of a novel. This character is Persephone, who darts forward again and again in the early chapters, showing Herself and then retreating once more until the proper time for Her full appearance.

In the myth, the unnamed Goddess appears first as an innocent Kore ("maiden" or "daughter") gathering flowers when Death roars out of the ground to drag Her down into the Underworld. Rather than accept what the Gods describe as irreversible, even proper, Persephone's mother, Demeter the Grain Goddess, stops all plant life from growing until Zeus agrees to order Death to allow Persephone to return. But Persephone does not come back the same as before. Instead, She has found Her true power as the Queen of the Dead, going back underground for part of every year to shine in the darkness. The more we ponder this story the more we discover so many of our own issues: the cycles of the year; our own fear of death; separation and reconciliation with our mothers; struggle against the brutality of rape and incest; the courage to face institutionalized authority; and even wider issues. The myth symbolizes that very return of the Goddess religion from the seeming death of 5,000 years of rule by a transcendent God separated from the world. Finally, we can discover in this tale of the Mother and Daughter separated by an intruding male the coded origin of sexuality and death.

The discovery of biological realities in the story of Persephone leads to the final chapter and the "Gaia Theory" of contemporary science. In this idea of the Earth as a single living organism we discover that the spiral has truly turned round and opened, bringing back the prehistoric Goddess in a new and vital way. Both the Eleusinian Mysteries and the Gaia Theory address our very deep sense of the world as composed of isolated fragments, each one seemingly alone, and yet all of them, all of us, connected at some fundamental level. Modern biology returns us to the same idea as that represented by the Goddess Persephone rising from the land of the dead – that we are all alive, all joined with each other, with the animals and the plants, with the stars and the dust, together in the body of the Goddess.

How Can the Goddess Have a Body?

How we remembered. How her memory brought me my memory.
How I knew what she knew, how her breasts felt then, her body,
how we were flooded with memory.

Susan Griffin

*W*e enter the body of the Goddess as we would a strange country, uncertain, excited but confused, marveling at unknown customs and an alien language. How do we speak of these things? How did the ancient people regard the divine body and its physical reality? And what will we discover of ourselves and our own bodies when we open our awareness and our lives to the Goddess?

Artemis's Birthday

What does it mean to write about the body of the Goddess? To concern ourselves with the body, to think the idea, to try to conceive (a word coming out of women's bodies) of God(dess) having a body? For many people the idea is alien, almost unthinkable. In the years I spent writing this book, I would sometimes tell people what I was working on, only to get back a puzzled look and the question, "How can the Goddess have a body?"

A sacred calendar published some time ago listed, among pagan seasonal rituals and the holidays of the established religions, the birthdays of various deities from ancient Greece and other cultures. April 28th was given as the birthday of the Buddha and the Goddess Artemis (whose body fills these pages even as Her body rises still in the hills and mountains of Greece). To celebrate Artemis I went to a waterfall in the mountains near my home. When I told people what I had done, many of them looked surprised, or even laughed. "Artemis has a birthday?" they asked. Now, some of these people were pagans, who actually worshipped Artemis as the Roman Moon Goddess Diana. Others would have had no trouble with the Buddha having a birthday, since, after all, he was a mortal man, Prince Siddharta. And most of these people have celebrated the birthday of Yehoshua ben Miryam, a radical Judean who claimed to be God's son, and whose followers claimed was the Messiah, or Christ. And yet, the idea of a Goddess, a wholly divine being, actually being born struck them as bizarre. They may have read myths of Her birth, along with her brother Apollo – but an actual birthday?

Who Is the "I" that Has a Body?

For most people who think about these things at all, mortals have bodies, Goddesses do not. This is what makes us mortal, that we are "trapped" in our bodies. Many years ago, a friend of mine (who spent a great deal of time meditating and chanting) wrote on a wall, "If you have a body, you must have done something wrong. P.S. I am a woman."

But who is this "I" that has a body? In what way are we separate from these bodies that move, and sleep, and eat, and make love, and cry, and give birth? The very language we speak isolates us from the reality of the body. We talk of "my" body, "my" arms, or lungs, or face. Who is it that owns these physical objects?

The body is our basic reality. It gives us everything from our connection to the outside world to our artistic and intellectual systems. For example, people who study symbolism have often noted the way the number four appears in many cultures – the landscape divided into quarters, four seasons, four "elements" (usually fire, water, air, and earth), four basic spiritual colors (usually attached to the four directions), and so on. And seeing all these fours, they will comment that the number four is somehow fundamental to the human mind, or possibly embedded somewhere in the lobes of the brain. But there is a simpler explanation of the importance of four, one connected to our bodies, and the physicality – the *body* – of the Earth. There *are* four seasons, or rather four solar points of the year, the solstices and equinoxes. These are not inventions but facts of our existence. If we stand upright, our bodies lead us to four directions, for we can look before us, turn and look behind us, and stretch out our arms to the right or to the left.

And, in fact, four directions exist in nature as well, independently of us. The Earth spins on an axis, creating north and south poles. On the equinoxes the Sun rises due east, which is to say at a ninety degree angle from the polar axis, and sets due west, again a ninety degree angle. If the full Moon falls on the equinox you can experience the four directions directly in your body. At sunset, stand with your arms out to each side. If you point your right hand towards the setting Sun, your left will point to the rising Moon and your face will look due north, with south directly behind you.

We can think of a "symbol" as an image that opens our awareness to different ways of understanding. A symbol suggests ideas, it brings together different concepts and perceptions. It touches some part of us which we cannot easily explain or put into words. Symbols, images, do all all these things because they arise from bodies – our own bodies, those of animals, or aspects of the sky or Earth. We know a symbol affects us at that deep level when it affects our bodies, when the hair stands up at the back of the neck, or we get goose bumps, or become sexually aroused. And yet, we still describe symbols as intellectual abstractions.

Just as our language tends to separate the body from the mind, or the soul, so it also includes, almost as some buried layer, an identification of nature and women's bodies. We speak of Mother Earth, or Mother Nature, we refer to nations (not to mention battleships) as "she," we even call hurricanes by women's names. (Complaints from women have changed the practice to alternating men's names with women's, but no one has suggested taking the names away altogether.) The link between nature and women's bodies moves in the other direction as well. Women's breasts are described as hills, vaginas as jungles, or swamps, or even volcanoes. For most of us, however, these are all metaphors, turns of phrase. The Goddess cannot have a body.

A Religion of Basic Realities

To think about the body of the Goddess is to think about our own bodies. To recall the birth of Artemis is to recall our own births. At its best, the newly (re)awakening religion of the Goddess is a religion, and a movement, of basic realities, of birth and death, of the cycles of the Moon and Sun, of menstruation and pregnancy, arousal and orgasm. Gertrude Rachel Levy, author of *The Gate of Horn,* characterized religion as "the maintenance of an abiding relationship." This relationship breaks down, and religion becomes superstition, or perhaps philosophy (or psychology), when we lose that original relationship to the divine in the physical world, when ideas and symbols become detached from bodies.

The body remains our fundamental truth. I do not mean by this only the *human* body. The African Goddess Oya expresses Herself as lightning, and as rivers. The prehistoric Goddesses of Europe and the Middle East took the forms of fish, or bees, or trees, or toads, or vultures. To us today these images seem strange, even childish. We are used to thinking of God as an abstraction. But these images were not arbitrary, let alone trivial. They came from a deep and specific knowledge of animals and plants and the processes of life. That knowledge joined with a spiritual awareness, a sense that divine reality moved in people's lives at all moments. How natural, how *real*, to bring together the understanding of physical existence and the intuition that spirituality flowed through all experience.

This abiding relationship extended to all aspects of life, including daily existence. Today, we rarely think of the act of cooking as something sacred. We may put together special meals for religious holidays, but usually only as a family tradition. But when James Mellaart and others excavated a 10,000-year-old city near the village of Çatal Hüyük, Turkey they found Goddess statues shaped like pregnant women set on top of ovens for baking bread. This may strike us as bizarre, but think – isn't bread, and all cooked food, a miracle? Various ingredients get mixed together, shaped into some particular form (how wonderful it would be to know the forms Neolithic people chose for bread), the mix goes into a hot, closed container, and something totally different emerges, something life-giving and sensually satisfying. And think of the miracle of pregnancy, of a fetus forming and growing like bread in the hot darkness of a woman's body. Bread and babies are miraculous – divine – in the same way. We have lost the sense of the wondrous in the everyday things of life precisely because we have tended to see God as abstract, remote, somewhere out there – detached from bodies.

And yet, is the link between bread and babies really so far-fetched? We describe a pregnant woman as having "a bun in the oven." Might this phrase go all the way back to prehistoric Turkey? Or does it simply show that the modern imagination has made the same association, babies and bread, as was made in the Stone Age? There is a difference, however. The modern expression does not include the missing link, spirituality. The statues on top of the ovens did not show ordinary women. They showed pregnant *Goddesses*.

Love, Sexuality, and the Divine Body

Even love has become abstract. We think of "true" love as a pure essence, and physical love as suspect, a trick or illusion, even dirty. "God is love" we say, but since God does not have a body, we must not contaminate divine love with physical desire and satisfaction. Sexual love makes us like animals, we say, and consider that a reason to suppress it. In other cultures and times, people did not separate sacred love and sexuality. In Her early form, Aphrodite, Goddess of sexual passion, was also a Goddess of birth, of death, of the surging sea and the birds of the sky. She was a mother of change and becoming as well as desire, and she had historical connections to those ancient female-centered cultures of the Anatolia region of western Turkey. Over the centuries the patriarchal Greeks narrowed her power, limiting her image to a petty courtesan.

Paul Friedrich, in *The Meaning of Aphrodite*, tells us that Aphrodite inspired passion in heterosexuals and lesbians, while her son Eros inflamed homosexual men, that is, men without women. It says something about our culture's attitude to women that the term for sexuality is "erotic" and not "aphroditic," and that the names Aphrodite and Venus – Venus is the

Roman name for Aphrodite – survive in such negative or trivial sexual terms as "aphrodisiac" and "venereal" disease.

When the Christian religion took over, the Church fathers banished Aphrodite. According to Friedrich, most of the Greek deities became saints in the new religion – except for Aphrodite, who simply disappeared (though aspects of Her worship – without the sex – were grafted onto Mary, Jesus's mother). Even diminished, the reality of Aphrodite's (female) body threatened the Christian paradox, that of an all-male deity who at the same time had no body.

Christian myth describes angels as disembodied, sexless. And yet they are also male, with masculine names still in use today, such as Gabriel and Michael. Under Christianity maleness became separated from sexuality. "Reason" became the primary male quality, detached, in control of the body which stood always in danger of pollution, especially from women. The new religion considered the body, and its animal desires, as the enemy of true reason. The Church saw women as closer to animals. Women tempted men and led them away from God.

Measuring the Body of God

After several thousand years of an abstract, impersonal God, it becomes almost impossible to think of God's body, certainly as anything more than a metaphor. In many cultures, however, such as the Jains of India, there is a tradition of seeing the universe as a single body. Jain scriptures describe this body in extreme detail. The idea is not limited to Asia. In the Jewish esoteric tradition of Kabbalah we find the image of Adam Kadmon, the cosmos as a great primordial being in the shape of a man. Sometimes the Kabbalists described Adam Kadmon as hermaphroditic, with female qualities as well as male. (*See* Chapter 5 for more on androgynous Adam and other mythic hermaphrodites.)

Adam Kadmon is God's creation, not God Himself. The Kabbalah, however, goes further. It describes an idea called "*Shiur Komah*," Hebrew for "Measurement of the Body," in which mystics attempted to discover God's physical measurements. Gershom Scholem, the great scholar of Kabbalah, described this idea as "absurd" and "monstrous," though he also describes

14

it as inspired by the Song of Songs and its description of the Body of the Beloved. Despite his exploration of ancient mysteries, Scholem was still a modernist, heir to the Western tradition of God as pure thought without a physical body.

Presumably, Scholem knew that the idea of *Shiur Komah* was not unique to the Jews. As well as the Jains, with their very precise measurements of God's lips, toes, elbows, and so on, we find a tradition of the physical world having been formed out of a single body in many cultures. Usually, the body is that of a Goddess. In many versions of this myth, She is dismembered, broken apart into millions of pieces, often by male violence. These are myths from male dominated cultures, and they raise many complex issues (some of which we will look at in later chapters). Still, beyond the tearing apart, or the Goddess breaking in pieces, we find a deep intuition – that the cosmos and everything in it, every rock and drop of water, is alive, like we are, and is female, like the mothers who gave us life.

The medieval Kabbalists, in fact, followed their own intuition of feminine divinity. They described an androgynous God, "both male and female" as Genesis says, splitting off part of "Himself" so that something might exist to regard and mirror God's splendor. This something is usually thought of as female. Some identified it with the *Shekinah*, a Biblical term that originally meant God's "indwelling presence," which is to say God's physical manifestation within the holy of holies. In the Middle Ages and later the *Shekinah* became a female presence, shielding the faithful with her wings. God's female half has also borne the name *Chokmah*, or Wisdom. The Greeks gave this Goddess the Greek word for wisdom, *Sophia*.

Body Forms in Landscape and Temples

This book began as an idea for a series of journeys. Over a period of years, and through the influence of friends, and books, and my work with the imagery and symbolism of the Tarot, I had become interested in the religion of the Goddess, and wanted to deal with this subject in my work. I knew that many people were reviving the practice of pilgrimages by traveling to power places and ancient temples in many countries. Some ten years earlier I had visited several of the caves in France containing engravings and paintings as much as 20,000 years old. That experience had moved me deeply, and I knew I wanted to go back and see these works in a context of sacred knowledge, especially the idea of the cave as the Goddess's womb.

When I began to do research I came across a startling idea. In various places, particularly the island of Malta, the temples dedicated to the Goddess were themselves shaped like a simplified drawing of a woman's body – that is, with rounded chambers, like breasts and hips, with a smaller chamber at the back for a head (see *Figure 1*). The worshipper who entered them felt as if he or she were entering a divine body. Contemporary people who had traveled to Malta described an overwhelming sense of protection, even love.

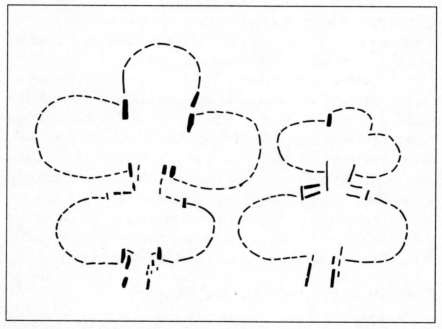

Figure 1 The structural outline of Ggantija temple, island of Gozo, Malta, c.4000 B.C.E.

It was not just human constructions that were seen to carry the shape of the Goddess's body. The land itself could take such a form when viewed in the right way. In an article by architect Mimi Lobell (the same article in which I read about Malta) I came across an idea first put forward by Vincent

16

Scully, professor of architecture at Yale. Scully found that the so-called "palaces" of ancient Crete (the term "palaces" derives from Greek assumptions of monarchy which have never been proven) were set in particular landscape formations. The Cretans sited each of the large buildings on a (roughly) north-south axis facing a conical hill and beyond that a horned mountain containing a cave used as a religious sanctuary. In Lobell's words:

> The proper siting of the palace accentuated the meaning
> of the landscape as the body of the Goddess. The valley
> was her encircling arms; the conical hill, her breast or
> nurturing function; the horned mountain, her "lap" or
> cleft vulva, the Earth's active power; and the cave
> sanctuary, her birth-giving womb.
>
> (Lobell, "Temples of the Great Goddess," **Heresies,** Issue 5)

This idea captivated me. Like many people, I had earlier suspected that the concept of the Great Goddess was a modern invention, a feminist myth. Though my early reading changed my mind and showed me the solid research behind the image of the Goddess, it was the ideas of Lobell and Scully which gave the Goddess a physical reality. I had never experienced such a reality in the traditional religious ideas of my own society.

I began to read, and to think, about the Goddess, about Her body, Her presence in the world, the connection to my own body, and to women's (and men's) bodies in general. The Cretan use of caves as sanctuaries suggested a link to the prehistoric art caves of France and Spain. If the Earth is our Mother, then a cave becomes an image of Her womb and a place to enter Her actual body. Was this why the Cro-Magnon artists chose to paint and engrave their work in caves? There is no way to know. They left no record other than the art itself. Nevertheless, when I read more about the caves, I found it natural, as so many others have, to compare them to the inside of my own body. And when I and a friend visited the cave of Pêch-Mèrle, with its huge tunnels and chambers, and its walls dripping red, both of us (independently) felt like microbes inside a gigantic body.

In many mountainous areas certain peaks will resemble a face in profile, or a woman lying on her back, and folklore will often make this link explicit. This use of a fixed image can become simplistic. Other ways exist to see the Goddess as physically present in the land. The indigenous people of North America have always considered the Earth the mother of all her people – with "people" including the plants and animals as well as humans. When I was growing up I learned in my history classes that Native American men refused to become farmers because farming was "women's work." In fact, as I learned much later, some native people resisted farming because it involved cutting the Earth with plows, an act they considered the same as cutting their mothers' breasts with a knife.

The Moon and Women's Bodies

As well as the idea of the land as the Goddess's body, I knew of traditions that saw specific aspects of nature as essentially female because of their symbolic resemblance to women's physicality. Many cultures have identified the Moon as a Goddess, directly linked to women's bodies. (Some books will describe this connection as a universal idea; however, universal ideas rarely exist. The ancient Japanese and Germans were among the minority of cultures that saw the Moon as male and the Sun as female.)

Most obviously, most women's menstrual cycles are roughly the same length as the Moon's cycle from new to full to old to new. Studies in college dormitories and isolated villages have suggested that a group of women living closely together will tend to menstruate at the same time, often during the full or new Moon. Some researchers believe that this ability of women to unite their cycles may have started the process of human community and culture. (For more on this subject, *see* Chapter 5.)

There is a more subtle connection as well. The Moon moves through three distinct phases. It is born out of darkness as a sliver which steadily increases until the magnificence of the full Moon, and then, after three days, it dwindles and dwindles until finally it dies, vanishes for three days, and then is born once again. Women and men arrive in the world out of the darkness of their mother's womb. Women, however, cross from childhood to adult fertility by means of a sharp division in their lives – menarche, the first menstruation. They remain fertile, capable of the miracle of growing children in their own bodies, until another distinct break (though a gradual one) – menopause.

These phases, maiden, mother, crone, form a natural comparison with the waxing, full, and waning Moons. The various Triple Goddesses in different mythologies (especially Western European mythologies) have given the identification a powerful presence in the modern religion of the Goddess. Wiccans (modern witches) worship the Moon, not as a celestial body but as a manifestation of female truth and power. Aware as anyone else that the Moon is a rock orbiting the Earth, they have looked deeper into the Moon's importance in our lives. Like the ancients, they have embodied the Moon as a symbol of women's fertility.

But is it "only" a symbol? Or does some physical quality of the Moon directly affect women's bodies? People sometimes assume that since the Moon's gravitational pull controls the tides, why should it not control the monthly tide of menstruation? However, the tidal effect on the oceans comes because of the great size of the Earth. That is, the Earth is so large that the Moon's gravity affects the side closest to the Moon in a different way from the side furthest away. This difference in the force of gravity causes the tides. Women's bodies are not massive enough to create such a huge difference. But a more direct way exists for the Moon to influence fertility. That way is the special quality of lunar light. When women experience problems with their menstrual cycles, such as irregular periods, doctors often give them hormones. In recent years, however, a number of doctors (and women on their own) have tried a different approach. The women sleep in moonlight or under a lamp that gives the same kind of light as the Moon. In many cases, their cycles have evened out within a few weeks.

When we think of the Triple Goddess we tend to think of ancient Greece, or Celtic Ireland. However, Marija Gimbutas has pointed out that the image goes back at least to the Magdalenian period in France, some 12,000 years ago, for the cave of Abri Du Roc Aux Sorciers, at Angles-sur-Anglin, France, contains a relief of what Gimbutas terms "three classical female presences with exposed vulvas." From 3200 B.C.E. we find a more abstracted triple image, a magnificently carved triple spiral on the kerbstone at the entrance to the huge passage mound of Newgrange, in the Boyne river valley of Ireland (see *Plate 1*).

We cannot claim with certainty that such prehistoric forms represent a lunar Goddess, or the phases of a woman's life. However, they do show the astonishing longevity of triple images. And spirals have been found on many Goddess statues and temples, possibly as symbols of birth, death, and rebirth. The spiral is not just philosophical. Though it often appears in art as abstract, it actually is a fundamental form of nature, found much more commonly than the circle, which other than as an image of the Sun or Moon hardly appears at all. Snakes coil in spirals, water moves downward in a spiral, birds will sometimes spiral upwards to make use of wind currents, the galaxies are spiral shaped, and the horns of rams and other creatures often spiral out from the head.

But what of the fourth phase of the Moon, the dark? The obvious answer is that just as a woman dies, and goes back into the ground, so the Moon dies as it vanishes into the dark. But the Moon is reborn after three days (the same length of time as the full Moon), which suggests powerfully that death is not final, that the Goddess promises rebirth. Joseph Campbell has pointed out that many pictures of Triple Goddesses will show a fourth figure to the side, often, though not always, a God or mortal man. Jesus remains in the ground three days, until He is resurrected on Easter Sunday. The name "Easter" derives from Eostre, a German Goddess of spring, whose name in turn is connected to "estrus," female fertility. The Earth gives forth plants in the way women give forth babies, out of a hidden darkness. Here too we find a promise of rebirth, for the very plants that "die" in winter return in the spring.

Water, Women's Bodies, and the Goddess

Just as the length of the Moon's cycle connects the Moon to women's bodies, so strong resemblances exist between the female body and bodies of water. A baby growing in its mother's womb floats in a sac of liquid, and when the woman gives birth the "waters break." Birth itself involves bleeding so that we find two red flows, during menstruation and birth.

The sea surges and falls like a woman's inner rhythms. The very Moon that appears to govern menstruation causes the rhythm of the tides. The seas are salty, like the tears and blood of women and men. And as far as we know today, all life originally came from the seas, making the sea our Great Mother.

Before beginning this work, I had written of some of these things in earlier books, especially in a commentary on a Tarot deck painted by German artist Hermann Haindl. There I tried to make the point that these things formed a fundamental reality. Here is what I wrote at that time:

> Many modern people can acknowledge all these correlations. They may even believe that the Moon's gravity somehow "scientifically" affects a woman's childbearing potential. But the ancient peoples saw it differently. They looked on the Moon, the seas and women as *all the same thing*, a mystery of life which they worshipped through Moon rituals and statues of pregnant Goddesses.

As I continued my reading, and began my travels, I began to find still further connections between the female body and water. One of the first places I visited was the English city of Bath, with its elegant spa, used by the Romans and, much later, the Victorians. Though arches and columns obscure most of the original form of the site, the visitor still can watch the steaming waters pour out from a large hole in the native rock. Writer Marian Green, who guided me at the site, pointed out that the water was tinted red, from iron deposits in the stone, and that the combination of heat and redness produced an intense image of birth waters surging from the womb of the Earth.

Later, I visited Glastonbury, where the spring also flows red. And I read that many cathedrals were built on ancient pagan sites, which in turn were built over underground streams. When I researched Silbury Hill, a giant human-made hill in England, thousands of years old, I found that the Stone Age people built it at the confluence of two such hidden waters.

The Body in the Sky

To many people who seek the divine body in mythology it has become a commonplace that Earth = Goddess, Sky = God. In European culture this idea comes largely from Greek and Roman mythology, with the Sky God, Ouranos, impregnating the Earth Goddess, Gaia. Some Native American cultures speak of Grandfather Sky and Grandmother Earth. Obviously, the duality acknowledges the "facts of life," an interesting, if old-fashioned expression. But are these "facts" of male and female involvement in reproduction the final truth of creation?

Greek myth does not speak of Ouranos as coming into existence the same time as Gaia. On the contrary, existence begins simply with Gaia, who then gives forth Ouranos out of her body that she might have a partner and consort.

The body of the Goddess becomes the origin of all things, including the Sky God, whose downfall, in fact, begins with his arrogant assumption of superiority over his creator. (This downfall, according to some versions of the Greek myth, involves the severance of Ouranos's genitals, out of which emerges Aphrodite – for more on this astonishing story, and its implications, *see* Chapter 7.) Many cultures have seen the Milky Way literally as milk streaming from the Goddess's breasts. Elisabet Sahtouris, in her book *Gaia: The Human Journey from Chaos to Cosmos*, describes a Greek myth of creation in which Gaia dances and the Milky Way spirals out from Her body. This is a remarkable image when we consider that the Milky Way is actually our galaxy, and modern telescopes have shown that galaxies originate in a spiraling movement, something not apparent from observing the Milky Way alone.

The Emergence of the Male

The findings of biology and evolution reinforce the primacy of the female. Biologists describe the earliest organisms as female, reproducing by splitting the "daughter" off from the "mother." In the long run of evolution the introduction of the male comes rather late, and can be called a mutation out of the female.

Several decades ago, biologists discovered that all human fetuses begin as female, and for the first two months follow a pattern of development that would result in a girl baby. In the fifth week an undifferentiated gonad develops which will eventually become either female or male sexual organs. A fetus with XX chromosomes will then develop ovaries by the sixteenth week. However, if the fetus contains XY chromosomes, the Y chromosome will cause the gonads to secrete a "testicular organizer." This chemical promotes "differentiation," that is, it sends the gonads into a new line of development, forming testes. An article in *The New York Times* of 4 August, 1992 describes how the process begins with the protein known as "testis-determining factor" bending the DNA so that different genes will come into communication.

According to Monica Sjoo and Barbara Mor, in their book, *The Great Cosmic Mother*, the early fetus bears both female and male reproductive possibilities. As one set develops, the other degenerates. Externally, however, the organs initially are the same in both male and female. Under the influence of the androgens, we might say, the clitoris becomes a penis and the labia majora becomes a scrotum.

There are two ways to look at this reality of fetal development, these facts of life. A female chauvinist approach might be to describe men as a kind of afterthought in the scheme of existence. If males are offshoots of a fundamental reality, then men are clearly inferior. Implicit in the modern Goddess religion, however, is a respect for all beings, and a rejection of what Riane Eisler calls the "dominator" model in favor of a "partnership" model. Therefore, we can choose to find a more subtle view of evolution, one I believe is supported by the Goddess religion of our earliest ancestors. This is the idea that men and women are not alien species, not eternal enemies, but part of the same sacred being.

The representations of the Goddess in Stone Age religion show a deep understanding that the body of the Goddess contains the male as well as the female. The so-called "Venus" figurines from as much as 30,000 years ago are well known for their exaggerated female forms: mountainous breasts and hips, overlarge vulvas, sometimes abstracted into triangles across the pubic area, pronounced steatopygous buttocks. Less well known are the figurines of women with long phallic necks, or the cave engravings showing only a very long neck, pendulous breasts, and large buttocks, as if reducing the human form to essential female – and male – characteristics. A carved reindeer antler from 15000–13000 B.C.E. in France appears simply as a vulva below a long neck marked with diagonal strokes of different lengths. Alexander Marshack has demonstrated the possibility that these marks (and others on similar bone carvings) may have counted the progression of lunar phases and/or menstrual cycles (*see* Chapter 3). A much later carving, from 5600–5300 B.C.E., in Hungary, is more clearly hermaphroditic. The cylindrical body, with small pointed breasts and a flat face, has a distinct phallic quality, while the prounounced buttocks at the bottom (there are small feet but no legs) clearly resemble testicles. The result is an elegant merger of male and female imagery (see *Figure 2*). (For another view of the phallic Goddess, *see* Chapter 3.)

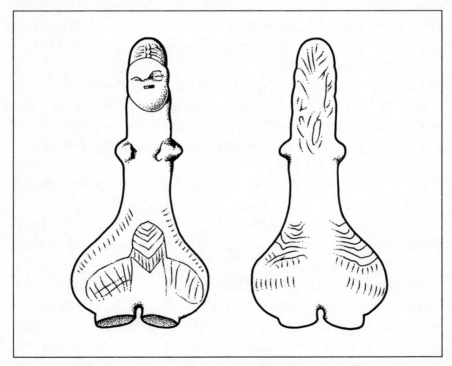

Figure 2 Drawing of the front and back of a phallic-shaped female figurine from Starçevo, Hungary, c.5600–5300 B.C.E. (after Gimbutas).

24

The figurines date primarily from the Paleolithic, or Old Stone Age, the time of the caves. In the Neolithic, or New Stone Age, we find the beginning of temples, stone circles, and monumental earthworks. Here, too, we find subtle combinations of male imagery with essentially female forms. Artist Michael Dames has demonstrated the strong possibility that Silbury Hill formed a gigantic Goddess sculpture. (Seen from overhead, the hill, with a surrounding irregularly shaped ditch, greatly resembles a figurine of a pregnant Goddess found in Bulgaria.) And yet, excavators have found stag antlers within the hill, as well as evidence that the workers used red stag antlers as picks. The stag is a primal male creature, filled with force and dynamism.

Earlier (p.16), we looked at the idea that the prehistoric temples on Malta formed the outline of a female body. This outline is fairly abstract, consisting of oval shapes connected by narrow passages. Statues found within the temples show a more realistic interpretation of the Goddess's body. And yet, the statues, some of which are very large, often appear androgynous, with wide female hips and feminine faces but completely flat chests. Long flounced skirts conceal any suggestion of genitals. These Maltese figures may represent a mingling of male and female imagery, but they also may show a more literal blending of the sexes. Many ancient cultures chose their priestesses from emasculated males who took on female dress and roles. These "transsexual" priestesses (to borrow a contemporary term) may have demonstrated the merger of male and female forms within the divine body (for more on these practices, *see* Chapter 7).

In Çatal Hüyük, carved breasts on the walls sometimes show boars' heads and tusks emerging from the nipples. Bulls' heads often appear on the walls, particularly in the birthing rooms. Here we find the most remarkable link between a powerful male animal and the Goddess's body. We might assume that the bull represented male generative power, just as a single bull in a herd will impregnate the different cows. Quite possibly this idea was partly behind the prominent bulls' heads at Çatal Hüyük. The link, however, becomes more intimate, more directly of the *body*, when we look at anatomical drawings of the human female. For there we discover that the uterus and fallopian tubes bear an astonishing resemblance to the head of a bull (see *Figure 3*).

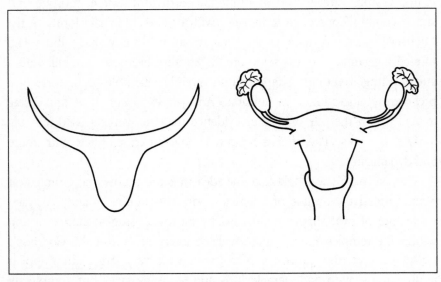

Figure 3 Drawing of a bull's head from a Mediterranean tomb at S. Lesei, Bonnanaro, Sardinia, c.4000 B.C.E. (*left*), compared to the form of the human uterus and fallopian tubes (*right*), (after Gimbutas and Cameron).

Some feminists have argued that this means that originally the bull did not represent male power at all, but *only* the Goddess. And yet, it is impossible to look at a bull in a field and not be struck by its masculine force. The bull, then, becomes an example of the unity of male and female experience within physical reality.

All of this – the biological facts as well as the sacred images – suggests a way out of the duality in thinking about gender, the tendency to argue over whether the genders are equal, or whether one is superior to the other. Both these positions accept the assumption of female and male as fundamentally different, but in the womb, however, all fetuses begin as the same. Instead of seeing an essential separation and conflict between men and women (who may cooperate, but remain separate) we can see them as united within the divine body. Not united metaphorically, or even just in partnership, but on the most fundamental physical levels.

What Is the Goddess? What Is the Body?

When I began this work I sought the Goddess's body in the most literal way, looking for mountains that appeared like breasts, or the profile of a woman lying on her back. Very soon the research opened my mind to more subtle ideas. Landscape formations of the Goddess might display other characteristics, such as cone-shaped mountains, or the Cretan alignment with north and south. Temples and stone circles might form a woman's body, but they also might function as landscape markers or as astronomical observatories to record the solstices, equinoxes, or other moments of the year.

Just what do we mean by "the Goddess?" And for that matter, what do we mean by "the body?" Through working on this book, through the research, through the travels both alone and with friends, and through thinking of what these things mean to me and to others, I have come slowly to a much wider understanding of those two terms. "The Goddess" to me means the historical female deities from different cultures. But it also means the divine being, or spiritual power, as it comes into existence in ourselves and in the universe around us.

Some would call this fundamental spiritual reality "God." Others see it as impersonal, transcending gender. I use the term "Goddess" for two reasons. First, it joins our recognition of the divine to that long tradition going back to our earliest ancestors, with their elegant female carvings. Second, giving the divine a female title – Goddess – emphasizes the power to give life, and to feed us with the milk of spiritual beauty. Hallie Inglehart Austen writes, in *The Heart of the Goddess*, "Ultimately, I see the Goddess as incorporating the full spectrum of existence, not just the 'feminine.'" She goes on to say, "The Goddess represents a unity and wholeness ... All of us, all of existence, are the Divine."

In the Stone Age, the Goddess was the giver of birth but also of death, the Goddess of nature but also of art, of planting and growing but also of dreams. The Goddess is fundamental reality.

Language becomes a looking-glass here. In recent years, many feminist linguists and social critics have pointed out the powerful effect language has on the way we formulate our very thoughts. Most European and Asian languages come from patriarchal structures where men and male experience form the ground of reality. The word "Goddess" clearly derives from "God," just as "female" and "woman" derive from "male" and "man." The derivative quality of the word "Goddess" makes it hard not to see the word as narrow, and exclusive of anything from male experience. And yet, if we use the word "God" we become caught in the cultural dismissal of *female* experience.

If we speak of the Goddess, and femaleness, as fundamental truths, it may appear that we are just turning things upside down. But the newness of the modern Goddess religion gives us a chance to see things in a new way – to include rather than exclude, to explore spiritual experience, not simply to limit it.

And the *body*? Slowly, I have come to see the body as whatever comes into existence in the world. Sitting in the hills of Delphi in Greece, or walking among the limestone crevices near the "Teaching Rock" of Peterborough, Canada, or entering the darkness of passage mounds in Northern Europe, or taking part in a ritual in a city apartment to celebrate the coming of spring, one becomes aware that the body is more than an object. The body encompasses all our experiences. The body of the Goddess is not just the forms of the Earth, or the stars, but their qualities, and their meaning. The *body* is whatever we experience as real, and present, in our lives.

The Visible and
Invisible Body

Whoever you are,
howsoever you come
    across her sacred ground
    you of the sea,
    you that fly,
it is she
    who nourishes you

        Homeric Hymn to the Earth,
        translated by Charles Boer

*A*s with any radical idea, the body of the Goddess attracts us by the strangeness and wonder of its basic theme, calling to something ancient in ourselves we did not know existed until the moment of its awakening. But once we enter this world it begins to open up, revealing greater and greater subtleties. The people who worshipped the Goddess did not see Her only in the most impressive heavenly bodies, the most obvious conjunctions of nature and human reproduction. They sought to find Her in the terror of death, or the coiled energy of snakes. They brought Her into being in the shapes of their temples. And when we begin to follow these paths we discover our own branches and turnings as we discover the reality of the Goddess's body in art, in the mysteries of desire and the joy of contemplation.

The Visible Body

The Goddess has both a visible and an invisible body. The visible is whatever is physical and substantial. The invisible comes into being as whatever is real, but cannot be touched. The invisible includes such aspects as imagination, desire, and thought. The sacred body involves the Sky and the Earth, not only in their physical existence, but also as expressions of the mythic imagination. That is, the world simply exists. When we *regard* that existence, and begin to perceive it in spiritual terms, we ourselves allow the Goddess's body to become visible.

Both the visible and the invisible are mediated by culture. That is, humans have designated certain animals, or certain landscape forms, or certain artistic images, or certain ideas and expressions, or certain kinds of speech and writing, as especially evocative of the Goddess's physical reality. The visible body takes form in the landscape, in the temples, and in trees, especially sacred groves and particular species of trees, such as cypresses and sycamores. It lives in all animals, but especially those seen as Her companions or as expressing Her special qualities. These include pigs, sheep, fish, bears, birds of prey, and especially cows, bulls, and snakes. The visible body surges in the sea, source of all life, whose salt water matches our blood. We find Her body in rivers and streams, and in the rain, without which we cannot live.

We find the Goddess's body in birth, and in menstruation, especially when we give these physical functions a sacred and ceremonial value. But we also find Her body in disease, and death, for these are not mistakes, or punishments, but are part of existence. Here we come to a crucial difference between the Goddess religion (especially as it emerges today) and the religions familiar to us from our upbringing and official history. If we see God as perfect, immortal and never changing, then death becomes a violation and a mark of our distance from God. To paraphrase my friend's graffito "If your body dies, you must have done something wrong." But once we accept death as a genuine aspect of the sacred body, we begin to accept our own death as well. Acceptance does not come automatically. We cannot banish the terror of death simply by telling ourselves that everything dies and returns to nature. But we can move in that direction, and we can take away the assumption of guilt in the fact of inevitable death.

These are not just modern speculations. If we compare the mythologies of Goddess-centered Crete and the later, patriarchal religion of the Greek mainland, we get a sense that the idea of the "immortal Gods," forever alive, forever the same, apart from nature and human suffering, developed only when society separated itself from the cyclical Goddess of death and rebirth. Zeus, the Sky Father of Olympus, actually began as a seasonal vegetation God on Crete. Folklore still claims the Cretan horned mountain, Mt. Dikte, as Zeus's "burial place." Though I was not able to visit the cave during my visit to Crete, I have this description in a letter from writer Samuel R. Delaney: "The cave mouth, when you come upon it, is a great, back-slanting, natural vagina with a huge stone clitoris hanging down, back behind the stone labia, from its center."

Death

The visible and the invisible move in and out of each other. We find this movement in the play between birth and life and death. However much we know of the sperm and the ovum and the development of the fetus, each birth still recreates the miracle of something visible – an individual human being – emerging from a vast invisible mystery. And with each death, the soul, the *person*, returns to nothingness.

Plants vanish into a seeming death in the autumn, disappearing into the invisible underworld, only to become visible again in the spring. When we contemplate death, we gain a sense that the Goddess's invisible body is vaster, and perhaps truer, than the visible. Over 90 percent of all species who ever lived on Earth are extinct, and of living species, the number of individuals living at any moment is a small fraction of those who have lived.

This holds true for all species except one – human beings, of whom there are more alive now than have lived through all of history. This simple fact probably distorts our relationship with nature, and with our own existence, more than any other aspect of our lives. Not only does it crowd those parts of the world hospitable to human life, it allows us to deny the dominant place of death in the natural world.

31

The distortion, however, is a modern phenomenon. Throughout most of human history, the dead far outnumbered the living. And if they are more numerous, then maybe the dead possess more spiritual power as well. After all, life is short but death is forever. And life is filled with limitations. We cannot control the weather, or such disasters as earthquakes. We cannot know the future. But if the living cannot do these things, maybe, just maybe, the dead can. Most cultures have ascribed great power to ancestors or other long-dead figures. In myths, the hero often will visit the Land of the Dead for knowledge, or help. The greatest magicians are those who can raise dead spirits.

The primacy of death emerges in an unusual way in the cosmology of the Bella Coola people of British Columbia, as recounted by Joseph Campbell in *The Way of the Animal Powers*. For the Bella Coola the Sun, known as "Our Father," generated mankind acting together with a Goddess named Alkuntam. Alkuntam Herself, however, was the daughter of a more primal Goddess, a cannibal figure who devours the brains of human beings. And Alkuntam's two sons inspire a cannibalistic frenzy in living humans, so that human society becomes surrounded by destruction.

Through cannibalism the invisible terror of annihilation emerges into the visible world. The act of eating a dead person destroys the integrity of visible bodies. But something more happens as well. It is not just life that breaks down, but social structures and mores, the whole container of civilization. Our modern civilization has convinced itself that the morality and conventions of civilization are somehow basic reality. Most people have recognized that we impose social structures on ourselves in order to allow us to live together. Through the actions of tricksters or sacred clowns – or cannibalism – people allow the unrepressed wildness of life to exist alongside civilization.

Campbell recounts Ruth Benedict's description of a Kwakiutl cannibal society initiation (like the Bella Coola, the Kwakiutl come from the Pacific Northwest). The possessed initiate would bite spectators, and "in the old days," as Campbell says, would even consume portions of murdered slaves. But this very act which initiated him into the secret power of the Kwakiutl spirit world also defiled him for human relations, so that the initiate would be kept apart in a small room for up to four months, guarded over by a Bear Dancer. When he emerged, the initiate would pretend to forget how to be human, and would relearn how to walk, speak, and eat.

Various social tabus would last for several years until a winter ceremonial, during which an old man would act as "bait" for the cannibal. When he approached the old man, as if to bite him, the cannibal would find himself surrounded, and he would then be lured into a building by a woman dancing naked with a corpse in her arms – offering him, in other words, the double life force of food and sex. Inside the building a purification would take place, using, among other agents, "cedar bark impregnated with the menstrual blood of four Noble women."

Sexuality

The visible body further expresses itself, emerges into being, in sexuality – the procreation of animals and plants, the electric sex of sky and earth in thunder and lightning, and the vast variety of human sexual experience. And here the Goddess religion, both ancient and modern, differs sharply from the religion of the transcendent God. For if God has no body, and exists apart from the universe which He has created, then human beings become souls which either *possess* bodies, like objects or clothes, or else become *trapped* in bodies, prisoners in a cage of flesh. Religion becomes a yearning to escape the body, as well as a command to control it. In the religion of a bodiless, sexless God, human sexuality becomes a failure and a betrayal, a move away from God towards a despised nature, a sin.

A religion worshipping the Goddess's body does not need such a split between spirituality and sexuality. As something basic to life, sex takes its place as holy ... "All acts of love and pleasure are my rituals" writes the contemporary witch, Starhawk – a manifesto of liberation in a single sentence.

Scientists and philosophers often argue over what makes humans unique and separate from other animals. Some say language, others abstract thought, and so on. In a way, the question alone betrays an anxious need to isolate ourselves from nature. However, there is one human characteristic which does indeed make us unique – the clitoris. Human females are the only mammals for whom sexual desire and pleasure are not directly connected to reproduction.

This makes human sex cultural rather than simply biological. Sex becomes communication and an expression of our humanness. When fundamentalist Christians and others describe sex as the "animal" part of us, they actually have turned reality on its head. The idea that we should make love only to produce babies would reverse evolution, for this is what animals do. Sexuality is visible, involving touching and other sensations, including orgasm, which is a physical event in the body. And yet sex opens us to the invisible body of desire. How can a touch on the lips, or the breast, or the shoulder, produce a reaction in a part of the body not touched at all, the genitals? And why with some people, but not with others? And what of the response in our bodies when we see, without touching, someone beautiful, or "sexy" – a lover, or a total stranger, or simply a photograph? And what of the fantasies which do not exist physically in the world at all, but only in our minds? What invisible line connects *them* to our genitals? To say that sexuality exists in the brain simply begs the question. We cannot answer the mystery of desire with descriptions of biological functioning.

Just as death leads to the invisible body, so does birth. When a child asks, "Where do babies come from?" he or she is not inquiring about the mechanics of sexual intercourse. Our nervousness on this subject leads us to talk about biological reproduction, and "a mommy and a daddy loving each other," which perhaps satisfies the child, who at least has received an answer. The question, however, touches a basic mystery of life. Where *do* babies come from? We know how fetuses grow, but what makes a fetus a living person? How does an individual being emerge from nothingness to form itself around a physical body?

Birds, Snakes, and the Invisible Body

Birds, and the objects of the sky, shape one aspect of the visible body. The air, however, leads us into the realm of the invisible. We can feel it when it blows on us, and we know it in our body when we breathe. The breath carries life, and spirit, a word which derives from the Latin *spiritus*, which means "breathing, breath of life." But in our normal range of senses we cannot see or touch the air.

The idea of the Goddess's invisible body first suggested itself to me when I thought about the significance of birds in the world's religions and mythologies. In Neolithic art we discover a vast array of bird-woman Goddess statues, pots, and paintings. Many Goddesses, such as Aphrodite or Athena, have birds as companions. Other Goddesses and Gods transform themselves into birds, or receive messages from birds, such as the Scandinavian God, Odin, whose twin ravens, Hugin and Munin, Thought and Memory, bring him news from all over the world. And shamans in many lands dress as birds to travel into the lands of the spirits.

Birds represent the Goddess because they travel in air, Her invisible body, while humans can only travel on the visible body of the Earth (to travel on the sea we must create boats, which by their womb-like form acquire the character of females). And because birds "speak," in the form of *song*, they carry the Goddess's coded wisdom, as well as the inspiration for art, another way for Her invisible body to move into the visible.

Birds link us to snakes, even if only through their symbolic opposition. Birds move through the invisible air, but snakes, more than any other creature, slide through the invisible body of imagination. Mythologies all over the world describe the intimate connection, often antipathy, between birds and snakes. In almost every culture, these two appear as the Goddess's primary creatures. They are not always enemies. Many myths and fairy tales tell of a hero who tastes the blood of a snake (or dragon) and learns "the language of the birds," which is to say, all knowledge. The bird travels to the invisible worlds above, and the snake slithers into the mysteries below ground.

Birds and snakes seem to represent the split (or play) between conscious and unconscious, rationality and instinct. It is easy to understand the fascination with birds, and their ability to fly gracefully into the heavens. But what gives snakes their mystery, their dreamlike hold on almost every mythology?

We can think of several possibilities. In order to grow, snakes must periodically shed their skins. This gives them an aura of immortality.

Snakes have an androgynous quality – extended, they look like phalluses, while coiled they resemble the folds of the vulva. And yet, the snake's power is more than intellectual symbolism. Marija Gimbutas speaks of the snake as coiled energy.

Though we think of snakes as poisonous, they can act on the body in positive ways. The venom of many snakes, especially cobras, acts as a hallucinogen, producing ecstatic visions. In 1989, Dr. Richard Kunin of California decided to research snake oil, often used as a symbol of useless and fraudulent cures. He discovered that the oil from Chinese water snakes contained a high degree of important acids and other nutrients, including the highest concentration of omega-3 derivative eicosapentaenoic acid (EPA). According to Udo Erasmus, in his book *Fats That Heal, Fats That Kill*, *The New England Journal of Medicine* refused to publish Dr. Kunin's study.

One of the more striking descriptions of the snake comes from Roberto Calasso's book-length meditation on Greek myth, *The Marriage of Cadmus and Harmony*: "Where the snake is, there gushes water. Its eye is liquid. Beneath its coils flows the water of the underworld. Forever. Its scales are uniform, its mouth undulating and constantly self-renewing, like waves." Looking at snakes, we seem to be looking backwards in time and deep into our own primal selves. Snakes embody a stage of evolution still embedded in the root of our brain. With their mix of male and female imagery, snakes are sexuality incarnate. And when we see snakes coiled around the arms of the Goddess, or moving through Her hair, we see the force of our earliest beginnings joined to the image of divine power.

Aspects of the Sky

Light in all its frequencies, including radio waves, travels through the invisible body of space – and time – to bring us images and knowledge from stars and quasars and galaxies which have long since vanished. When we look at the stars, or even the Sun, whose light takes eight minutes to reach us, the past becomes visible. Time becomes a revelation of divine reality. The deeper we look into space the farther back we see into time, until we approach the very origin of existence.

Our bodies come out of past reality, for everything in our solar system, including ourselves, and the Sun, formed out of the dust of exploded stars. And we cannot live without the Sun, whose light travels to us through the invisible body of space, air, and time.

Remember the myths of our galaxy, the Milky Way, streaming from the breasts of the Goddess (often depicted as the visible body of a cow, or buffalo), or the stars as part of Her dress, or cloak, or dance. And think as well of stone circles and mounds marking the sunrise (or sunset) on special days of the year. They serve a purpose of time-keeping, of knowing when to plant, or harvest, but they clearly serve a ritual purpose as well. Part of that purpose may have been to bring the invisible body of the heavens into the most visible body of all, stone and dirt. When the midwinter shaft of light penetrates the artificial cave of Newgrange in Ireland, the light has taken form in the presence of the worshippers. For a few moments, the stone tunnels mold the light into a kind of sculpture, a form like a standing human being.

In a very different way of rooting the invisible Sky into the visible Earth, the Australian Aboriginal "Dreamings" are sometimes called Sky Heroes, ancestral beings who came down from the Sky, performed their stories on the surface of the Earth, and then went underground, appearing only as particular facets of the landscape: rocks, plants, animals, pools of water and so on. There is an interesting resemblance here to a meditation currently popular in the West. The person begins by imagining her or himself bathed in white light. This light serves as a medium to bring down particular qualities the person needs or desires – abstract qualities such as love, or healing, or strength. To make these qualities real, the meditator breathes them directly into the body. Finally, she or he then "anchors" these qualities by sending them symbolically down into the Earth.

Everyone knows the picture of witches traveling through the sky on brooms. Probably the image goes back to shamans and healers dressed as birds, or "flying" on drums – which is to say, journeying to the spirit world through a drum-induced trance. The link between shamans and witch brooms becomes clearer when we consider that European "witches" were often village healers or wise women with special herbal knowledge. The handle of the broom suggests a phallus, and therefore a union with male sexual power, either through actual sexual magic, or through the same kind of unity of the sexes found in those prehistoric statues of Goddesses with phallic necks. The broom also links the practical daily work done by ordinary women – yet another physical emergence of the Goddess's body – with spiritual mystery and ecstasy. We also should remember that the brush of the broom, when emerging from between the legs, resembles nothing so much as the tail of a bird.

Nature and Art

The visible reality of the world also leads us to the invisible. The power of the land lies partly in our dependence on it for life, and partly in the sense that something greater than we can see lives within and gives meaning to the world of the senses.

The act of making the Goddess visible becomes more than passive recognition. Works of imagination make visible the invisible body. The Neolithic (New Stone Age) was a time given to great monuments. Silbury Hill in England, the giant passage mounds of Newgrange, Knowth, and Dowth in Ireland, and Cahokia Plain in Illinois (whose "Monk's Mound" is the largest prehistoric earthen structure in the world, covering 14 acres) all act, among their other functions, to make visible a human sense of the cosmos as ordered, meaningful, and alive. They give physical form to ideas of beauty, rhythm, and purpose.

The builders of the early pyramids and ziggurats were probably imitating mountains. An earthen mound forms an even more direct imitation. The interior passage in Newgrange or Knowth (*see* Chapter 4) takes up a small portion of the huge construction. These passages mimic the cave sanctuaries in those mountains where the people of such places as Crete went to worship the Goddess. The giant mounds with their small narrow passages imitate the human form as well, for the uterus and birth canal make up only a small portion of a woman's body. Just as the Maltese temples may have outlined the image of a woman, so a mound or hill may have suggested the Goddess's body, especially Her pregnant belly.

As well as creating stone circles and mounds, Stone Age people in different lands (and times) created giant sculptures. The Serpent Mound earthwork in Ohio runs for a quarter of a mile from the tip of the tail to the mouth (see *Plate 2*).

A similar sculpture near Loch Nell in Scotland runs 300 feet and reaches as high as 20 feet. Both serpents have tails pointing west, and each originally held an altar looking east, to the rising Sun. In both cases, as in other such works, the shape of the land at that place suggested the form of a serpent. Nevertheless, this form existed only in the invisible junction of landscape and imagination – something people could "see" only in their minds – until the builders brought it into permanent visibility.

Modern Creations Imitating the Goddess's Body

Some contemporary artists have revived the practice of creating giant works forming the literal body of the Goddess. Among these, the American sculptor Christina Biaggi has created a concrete mound whose interior mimics the contours of the inside of a woman's body. For the last few years, Biaggi and architect Mimi Lobell have worked on creating a giant mound like Silbury Hill which will function both as an astronomical observatory and a temple. Worshippers will travel through the interior of the hill for an experience of rebirth out of the Goddess's belly.

Other artists have created even more literal images, on a huge scale. The French-American artist Niki de St. Phalle creates statues of Goddesses – "Nanas" as she calls them – so large they function as buildings. Where builders in earlier cultures formed their structures into abstractions of bodies, de St. Phalle uses modern technology to make her images very direct. For a fair in Sweden she created a Goddess lying on her back, 82 feet long, with a cinema (showing a Garbo movie) in the left arm, a moving wooden brain in the head, a planetarium in the left breast, a milk bar in the right breast, and so on. People entered and left through the vagina (see *Plate 3*).

More recently, she has built a giant sculpture garden of three-dimensional Tarot cards. Several of these are simultaneously Nanas and buildings. Traditionally, the Tarot card of the Empress signifies the Great Mother. For this "card" de St. Phalle made a sphinx, which also served as her home over the several years of work on the project.

Many artists have used their own bodies to express the Goddess's body. Some have made pilgrimages to re-enact ancient rituals in caves, others have dressed in costumes and objects evoking traditional Goddess images. People often think of such art as giving power to our bodies by comparing them to sacred beings and traditions. We also might say that when we use our bodies in Goddess art *we* give power to the Goddess. We help Her return from history to emerge once more into physical reality.

The junction of the visible and the invisible opens the way for art. Almost every artist has expressed the sense of being an agent for the work to create itself. We speak of the "medium" of a work of art, meaning the substances used, such as paint, or stone, or print, or recorded sound. The true medium is the artist, who opens the way for whatever needs to emerge from the invisible body.

Myths and folklore too are the body of the Goddess, as are prophecy and oracles, for all of these utterances give form and intellectual substance to an intuitive sense of sacred reality. This reality is formless until we embody it in words or pictures or stone.

And just as our bodies change and develop, growing and aging, shedding skin, menstruating or becoming pregnant, rising and falling with desire, so the visible body of the Goddess, in all its aspects, is not fixed or eternal, but changes, evolves, gives birth, dies and is reborn continually through the invisible body of time.

Human Participation in the Goddess's Body

In all these things we know them, and recognize them as the body of the Goddess, through the reality of our own bodies. In writing his vision of the purpose of Silbury Hill and Avebury Circle in England, Michael Dames wrote that we can understand these ancient constructions as a "code" based on the human body, especially the transformations of pregnancy and birth. Human experience becomes the means to comprehend and express our awareness of the sacred.

In the patriarchal conception of God, human beings are God's creation and subjects, with no real role to play in the divine except as rulers of God's lesser subjects, the plants and animals. When we see existence itself as the divine body we create a more reciprocal relationship. The full realization of this body requires human consciousness to perceive its presence, and human action to bring it most completely into being.

In Vincent Scully's description of the Cretan palaces and the Greek temples, the buildings do not just take advantage of particular landscape formations. They *complete* the landscape forms by their position in such a spot and with such a viewpoint that an observer sees all the landscape elements in the exact relationship that evokes that sense of a female body.

A Double-Peaked Mountain and a Rounded Hill

As part of his ideas about the sacred landscape Scully suggests that a hill between two peaks embodies the Mother. In her book *Earth Wisdom* Dolores La Chapelle extends this idea, pointing out that a newborn child emerges fully conscious (if not doped by drugs administered to the mother), and will see its mother's body first of all as the mons veneris and belly with the breasts looming beyond them. When the child is brought up higher, it then sees its mother's face. Thus, when we see the triple landscape formation, we unconsciously expect that the Mother Goddess's face lies just out of sight.

In Greece, the triple hill formation brings forth Artemis in particular. Artemis watched over women in childbirth. She also belonged to the mountains, where She lived with Her nymphs and both hunted and protected the animals. Archaic pictures of Artemis sometimes show Her with outstretched wings. This image may have arisen from that same triple peak, with the central hill as Her body and the mountains on either side as Her wings.

If we accept that such a landscape image embodies the Goddess, then it requires first of all a human to perceive and celebrate it, and secondly it requires that human to stand and look in a particular spot. I came to understand this best at a place in Greece where I was not particularly looking for it. Near the temple of Artemis at Brauron (Vavrona in modern

Greek), there is an example of Scully and La Chapelle's Mother image (see *Plate 4*).

The relationship between the three hills is best viewed from a spot along the road a mile or two from the temple. I do not know if the modern road lies on the path of the ancient one, but it certainly is possible that the young girls who came in procession from Athens to serve Artemis were led past this spot. Many current highways do indeed follow ancient routes.

Walking along the road from the Brauron temple you will experience a sense of the Goddess's body slowly emerging into reality. At first you see only the nearest hill and part of the further one. Then, as the two outer hills separate, you see a glimpse of the smaller hill that lies between them. But the view of this hill remains overlapped by the one near to you, so that the essential form, a mound in the center flanked by two equal peaks, only clicks into place (and that is the feeling, at least for a modern observer) at the precise spot in the road where you can see the middle hill rise equidistant from the two larger ones. Therefore, this small vision of the Goddess's landscape body comes into existence only when a human observer stands and looks from a particular point.

At all those places where we see the Goddess's body as a landscape form we need the proper viewing point. If we accept Scully's analyses, the Cretans built their palaces to give celebrants of the Goddess a permanent place to view Her body and so allow Her to emerge into physical reality. When I visited the palace of Phaestos in southern Crete I knew I had arrived before I saw the building or the road sign, for I drove around a bend and suddenly saw a cone-shaped hill in a winged hill setting, looming up almost from the side of the road. A few moments later the car reached a point where that landscape formation became free of surrounding low hills – and there stood the entrance to the palace grounds.

The transcendent God, separated from the physical universe, does not require human observers to bring Him into existence. Not having a body, He does not need participation to make that body real. Having grown up in a culture based on such a God, it may seem strange to us to worship a Goddess who can physically appear to us, but only when we stand in a certain place. And yet, such participation brings out a beauty and a power. I am not suggesting that the Goddess does not exist the moment before we reach the correct spot on the road from Brauron, and winks out of existence the moment we walk away. There is, however, a certain reality that does require an observer, one who has learned where to look, and especially how to look, with awe, humility, and acceptance of the Goddess's beauty and life-giving power.

In a curious way, quantum physics, the most intellectual of all the sciences, has revived the ancient play of the observer creating reality. According to quantum theory, elementary particles do not really exist until an intelligent observer measures them. Before that moment, they inhabit the various levels of probability, as described in a wave. Only when someone actually looks does the wave "collapse" into a fixed reality. Some physicists argue that the need for an observer holds true even for such massive objects as the Moon. Such a view flies in the face of what we call common sense. It sounds absurd to claim that an electron, let alone the Moon, does not really exist until a human looks at it. And yet, the most sophisticated experiments have proved quantum theory correct time after time. Maybe we should recognize that particle physics, like the Goddess's landscape formations, restores the human observer to a vital role in the very reality of existence. Perhaps "existence" itself, as a fixed reality, is really a function of the human mind.

The temples at Malta, the passage mounds, Silbury Hill, the giant Serpent Mound in what is now Ohio, these too manifest the Goddess's body. And these too could only come into existence through human awareness, human effort, and a continuing human action. For the shape alone does not constitute the body of the Goddess. The shape must be observed, and understood, and joined in an act of awe and worship. When Gertrude Rachel Levy and, later, Mimi Lobell suggested that the temples of Malta formed giant sculptures of a woman sitting or lying down, they took the first step towards bringing that aspect of Her body into contemporary reality. When others, inspired by this idea, traveled to those temples, and sought Her presence within the walls, and in the dirt and the stone, when they performed rituals there, or simply sat and contemplated the power of the Mother, they took the further step towards completing Her body at that special place.

In Michael Dames's idea of the body as code, the sacred power of Avebury Circle and Silbury Hill derives partly from the natural springs, partly from the sculpted forms of the stones and the human-made hill, and partly from the processions of young women and men Dames imagined as traveling along the megalithic avenues. The "sculpture" took shape from the land, the structures, and the precise ritual movement of human beings. Without that final element the divine sexual union and birth could not occur. Like electrons, the Goddess requires participation.

Seeing with One's Own Eyes

The Greek-derived word *autopsy* translates literally as "seeing with one's own eyes." In a medical autopsy, doctors dismember a dead body to investigate its parts. The Goddess is alive but appeared dead for many centuries. This has been the period of patriarchy, in which we have been told that a Father God created the world, and that civilization, if not existence itself, began some 5,000 years ago, with the first patriarchal king-centered societies of the Middle East. (In the 19th century a certain Bishop Ussher claimed to have calculated not only the year of creation – 4004 B.C. – but the day, 23 October, and even the hour, 9a.m.)

Now, through the work of archaeologists, mythologists, artists and art historians, priestesses, scientists, classicists, historians, anthropologists, philosophers, and psychologists, the fragmented evidence of the Goddess religion is coming together. Temples have been excavated, texts translated, statues and paintings and myths catalogued and analyzed and explored. But all these pieces remain separate, isolated from each other and from meaning, until they are "seen," looked at with awe and respect by people seeking that "abiding relationship" with the living Goddess.

Unlike the dead body, which an autopsy dis-members, the Goddess is a living body in fragments, and when we *see* the Goddess with our own eyes, when we go to Her temples, or find Her in the mountains, or in rituals created in our own homes, we re-member Her, restore Her to wholeness. And this act of seeing restores *us* to wholeness as well, for we heal the fragments of our broken lives by finding the links between our bodies and the body of the Goddess.

There is another sense in which the Goddess is fragmented. Earlier I mentioned the many myths of the universe created out of a dismembered body. They teach us that the Goddess is all around us, alive in all things, yet in so many pieces we do not realize we are walking and living in Her midst at every moment. When we go to Goddess sites, or perform rituals, when we see with our own eyes, we bring together the isolated aspects of Her reality.

Bringing Together History and Life

Honoring our own experiences at sacred places enables us (including those with whom we share our stories) to overcome the split between history and life. Too often we think of the Goddess as an aspect of archaeology, like an exhibit in a museum. If we can prove something historically we think of it as real or authentic. Anything we experience ourselves we consider frivolous, or sentimental. It is true we no longer live in the cultures that produced the great temples or stone circles or earthworks. And in many cases we know almost nothing about their actual beliefs and practices. But we still can give meaning to those places through our own experiences.

In her book *The Laughter of Aphrodite* Carol P. Christ defended what she called "story thealogy" ("thealogy" is the female form of "theology," the study of *thea*, or Goddess, rather than *theos*, God). "I can hear choruses of criticism," she wrote, "saying 'reductionistic,' 'self-indulgent,' 'narcissistic.'" And she added "I do not propose to 'reduce' thealogy to autobiography." At the same time, however, she insisted that women's knowledge and visions came from a ground of personal experience.

As Carol Christ points out, traditional academic theology follows a "myth of objectivity," as if by not writing about their own experiences theologians, historians, and indeed, archaeologists somehow produce works of absolute truth. This myth arises from the wider context of that bodiless God, all mind, detached from involvement with the physical world. Scholarship attempts to "transcend" the personal to mimic this supposed pure state.

In science, this mythic purity has fallen. Field workers who work with animals now recognize their own influence on the behavior of their subjects, and the need to minimize this influence by staying for long periods of time in the creatures' natural habitats. In physics, Werner Heisenberg's famous "uncertainty principle" demonstrated that we cannot study the universe as if we ourselves do not take part in it. When we "look" at subatomic particles the physical act of observing them changes their state. In other words, Heisenberg pointed out that bodies, not detached minds, perform experiments. And we have seen the further extension of the uncertainty principle: the idea that particles do not even exist until we observe them.

The Personal Is the Spiritual

In the early stages of the modern women's movement, a phrase became a touchstone for feminist thinking. "The personal is the political" has had various interpretations, but perhaps two of the main meanings could be described as firstly, individual women develop political knowledge and understanding through looking at their own experiences, and, secondly, this happens because what we experience in relationships, or at work, or in our families takes place in a political context. Put another way, a whole social structure exists when a man and woman argue about housework, or a woman seeks an abortion, or struggles for equal pay. When women start to examine and share their experiences, they gain knowledge of politics. Action in the community and change in our lives begins with this knowledge.

We also might say that *the personal is the spiritual*. Spirituality does not exist only in ancient times, or in books. It exists – it *emerges* into existence – through our own encounters with the sacred. Some of these encounters will take place at acknowledged sacred sites, others through our attempts to recognize the Goddess in our daily lives. When we celebrate our sexuality as part of nature, when we link the rhythms of our lives to the Moon and the Sun, when we find our own ways to commemorate the ancient festivals, when we explore our emotions at sacred places, when we see with our own eyes, we make the personal the spiritual.

The idea that the personal is political allowed women to recognize their own reality as valid, to escape the belief that only experts could tell us how to look at our lives. To say that the personal is *spiritual* validates the sacred experiences of individual women and men. It tells us that what we do, and the way we understand the world, matters. For those of us seeking to (re)create the religion of the Goddess this validation is vital. The established religions back up their authority with ancient texts, and rituals performed by official priests, and often great wealth and political organizations. In the Goddess religion we have recovered many of the myths and images, but we have lost many more. We need to respect the prayers and rituals we create together, the dances we perform under the Moon, the truths we tell in our circles, and the small miracles we encounter on our pilgrimages and in our daily actions.

The Spiritual Is the Political

As well as its other meanings, the phrase "the personal is political" means that whatever we do has a political value and impact. Politics does not occur only in voting booths or demonstrations. How we live our lives carries political meaning, for society as well as for the people around us. The same holds true with the phrase "the personal is spiritual." We do not experience the Goddess only when we go to temples or perform rituals. Instead, we do those things in order to become more aware of the sacred within and around us at all times, to recognize the sacred in our relationships, our families, the food we eat, the way we walk on the Earth. The Goddess did not create human beings as a one-time event thousands of years ago. She creates each of us, every day. Just as we create Her.

If the personal is the spiritual, the spiritual is also the political. The established patriarchal religions often depict their revelations and teachings as transcending (that word again) politics. But there is no religion without political effects. To worship an all-male yet bodiless Godhead (a head without a body) sets up a society which treats women as inferior, or as the property of men. To worship an angry warrior God, a monarch, may lead to a society based on slavery (as in the Greece of Homer). To worship a monotheistic "jealous" God encourages a monolithic view of personality, in which people can never change a supposed basic personality, and each person is judged on the basis of gender, race, or class.

As Carol Christ says, "Symbols have both psychological and political effects." And when we compare different societies based on different religious structures we discover basic political differences. In those cultures which worshipped the Great Goddess we often find evidence of highly developed communities existing for hundreds of years without fortifications, without war or weapons, with virtually no sign of violent death.

The Teaching Rock

When we travel to a sacred place we discover its spiritual power within its actual setting. One of the first journeys I made in this work was to a large boulder in the woods near the city of Peterborough, Canada. Discovered in 1956 (a year after the Canadian government rescinded a law forbidding native Canadians to practice their own traditions), the rock contains some 900 carvings (300 of which are clearly distinguishable) incised into the rock by removing the outer layer of white crystalline limestone so that darker rock shows from underneath. The Provincial Park Service refers to the site as the Peterborough Petroglyphs, but the Indians call it "the Teaching Rock," believing that it exists to give a message of peace to the world.

The images on the rock include abstract symbols, such as a large arrow chevron, stick figures which may be shamans in trance, solar images, birds, turtles, snakes, and a spirit boat apparently with masts, which indicates the possible influence of encounters with Viking ships arriving from Europe.

The largest figures include a carving of a woman, her breasts seen in profile, her abdomen from the front (*see* Chapter 3 for the "twisted perspective" of the bulls at Lascaux cave). According to archaeologists Joan and Roman Vastokas there are four female figures, all emphasizing the genitals, plus seven isolated vulva signs. What is remarkable about the large figure is that she was carved around two large holes in the rock, one at the level of the heart, the other at the womb. A red mineral seam runs along this image, so that we get a powerful sense of the lifeblood of Woman, pumped by the heart, and flowing out of the vagina with menstruation and birth.

This large Goddess image gives the entire rock a female, life-giving quality. I visited the rock with Tana Dineen, who mentioned to the guard/caretaker, Lorenzo, that I was writing a book about the Goddess.

Lorenzo told us that many people believed that women made the carvings, since none of the hundreds of images show any sign of violence, neither war nor hunting. (The same point has been made about the prehistoric French cave, Pêch-Mèrle.) The Vastokas, too, describe the entire site as possibly a symbolic womb, the center of the world (like the Greek *omphalos*, or navel, at Delphi), and an entrance to the Underworld.

There is a sense, a *body* sense, something we know deep down in our bodies, that the Underworld, the Land of the Dead, is also the source of life, of birth and rebirth. Though we try to forget it, with our focus on the outer world of light, we know, both rationally and at a much deeper level, that we come from the darkness and blood of the womb. The Vastokas comment that the Amazonian Pesana see cracks in hills as "the uterus where the gestation of fauna takes place."

At the Peterborough site, a placard reads, "The rock itself, pierced and perforated, may have been seen as an idealized feminine symbol, and a means of access for the shaman to the hidden powers or sexual energy of nature."

Carvings and Natural Fissures

What made the Algonkins of a thousand years ago (ancestors of the modern Algonkin people living in the same area) choose this particular rock for their carvings? Besides the suitabilty of the limestone, and the large flat surface, we need to look at the surroundings. The Teaching Rock itself, and all the smaller rocks around it, are cut with deep natural fissures. When I examined them I took compass readings and discovered that almost all of the fissures ran on a north-south or north-west to south-east axis. Moreover, an underground stream runs below the rock. Just as at Silbury Hill, the invisible current gives a sense of the Goddess's life force. Underground streams evoke the blood flowing under the surface of our own bodies. At the Teaching Rock, the fissures allow us to hear the stream running in the darkness beneath our feet.

But there is something else about these fissures, something that needs to be seen, even felt. The crevices form natural images of great beauty. There are vulvas, clear human figures, a praying shaman, and a Goddess-like form, with green ferns growing at the heart, and multi-colored flowers at the genitals – a perfect match for the human carving on the Rock (see *Plate 5*).

Natural processes had "carved" all the images on these smaller rocks. Did they inspire the Algonkins who came there to create their own pictures on the large stone that would later bear the title "Teaching Rock?" As well as the two holes with the red seam running between them the Teaching Rock contains several natural fissures of its own, including a crack in the shape of a bird running the entire length of the bottom of the rock.

Carrying Sacred Meanings to New Places

When we travel from our own country to experience sacred places in other lands we act like bees bringing pollen from one plant to another so that the plant species can continue to live. We bring our knowledge from one culture to another, and we take back with us experiences we can then apply to our own lives and society.

Originally religion constituted an abiding relationship not only with deity, but even more with place. People understood the sacred as inseparable from the land. Dolores La Chapelle writes that early European explorers often thought that indigenous peoples lacked any religion because they couldn't give a specific name for God; but for the people in those places, God lived all around them, in nature and in their own rituals.

With the rise of empires, such as Hellenistic Greece and Rome, religion became something to export. The evangelist religions of Christianity and Islam made religion a matter of doctrines and laws, a religion of books rather than nature. It can be almost disconcerting for a Jew or a Christian to visit Israel and discover that the places described in the Bible are real places. For example, the Christian idea of Hell derives originally from a Hebrew myth of "Gehenna." Gehenna, however, is an actual desert valley south-west of Jerusalem.

For those of us who look to Artemis or Inanna or Oya, or go from America or England to the temples of Malta, we risk importing alien spiritualities into our native lands. This problem is acute for Euro-Americans. Our ancestral spirituality derives from places we have never inhabited, often never seen. What are we creating when we celebrate the

Celtic festival of Beltane in North America? If we have no Greek heritage but feel a kinship with Greek or Roman Goddesses, such as Artemis/Diana, or Aphrodite/Venus, then we are taking Goddesses from a place alien to ourselves and bringing them to a place alien to them. On the other hand, if we seek out the indigenous traditions of the Americas, and try to follow those ways, with their sweat lodges and vision quests, we may be attaching ourselves to a spirituality alien to our cultural upbringing. And the Native Americans themselves may find it exploitative of us to be using their traditions. This is particularly the case when white people charge high fees to conduct native-style ceremonies

Perhaps an answer to this dilemma lies in approaching the various cultures and native traditions with humility while still trusting the truth of our own experience – what we see with our own eyes.

Just as bees carry pollen from plant to plant, so migratory humans carry spiritual ideas and experience from one land to another. Hopefully we can learn to do this without the imperialism of Christians or Moslems who have tried to force indigenous peoples around the world to abandon their own Gods and Goddesses. The value of cross-pollination is to see things in a fresh way.

Survival of the Goddess in Maltese Daily Life

When we go to sacred places we sometimes may find something that is not described in texts because it does not belong to the archaeological evidence. Sometimes this is a cultural juxtaposition. In the west of Ireland a small roadside shrine to the Virgin Mary stands almost alongside an equally modest stone circle. Both of these sacred places sit in the quiet pasture of a modern farm, where cows – a form of the Goddess recognized worldwide – graze on the grass.

The island of Malta contains only a very few dolmens amidst its many temples. At one of them, however, we can kneel down and view a modern church through the frame of the prehistoric arch. On the neighboring island of Gozo there is a still more fascinating juxtaposition. Gozo is the site of "*Ggantija*" (the name means "female giant"), the oldest of the Maltese temples and one of those most shaped like a woman's body (*see* the structural drawing on page 16). Ggantija is 6,000 years old, which gives it a claim as the oldest free-standing building in the world. As in so many prehistoric and indigenous traditions, the temples and statues were often colored in red ochre, a suggestion of the Goddess's life blood. The stone fences built by farmers in the fields will sometimes contain stones with traces of red ochre from thousands of years ago.

A similar red dominates the architecture of contemporary Gozo. The churches are painted an earthy red, with red domes and cupolas, and thick red velvet curtains decorate the insides. Even the interior decorations of the houses seem to feature that same deep red. And the forms of the churches, with an emphasis on domes and rounded walls, evoke the female body in much the same way that Ggantija forms the image of a woman. The experience of seeing the temples and then the contemporary buildings implies an unconscious link between the prehistoric inhabitants and their modern counterparts – a body memory contained within the land itself.

Snail Shells and Butterflies – Symbols Emerging from Experience

During my stay on Gozo I went to Ggantija virtually every day. One day while examining the enclosed altar at the "head" (the chamber in the back of the temple) I found a group of four snail shells. Snails abound on Malta. Walking through the fields, or among the ruins, one finds elegant shells, often gold with brown dots that become smaller and darker as the curls of the spiral tighten towards the center. As I sat looking at the perfectly carved spirals on the large blocks at the temple of Tarxien one afternoon, it struck me that even though the spirals had developed into complex abstractions, they might have come originally from snail shells (see *Plate 6*).

Later, at Ggantija, I found a faint carving of a spiral that was much closer in form to that of a snail shell. And when I went to the museum on Gozo I discovered a block with a carved snail shell.

On the day I found the four shells I picked one up and took it with me to give to my friend Eva when I met her and her family that evening. When I told her where I'd found it, Eva began to laugh. She herself had placed the snails there, five of them originally, in the form of a pentacle, or five-pointed star. The pentacle has become the primary symbol of Wicca, the revived "witchcraft" religion of the Goddess. Wicca bases itself partly on the Triple Goddess of Maiden, Mother, and Crone. Earlier that day, someone had taken one of the snail shells, and I had taken a second, leaving three to form a triangle.

On Eva's last day on Gozo we went together to Ggantija, to give thanks to the Goddess, and to ask for healing for ourselves and for the Earth. We wore fresh clothes and blessed each other with dirt from the temple ground, tracing a pentacle on each other's forehead. We chanted, and then asked the Goddess for gifts, not for ourselves, but for each other, and for the people we loved.

For most of our ritual, Eva and I stood in the "head." When we started we were the only ones at the site. Midway through our ritual, however, a woman came and sat down not far from us, on a block of stone in the passage between the head and the upper body. She sat smiling, with her eyes closed, as if to drift back in time to the days of the temple's glory. She still remained there, eyes still closed, that sweet expression on her face, when Eva and I finished our prayers and when Eva's two young daughters came running up with their own adventures to tell, followed by Eva's husband. When we all left, the woman remained, journeying into the stones and their 6,000-year-old stories.

Two days later, on my own last day, I returned one last time to Ggantija, on my way to the ferry. That morning, the entire site had come alive with butterflies. In the sandy monochrome of the temple ruins the butterflies appeared like a miraculous burst of life. I went to the altar in the head, to look for Eva's snail shells. The snails had vanished, but now someone seemingly had traced a picture of a butterfly in the dirt. The picture was simple, with part of one wing rubbed out.

Days later, having left Malta, I thought about that drawing, and the connection it seemed to make between the snail shells and the butterflies. With the side of the drawing open, it appeared like an entry to the spirit world, the Goddess's invisible body, just as the temple opens Her visible body. History too is an invisible body, for the actions, and the people who performed them, have vanished. And yet the ruins and the other remains, the figurines and the pottery, the Goddess statues and the spirals on the stone blocks, these all bring history into visibility.

The temples appear at first like an empty snail shell. Just as the snail has long since died, so the prehistoric religion of the Goddess seemingly has died with the people who moved these huge stones into a form like a woman's body. But the discovery of these temples, and the wonder of their form, has inspired people like Mimi Lobell, or Eva and myself, or that silent woman, or the many others who come in groups or alone, to awaken our own knowledge of the Goddess, in our lives, in our bodies, in the world around us. The invisible body of history changes to the visible body of celebration, ritual, and changing lives. Instead of snail shells, the temples, caves, stone circles, and all the other sites have become chrysalises, with the religion of the Goddess a butterfly as it emerges once more into the bright light of the living world.

3

The Painted Stone Body

Sometimes I sleep, I go back to the beginning, falling back in mid-air, wafted along by my natural state as the sleepyhead of nature, and in dreams I waft on, waking at the feet of giant stones.

Pablo Neruda

Ways of doing things may be new,
things to be done are generally not.

Judith Guest, Miss Manners

They lived beneath the shadows of glaciers as much as a mile thick, sharing their world with herds of reindeer and wild cows and bulls called aurochs. We have picked apart their camp-fires and catalogued their tools and excavated their remains to examine their bones under microscopes. We have created fantasies of their lives, picturing savage men clubbing women over the head to drag them back to dark caves. And yet, one aspect of the lives of our earliest ancestors still astonishes us. Against everything we might expect, these Stone Age tribes tens of thousands of years ago created magnificent art, from huge pictures of bulls and horses to delicately carved figurines of the female body, many of them highly stylized and abstracted.

How do these pictures speak to us? What stories can we discover (and create) about them? When we think of the Goddess's body we think most often of Mother Earth, so that painted caves become a return to Her womb. Did the painters themselves look at it this way? The vulva signs carved on the walls suggest this. So do the figurines, for even though their creators made them small enough to hold in one hand, they also carved them in a massive style reminiscent of the mountains themselves. In the cave, the image of the human female, the wild power of animals, and the eternal presence of the mountain all merge together.

Primitivism

To look at the mystery of cave art means first of all to look at our own prejudices. When European ethnographers first began to investigate the beliefs and behavior of nomadic and other traditional peoples they invented the term "primitive," that is, people who had not evolved past the earliest stages of human development. By examining Africans of the Kalahari Desert, or Australian Aborigines, Europeans supposedly could look back in time at their own simple beginnings. Some texts compared the world-view of "primitive tribes" with that of Western children.

It is no accident that this approach to anthropology developed in the period following the publication of Charles Darwin's *Origin of Species*. The concept of evolution changed the way Europeans looked at other cultures. Previously, even Europeans who rejected Christian doctrine that God created the world 5,000 years ago still tended to think of non-European cultures as ignorant and wretched. After Darwin, Europeans began to describe humanity as evolving from one stage to another.

European culture itself certainly seems to have done this. The Old Stone Age changed to the New Stone Age with the development of agriculture and monument building. Metals produced first the Bronze, then the Iron Age. Patriarchy and centralized governments seemed to replace tribal communities, and so on.

For Europeans, then, it becomes natural to see each change as an advance to a "higher" culture. In fact, this is literally true in archaeology, since one finds evidence of older cultures by digging deeper into the Earth. Possibly, however, that is the only way it is true. For as we explore the knowledge, sophistication, and daily lives of Stone Age people, both Old and New, we begin to question whether changes necessarily advanced human society, or human knowledge. Only with computers and microscopes have we begun to recover some of the knowledge lost with the Stone Age. And we have a long way to go before we recover the wisdom.

Since European culture seemed to have "evolved" from primitive roots, Europeans viewed tribal, and especially non-agricultural societies as undeveloped, ignorant. People such as the Australian Aborigines seemed to have become stuck in the Old Stone Age. Europeans used this attitude (and still use it) to justify the conquest of tribal territories and the destruction of indigenous peoples.

Today, we may find it natural to make cross-cultural comparisons between different tribal cultures, or to look to contemporary hunter-gatherer cultures to understand the European Old Stone Age. We need to recognize the limitations of such an approach, for every culture is unique. We can find inspiration and possibilities in the Australian Aborigines, for example, but not explanations for our own past. The Aborigines have a highly complex civilization, one that has existed for 60,000 years. It also is alive and dynamic.

For many decades, people considered the art in the prehistoric caves of France and Spain a jumble, with no sense of composition. The painters were assumed to have painted whatever they wished in whatever seemed a suitable space. Experts also assumed that isolated people did the paintings over long periods of time, with little regard for what had gone before them. After all, these were the most primitive people of all, our earliest ancestors.

Since the 1950s prehistorians such as André Leroi-Gourhan and Annette Laming have studied the layout of the paintings, using both statistical analysis and a sense of aesthetics to demonstrate the possibility that Lascaux and other caves were created as a whole, a gigantic composition by a single dedicated team of artists. Animals of one kind may have complemented another – Leroi-Gourhan cited particularly the balance of horses and bovines. Groups of animals create special effects. A series of five stag heads drawn at varying heights and varying angles suggest the rhythm of a wave, as if the animals are crossing a stream.

The Power of Lascaux

One advantage of seeing with our own eyes is that it can help us let go of the ideology of primitivism. For ironically, when we do look at monuments of European prehistory – the circles such as Stonehenge, or the much older caves, such as Lascaux or Pêch-Mèrle – we may emerge cleansed of the idea that there *ever* has been such a thing as a primitive human being.

To see Lascaux is to see, overwhelmingly, the brilliance and complexity of the Cro-Magnon humans of 17,000 years ago. In 1963 the French government closed Lascaux due to bacterial contamination from the many visitors. (They have created a copy, as accurate as possible down to the pigmentation and the contours of the walls, by blasting out a second cave in the same hillside, a few hundred meters away. One wonders what archaeologists of the future, unable to decipher our languages, would make of such a duplication, nearly 20,000 years apart.)

It is still possible to see the original, if one requests permission far enough in advance. Because the original only receives four or five people at a time, the guides have developed a dramatic way to show the cave in its glory. They first lead you down into an antechamber cut into the hillside. Then they turn off all the lights before opening the door to the cave itself. If, as some people surmise, the cave was used for initiations, this may have been much the way the original tribal members entered into the secret – that is, in pitch darkness until their leaders fired up their torches or oil lamps.

The guides lead you into the chamber and throw the switch for the electric lights. And there you stand, surrounded by huge white walls covered in leaping, running, snorting animals, some as much as 18 feet long, seeming herds of horses, or bulls, some with other animals emerging from their bodies, and all of them in hard bright colors. The effect is a desire to shout or weep with amazement and joy, while all the while you are thinking, "This is 17,000 years old. People painted these masterpieces *17,000 years ago*" (see *Plate 7*).

It is not just the size of the paintings, or the bright colors, or the magnificent setting that liberates one from ideologies of primitivism. It is the technique and beauty of the work. The anatomical details are precise and elegant (in other caves, prehistorians have been able to distinguish three breeds of horses, as well as brown and black bears, by their anatomical differences). At the same time, some of the bulls display a kind of double perspective, with the head in profile and the horns seen as if from three-quarters. As in other caves, the painters used the shape of the walls to give a three-dimensional effect to the painted forms. On some figures, the artists engraved the outline of the animal, painted over the engraving, then engraved around the painting, all to increase the sense of dynamism. Unlike the figures in some of the other caves, the Lascaux animals appear in wild movement, including a horse painted upside down with its legs apart so that it seems to be falling helplessly through the air.

An old joke calls prostitution the world's oldest profession. To see Lascaux is to recognize that the oldest profession may very well be artist. There is virtually no possibility that a group of wandering people, without tradition or training, found an interesting cave and decided to make some pictures. These were people first of all with talent. Get a book of Lascaux photographs. Try to reproduce some of the pictures on an ordinary sheet of paper – and then imagine people painting and engraving them, 12 or 18 feet long, on an irregular stone wall, often while sitting or lying on scaffolding. The Lascaux artists had to have been talented people, special people in their community. And they had to have received training in the special techniques – and artistic tradition – used in their massive project.

Nor is Lascaux primitive intellectually. Less noticeable than the massive animals are a complex series of abstract signs dotting the walls. Leroi-Gourhan and his followers have catalogued some 400 of them.

For those of us without Leroi-Gourhan's training it is still the act of looking, of opening ourselves to the wonder, which dispels the ideology of primitive humanity and allows us to recognize the miracle of art embodying the sacred.

Beginnings of Art

Before we examine the possible purposes of cave art we should look at that art's development. Not only will this ground us in what scientists have learned of humanity's early history, it also will help demonstrate the primacy of art in human culture. Perhaps that last sentence should read "primate" culture. John Pfeiffer, in *The Creative Explosion*, tells of a London Zoo chimpanzee named Congo who produced 384 drawings by the age of four, "progressing from scribbles to rough circles and crosses," with some even selling in an exhibition. A chimpanzee in the United States, named Moja, aged three and a half, drew a picture of "four line segments, a right angle, and a sweeping curve." Moja was part of an experiment in interspecies communication, and had learned a limited vocabulary of American Sign Language. When Moja stopped drawing, the human watching signaled "Try more." Moja signed, "Finished." The human asked, "What that?" Moja replied, "Bird." Later, Moja went on to draw "grass," "berry," and "flower." Possibly the impulse to create language and art develop together.

Among the first human creations are "hand-axes," stones chosen for their elongated, rounded form, flattened by knocking off flakes, and then trimmed on the sides to produce both a cutting edge and symmetry. They appear around 1.5 million years ago. Did the makers shape them symmetrically for aesthetic reasons? An example found in Norfolk, England contains a fossil shell precisely in the middle, as if placed there for artistic beauty.

Prehistorians refer to these objects as hand-axes, but in fact, as Pfeiffer says, "they were not axes, and were not used for chopping or any other sort of heavy-duty work." Were they tools at all? The famous double axes of Crete were made of metal too soft for use as tools or weapons. Ranging in size from a few inches to over six and a half feet high, they served as votive offerings, devotional objects for the Great Goddess. The many seals and other pictures of them show them associated only with women, never with men. The name for the Cretan axes, *labrys*, is connected to "labia," the lips of the vulva.

We cannot compare Crete of 4,000 years ago with *Homo erectus* 1.5 million years earlier. But it is worth noting that evidence indicates that for a long time after humans discovered how to make fire they did not use it to warm themselves or to cook food, but to perform rituals. In a moment we will look at the work of Alexander Marshack indicating that art and "story," not tools, distinguish the first humans.

Early Female Images

Marija Gimbutas writes, in *The Civilization of the Goddess*, that flint sculptures of female figures appear as early as 500,000 years ago. According to John Pfeiffer, the oldest carefully marked object, found in France, dates from 2–300,000 years ago. It consists of an ox rib about six inches long, with what looks like a pair of curved parallel lines. Only when examined under a microscope do the lines reveal themselves as double lines, precisely executed. Professor Gimbutas has traced the prominence in later Goddess art of precisely that image, parallel curved lines. They appear over and over again, on pottery and statues.

Humans of today descend from the evolutionary strain known as Cro-Magnon. Our early competitors, the Neanderthals, also appear to have contributed to the development of art and religion in human culture. A cave in northern Iraq yielded remains of a 60,000-year-old Neanderthal funeral, with bodies laid out, as if asleep, on a bed of flowers, possibly healing plants. Some Neanderthal remains indicate that they painted the corpses in red ochre. We know from later cultures that red ochre symbolizes life, and especially the menstrual/birth blood of the Goddess. Ochre often appears in tombs or tomb art, especially on buried carvings emphasizing the Goddess's womb. Similarly, many of the figurines and relief sculptures of the Goddess found in the later caves were painted in red ochre. So were the statues and temple stones in Malta and other places. A recent article in *U.S. News and World Report* describes a four-walled rock structure built by Neanderthals deep in a cave. The idea of a building in a cave suggests some ritual purpose.

Very early art includes "cup" marks, from about 125,000 years ago. These engraved concave circles have proved to be an astonishingly enduring symbol, found in rock art throughout the world, from Europe to North America to Australia. The concave form suggests the interior quality of the female body, the womb. The Pomo Indians of Northern California call such carved pitted rocks "baby rocks." Couples desiring children would come to the rocks with offerings and prayers to the Spirits. They then would chip a small amount of steatite from the holes, grind it fine, and mix it with water to make a paste which they would paint on the woman's abdomen and pubic area.

The "Creative Explosion"

Approximately 35–40,000 years ago Cro-Magnon humanity underwent what John Pfeiffer calls a "creative explosion," with the appearance of wall engravings, delicately incised bones, and elaborately carved figurines, all of which continued to be created over thousands of years.

This does not mean that human culture began only in Europe. Most of our knowledge of the Paleolithic comes from a small area of southern France and northern Spain, particularly the Dordogne and Vézère river valleys of France. However, China and India at least are also known to have experienced Stone Age development, though little art has been found, possibly because of less extensive exploration. Rock art appears virtually everywhere, with the richest source being southern Africa, where some 6,000 sites have been found, containing as many as 175,000 paintings. Recent archaeological research has shifted the beginnings of art – and commerce – from Europe to much earlier times in Africa. At least 100,000 years ago, humans in Africa developed long-distance trading networks for various goods, including beads.

Early art, especially the wall art and the figurines, show the spiritual power of the female body. The European wall engravings began with vulva images, and even though the animals later became more prominent, the vulva remained a powerful symbol, in caves, in rock shelters, and on carvings. Prehistorians in Europe have found more than 770 slabs engraved with drawings of vulvas. At the cave of La Bastide, stones engraved with vulvas were found placed face down in a circle. (The idea of a stone circle inside a cave is fascinating when we consider the recent fashion for assuming all stone circles serve as astronomical observatories.)

At Les Eyzies, in the French Dordogne region, excavators discovered corpses painted with red ochre and buried with cowrie shells. We usually associate cowrie shells with Africa, where they became used for religious bead art, necklaces, headdresses, and money, as well as symbols of power and divination. Cowries form a natural Goddess image, for the slit side resembles the vaginal opening, while the rounded side suggests the swelling of a pregnant belly. Held vertically, the cowrie resembles the labia. Horizontally, the shells look like eyes. The distinctive large almond eyes of some African sculpture and masks derive from cowrie shells. A symbolic relationship exists between the eye and the vagina. Both open into the body. By its link to the mind, the eye gives forth creative ideas in the way the vagina gives forth babies. According to R. J. Stewart (writing about the term "Sil" in Silbury Hill), *sul* or *suil* in Old Irish meant "eye" or "cavity" and also "vagina."

Symbolic Abstraction

The carved vulvas were not realistic images of women's genitals, but abstracted clefts or triangles. In other words, they were symbols. And where we find symbols, we can talk of ideas and a sense of the sacred. The people of that time did not live in the dark inaccessible caves, but rather in rock shelters, which they also painted and engraved. In the rock shelter of L'Abri Pataud archaeologists found a woman and child buried in front of a vulva incised in the rock. Over and over again that same conjunction appears before us: the corpse and the vulva; ochre – the color of life – and the dead; death and rebirth; going back thousands of years.

Later wall engravings of women show even more symbolic abstraction. Images become reduced to essentials of breasts, buttocks, and vulva. Sometimes we find no head or feet. The figurines, too, show the female body abstracted. As noted above, the buttocks appear exaggerated, the feet often disappear, the hips and breasts appear mountainous, and the head may appear smooth, bird-like, or marked with holes. Archaeologists have found more than 1,000 Stone Age figurines. Almost all of them represent female images.

One of the earliest known carved figures in the world, the so-called "Venus" of Willendorf, from about 30,000 years ago, appears as a woman with large belly and breasts, truncated arms disappearing into the sides (or changing into narrow lines across the top of the breasts), stubby legs without feet (possibly to set into dirt, or the ash of a fire), and a large honeycomb-like head without a face (see *Plate 8*). The honeycomb image foreshadows the Bee Goddess found thousands of years later in Crete, Canaan, and elsewhere. Significantly, the statue appears to have been colored with red ochre, a clue to her status as sacred art.

Despite the title "Venus," the Lady of Willendorf (if we might change the expression) is not carved as pregnant. Nor are most of the other Goddess figurines. While they represent female power, with their huge breasts and hips and buttocks, they do not represent fertility only, but something wider, more abstract and all-encompassing. The vulva does not signify birth alone, but the sacredness and creativity of the Goddess's body as a whole. William Irwin Thompson writes (in *The Time Falling Bodies Take To Light*) that the link between menstruation and the lunar cycle makes the vulva a symbol not of physiology but of the cosmos. But why should these two things oppose each other? The power of the Goddess religion lies in the truth that the female human body mirrors – and gives meaning to – the cosmos.

Handprints

Two other forms of art appear early and continue through the Paleolithic: carved sticks and handprints. Like cup marks, handprints appear in rock art throughout the world. Sometimes we find them with other images, at other times just by themselves. The artists used two methods. "Positive" handprints come from dipping the hands in paint and then pressing them against the wall. "Negative" handprints seem to have been made by holding the hand against the wall with the fingers spread, and then blowing paint through a tube at the area around the hand. Some handprints appear with part of a finger missing. In the cave of Maltrevieso, in western Spain, all the handprints show the upper two joints of the little finger missing. Though this may have resulted from ritual amputation, perhaps as an offering to Spirits, Mark Newcomer, an experimental archaeologist, has demonstrated the possibility of faking such images by bending the finger before blowing the paint.

The size of the hands indicate women made the handprints, supporting the idea that women artists created the paintings. In rural India contemporary women painters often include handprints as part of their work.

As with all prehistoric art we do not know the specific meaning of handprints. We might guess at a generalized sense that would draw people to leave these kind of marks. When we go to a sacred place, where we experience awe, we often wish to touch the ground, or the rocks, or the trees. We want to press our hands as an extension of our consciousness, for the hands somehow carry a special charge of energy. Not only do our hands distinguish us from other animals, we use them to remake the world around us. Handprints make a powerful statement. They leave a mark of consciousness. They form both an act of submission and a daring gesture of taking part in the spiritual power alive within that place. With handprints we absorb the power of a sacred place and give back something of ourselves in return. We press the reality of our own body onto the body of the Earth.

In the cave of Pêch-Mèrle negative handprints surround a picture of two horses. The hands remain outside the bodies, giving a sense that humans may not penetrate something so awesome as a spirit animal. This strict separation becomes more interesting when we consider that cave artists often drew one animal emerging from another, as at Lascaux, or else superimposed many drawings on top of each other.

Marked Sticks

The marked sticks are a more complex subject, if only because they contain more information. The sticks consist of engraved and decorated bones or antlers, sometimes with a series of simple markings, seemingly abstract, but at other times with carefully incised pictures of animals and plants. Most have at least one hole bored into them, some have several. Archaeologists used to refer to them as "bâtons de commandant," assuming them to be the symbol of authority for a tribal chief – an assumption which perhaps says more about the archaeologists than about Stone Age culture. The cave art museum in Les Eyzies, France currently describes the few sticks on display as "enigmatic objects."

Of the various images of humans with animals in Paleolithic art, none of the humans carries weapons. Quite a few, however, carry ceremonial objects or discs, indicating that the people sought to *encounter* sacred animals, not to kill or overpower them.

The Work of Alexander Marshack

Alexander Marshack has pioneered the study of carved bones and antlers, working with objects from Africa and Europe. He has used two instruments in his work, a microscope and a mind willing to think about things in a fresh way. Unlike many writers, Marshack never claims absolute truth for his interpretations, but only that the prehistoric artists *might* (his italics) have intended such and such an idea.

The microscope has led to several discoveries. First, there is the remarkable technique of these artists from over 10,000 years ago. Carefully spaced markings in regular patterns mix with graceful images of deer and ibex, plants and sprouts, salmon and other fish. In many cases, it is only with the microscope that we can see the biological precision of the art, with particular species clearly distinguishable. (Flint knives were not the crude instruments we see in popular images of cave life. André Leroi-Gourhan writes, "Flint has cutting qualities which, for work in engraving or sculpture, can rival metal tools.")

The most common theory of cave art describes the pictures as hunting magic. The evidence supposedly includes pictures of barbed harpoons and arrows. However, the "harpoons" actually point in the wrong direction. Marshack has demonstrated the possibility that these barbed signs represent plants, thereby opening a whole new range of interpretation for Paleolithic art, which was thought to show only animals.

Plants are important for several reasons. For one thing, they show a concern for the dietary, and possibly healing, properties of growing things. In Lascaux the barbed signs appear alongside pregnant animals and vulva images. They might have represented medicinal plants for pregnancy. The herbal knowledge of non-agricultural peoples is often extremely detailed – far more so, in fact, than that of farming cultures. Farmers grow only a few crops, while gatherers pick from a vast range of wild plants.

Plant signs, especially alongside vulvas or pregnant animals, might symbolize the renewal of life in spring. Marshack has stressed this point, finding on one of the antlers studied a whole array of spring images: spawning salmon and seals, fresh sprouts, flowers. We might think of this as simply a pleasant picture, but Marshack has pointed out revolutionary implications. Prehistorians have always assumed that humans did not become conscious of the regularity of time until the invention of agriculture in the Neolithic. A group of spring images, connected to pregnancy, shows an awareness of the seasons, and of biological processes, thousands of years before agriculture.

Bone Marks

The study of the abstract marks on the bones suggests such awareness even more strongly. For if Marshack is right, these series of regular engraved lines, always thought of as meaningless scratches, actually represent a careful counting of days, or months. The lines may mark two kinds of time, both associated with women's bodies; firstly, the phases of the Moon, so vitally linked to menstruation, or, secondly, the duration of pregnancy.

Rather than being phallic wands representing a chief's power, the "bâtons" may have served as calendar sticks for midwives needing to keep track of pregnancies. If this were so, such a calendar would, amongst other things, indicate the knowledge that babies begin growing with the first missed period, if not an awareness of the connection to intercourse. Alternatively, the sticks might have helped women align the sacred power within their own bodies with the compelling spirituality of the Moon. An interesting conjunction of meanings from much later cultures supports this possibility. According to Elinor Gadon, in her book *The Once and Future Goddess*, the word "ritual" derives from Sanskrit *rtu*, which means "menses." *Klein's Comprehensive Etymological Dictionary of the English Language* traces "ritual" to the Indo-European root *ri* which means "to count, number." As with the cave art, we find the idea that sacred awareness goes back to awareness of the periodic time created by menstruation.

The Venus of Laussel

One of the most famous cave art images is the so-called "Venus of Laussel," a stunning relief sculpture over 20,000 years old, found in a rock shelter in the Dordogne river valley (see *Plate 9*).

As with a number of other relief works, the artist used the curve and swell of the wall to give the image three-dimensional quality. Evidence indicates that this figure too was painted with red ochre, that ubiquitous symbol of the Goddess's life-blood. Here the woman does appear pregnant. Her left hand rests on her belly, while the right holds a bison horn marked with thirteen lines. The horn holds immense symbolic significance. A year contains either 13 full Moons or 13 new Moons (a lunar month lasts 29.5 days), and the bison, or cow, horn resembles the waxing or waning Moon, just as a pregnant belly resembles the full Moon.

Remember that bovines, bulls and cows, are the commonest animals in cave art. And remember that in later cultures all over the world, the cow or buffalo embodies the Great Goddess, with such figures as White Buffalo Woman among the Lakota Sioux, Oya as a buffalo in West Africa, Europa in Greek mythology, Hathor in Egypt, and the cow in Scandinavian myth who licked a frozen block of salt-water to form the world. The Milky Way, our name for our galaxy, refers to the myth of the stars as milk from the (cow) Goddess streaming out into the sky. It is astonishing to find this complex conjunction of images and ideas so long ago, thousands of years before the beginning of animal husbandry. The conjunction of bovines and women in the image of the Goddess may have derived partly from the fact that bovine pregnancies last nine months.

Story and Time-Factoring

For Marshack, the distinctive quality that marks human beings is not tool-making but what he calls "story," and "time-factoring." This means the ability to perceive process and repetition – in other words, *cycles* – in the world around us and in our own lives, and to give these things meanings. I would add, to give them a *sacred* meaning. Such things as myths, symbolic art, abstract signs, and calendars all give meaning to raw experience.

Story and time-factoring come with brain development, and therefore belong to the body. If the first "stories" derive from menstruation and pregnancy, linking these experiences to the Moon and cows, then story, like creation itself, emerges from the Goddess's body – that is, from the female body perceived as divine.

We can trace so many of our fundamental stories back to the body, to the experience of birth, the awareness of death, the periodic flow of menstruation, the urgent rise and fall of the phallus, the fact of standing upright on two legs, and so on. This does not reduce spirituality to "mere" physical facts. Instead, it shows the unity of bodies and sacred truth.

Later Paleolithic art sometimes depicted the essential female images – breasts, buttocks, vulva – as a few marks, such as a circle with a line through it for the vulva. Some prehistorians describe this as a "degeneration" of the art. Marshack, however, suggests that the "story," the symbolic meaning of the image, had become so well known that a simple sign could carry the full weight of meaning (think of all the Christian meanings coded into the simple form of the cross). Marshack writes, "It is not the anatomic sexual origin that is being symbolized, but the stories, characters, and process with which the symbol had become associated." Experience, the facts of life, distilled into symbol and myth.

The standard view of human development assumes that myths of the Goddess did not arise until the discovery of agriculture. In other words, a technological breakthrough supposedly ushered in new symbolic meanings. And yet, the Willendorf statue is 30–50,000 years old. Just as the earliest artifacts appear to serve ritual purposes rather than practical uses, so technology may have followed art and not the other way around. The female images of the Old Stone Age continued into the New. Marshack describes them as part of an "intellectual, time-factored and time-factoring heritage that prepared the way for agriculture." That intellectual heritage came from recognizing the power and truth of the body.

Hunter-Gatherer Economics

For many years prehistorians described the cave paintings as "hunting magic." Concerned to ensure a steady supply of meat, the "cavemen" supposedly drew pictures of their desired prey and hoped that that would give them power over the creatures. And yet, the archaeological evidence undermines this idea.

First of all, from what we know of bone and fossil remains, game was not scarce at all, but plentiful. Most of us have grown up with the image of "cavemen" leading a miserable and desperate existence. This too belongs to the ideology of primitivism, for it tells us that we are so much better off with our advanced technological society, and that all history has followed a steady progress to better and better conditions. If we find our lives today unsatisfactory, we can tell ourselves we have no choice, and that earlier people suffered much more than us. Such a view of Old Stone Age life justifies not only the so-called "great civilizations" beginning with Sumer, but even late capitalism. When ecologists and others attack our consumption-based approach to nature, conservatives often cite the supposed misery that came before human dominance of nature. Research, however, has undermined this view of prehistoric life. In an article titled "The First Affluent Society" Marshall Sahlins demonstrated that Paleolithic people needed to work only 14 hours a week to feed, clothe, and shelter themselves.

This startling and revolutionary information brings into question our assumptions about our lives today, with people working 60 hours a week or more simply to survive. It reflects on various moments in history, such as the 18th-century Enclosure Acts in Britain, which transformed communal land into private property held by a small class of landlords, and which the landlords justified in the name of progress and economic efficiency. It helps us with the necessary and difficult task of questioning the very assumptions of human history as a march of progress from savagery and hardship to civilization and comfort. And it leads us to wonder, what do human beings do when they need work only 14 hours a week? Well, for one thing, they devote time, energy, and community resources to creating great works of spiritual art.

The proponents of hunting magic as the explanation for cave art have suggested that even though game was plentiful for most of the time, the herds would sometimes "crash," and that the hunters hoped magic would help them avoid such possible calamities. However, Stone Age people apparently did not hunt the animals they painted. By the evidence of bones and food remains, their meat diet consisted almost entirely of reindeer. But reindeer appear much less frequently among the paintings than other species, especially bovines and horses. It is as if the painters deliberately chose animals with whom they did not share a domestic relationship. (Leroi-Gourhan has pointed out that European heraldry depicts such animals as lions and eagles, rather than the cows and pigs eaten by the medieval nobility.) A similar situation exists with the carvings on the Teaching Rock in Canada, created some 16,000 years later. The rock contains many animal images, but not images of the animals the people actually ate.

We also should realize that many people, especially feminist scholars, have challenged the idea that meat dominates the diet of hunter-gatherer peoples. Meat is valuable, but daily life rests on the great variety of plants gathered by the women. We have seen how Alexander Marshack's microscope has revealed the neglected importance of plant images among the dramatic images of animals.

Thinking about Cave Art

If the images are not hunting magic, then why were they made? Why paint or engrave pictures of animals deep within a dark cave, where the artists had to work by the light of stone tallow lamps, often resting on scaffolding? Once again, we can never know, only guess. And those guesses will come more from our own sense of meaning and beauty than the actual beliefs of the cave artists. Objectivity lies only in recording the physical facts; any statement about purpose is a statement about ourselves.

In *Marks in Place*, a book of contemporary artists' photographs of rock art, Polly Schaafsma comments that there are no "universal meanings." There are, however, images that are almost universal, such as the cross or the spiral. And even though the species depicted change from place to place, animals seem to touch something in human beings that leads us to art. When the conscious mind struggles to make sense of powerful images, to make *symbols* out of them, then art takes on culturally specific meanings.

And yet, symbolic meanings do not derive only from cultures. Humans everywhere and at all times share the same conditions – roughly the same genetic structure, the same need for food and shelter and sexual fulfillment, the bond with children coming out of their mother's bodies, the relationships with the seasons and the changing phases of the Moon. In a very broad sense, we can claim that we do know the "purpose" of the cave paintings. For the purpose of all art is to mediate between the invisible spirit world and the visible body of nature. To make the invisible visible.

The various theories for cave art include the aesthetic joy of the work (art for art's sake), the creation of initiation chambers for young members of the community, and expressions of the ecstatic experiences of the painters themselves. This last idea suggests that the painters were "shamans" who

71

traveled in trance to the spirit world, encountered the divine beings in the form of animals, and returned to paint them. The word *shaman* comes via the Tungus people of Siberia. When the Ice Age ended in Western Europe and the reindeer herds moved east the people followed. Siberia became a center for the same culture that had produced the cave paintings.

Trance States

Did cave art come out of trance journeys? David Lewis-Williams has developed such a theory based on the neuropsychology of people in trance states, comparing their visions to the images in the caves. For instance, people in trance states will see geometric forms and abstract shapes similar to the hundreds of "signs" found in Lascaux and elsewhere. They will see, and talk to, powerful animal beings. They also may encounter "thieranthropes," creatures part human and part animal, or they themselves may become such creatures. While the cave walls display mostly animals, we do find a few mixtures of human and beast – for instance, a humanlike form with a stag's head and hooves. People in trance often begin their journeys by experiencing a descent through a downward tunnel. A cave brings this psychic tunnel into physical reality. Lewis-Williams studied the rock art of the !Kung, in southern Africa, as part of his research. Among the !Kung, shamans draw while in trance, often painting spots and other abstractions that appear to them in their altered states.

What is interesting about this trance theory is its grounding in the body. It looks to direct knowledge of the spirit world as the source of the paintings. But it does not treat such journeys as hallucinations. Instead, it recognizes them as body experiences.

There is a whole – body – of information concerning trance states. Much of it concerns measuring brain electricity and so on. Only recently have Western people begun to treat the journeys themselves as real experiences. Only recently have we started – very nervously – to see the spirit world as a real place, and the beings who inhabit it as something other than projections of our own fantasies. And yet, this is exactly the way people in all cultures have viewed the spirit world for thousands of years.

Believing in the reality of trance journeys calls for two kinds of trust. First, we need to trust that the people who made these journeys over a period of tens of thousands of years knew what they were doing. Second, we need to trust the experience of our *own* bodies. Felicitas D. Goodman, in her book *Where the Spirits Ride the Wind*, has documented a series of experiments using body postures to guide people into different spirit journeys. Goodman studied pictures and statues of tribal and prehistoric people in various positions – sitting with the feet tucked under, or to the side, lying at a particular angle, even wearing specific face paint and clothing. She then instructed her subjects to duplicate these postures as precisely as possible. Once they had done this, they used breathing and rhythmic rattling to induce trance states. Not only did the different postures produce different kinds of experience, but various subjects who used the same posture would report very similar journeys and encounters. Through the body, we can discover the spirit world as a real place.

The Lascaux Shaman

One of Goodman's postures came from Lascaux. The only human image in this great gallery shows a stick figure man lying on his back beside a bison (see *Figure 4*).

Figure 4 The Lascaux "shaman" and bison, Lascaux cave, France, c.15000 B.C.E.

At first he appears to lie flat, but when we look again we see that the body rests at a 37 degree angle. His arms stretch out and his penis stands erect. Goodman constructed platforms so that her subjects might duplicate this pose as closely as possible. In trance, both men and women experienced a great rush of energy, beginning or centered at the genitals, and sometimes emerging through the head or the chest to fly up into the sky. A picture from ancient Egypt, 12,000 years after Lascaux, shows the God Osiris rising to the heavens at the same 37 degree angle as the Lascaux stick figure.

What strikes us most forcibly when we look at the Lascaux drawing is the crude representation of the man. Artists who could paint animals with such anatomical detail that we can distinguish sub-species chose to depict their single human figure in the simplest manner possible – though as Goodman points out, great care was taken with the posture. (For comparison, Kwakiutl rock carvings of North America contain what Campbell Grant calls "small human stick figures" beside "rather realistic bighorn sheep.") This suggests that the artists did not consider their own appearance of any significance. In other words, they were painting journeys to the spirit world, not self-portraits. What mattered was the body's form – the arms out in such a way, the back at such an angle, the genitals excited.

The ideas of David Lewis-Williams and Felicitas Goodman may suggest that the cave painters lacked interest in the ordinary world, caring only for the trance world. But if the cave animals come from spirit journeys, they come from life as well. When we begin to see the divine body as all around us, we begin to heal the split between nature and the "other world," the world of the spirits. And we begin as well to gain a wider sense of "body." For if doing certain physical things – adopting particular postures, sitting in a dark cave, breathing deeply, not eating, and so on – will produce specific reactions, including a sense of *leaving our bodies*, then what we are leaving is really just a limited view of who we are and what is a body.

Fertility Cults and Venuses

The concept of "fertility cults" or "fertility magic" began as an offshoot of the idea of hunting magic. Supposedly, the artists depicted vulvas and created figurines of semi-abstracted women to magically ensure that the game animals would continue to give birth and replenish the herds. Again, we find the image of "primitive" people as simplistic, driven by crude desires, with no real sense of the sacred.

To this day, most texts on Paleolithic art refer to the wonderfully carved figurines, or the relief sculptures, as "Venuses." We read of the "Venus of Willendorf," or the "Venus of Laussel." The term refers to the Roman Goddess of sexual love, known as Aphrodite in Greece. Ironically, the name may carry more meaning than originally intended. For Aphrodite/Venus was a much more powerful Goddess than the playful sex character found in late Greek mythology. She was originally a Goddess of the seas, but also of the sky, of life but also of death. Elinor Gadon tells us that Romans called necropoli, mausoleums, and catacombs "dovecotes," in honor of Venus's sacred companion, the dove. Originally the Goddess of Love symbolized creative power as well as physical joy. We find Her archaic history hinted at in the myth of Her origin, for it describes Her as a generation older than Zeus and the other Olympian Gods.

In one version of Aphrodite's origin She emerges from the sea – with the dove – and comes first to Cyprus. Many mythologists consider that She was originally the Great Goddess of Cyprus, who later became assimilated into Homeric Greek myth. A clay image from Cyprus, dated to 3000 B.C.E. shows a Goddess with huge hips and thin legs coming to a point. This resembles very much those same Paleolithic "Venuses" blessed with Aphrodite's Roman name. The same Cypriot image bears a beaklike nose and huge eyes like a bird.

To call the Stone Age Great Goddess by the name of the Goddess of sexuality returns us to the realization that the Goddess means more than an intellectual abstraction. She is real and physical and present in the world. She has, she *is*, a body. Those figurines, delicately carved and small enough to hold in the hand (necessary for a nomadic culture), in form and style carry the weight and rough power of the mountains. Small as they are, they match the cave wombs in their intensity of meaning.

There is a paradox here. Huge as they are, the caves show us only an aspect of the Goddess's form, a localized vision of Her womb (or more generally, the inside of Her body). But the whole Earth is Her body. By contrast, the hand-held carvings give us an image of the Goddess complete.

Pornography and the Divine Body

A number of Paleolithic drawings and carvings of the female body show only the area from the breasts to the buttocks, without head, arms, or legs. Some prehistorians have suggested that these images constitute Stone Age pornography, like the pictures in contemporary men's magazines. Outraged by such a suggestion, others defend the Goddess's sanctity and insist that these partly abstracted figures signify creative power – as if creativity and sexual desire bear no relation to each other. A few years ago, one of the rougher men's magazines showed pictures of women photographed from the neck to the knees, drawing outrage from feminists about the ultimate objectification of women's bodies. Probably no one on either side of the battle thought of the many Old and New Stone Age carvings of headless and footless women. Is it possible that contemporary impersonal images of female sexuality actually reach back – in a very distorted way – to a sense of women as carriers of a vast power beyond individual lives? Maybe the images of female sex objects hint at an ancient truth, that the power of sexual creativity transcends personality. To show the female form in this way, torso only, raises the body to the level of a symbol, something of universal meaning that nevertheless still takes form and expresses itself within the actual bodies of women.

The problem with pornography does not come from pictures of naked women, but from the assumption that women's sexual parts somehow "belong" to men. The attitude that women exist solely for men's gratification drains the real power from images of women's bodies. It pushes women into unnatural shapes and ridiculous poses. Obscenity does not lie in women's sexuality. It lies in the idea of women as the property of men, to be used, with no identity or purpose of their own.

Rituals of Menstruation and Pregnancy

Most people who write about the "Venuses" and "fertility cults" assume that men created these figurines, to be used by men for men. But what if women created them, for women's rituals? In places as isolated from each other as Africa, India, and among the Eskimos, women use carvings of Goddesses, either without feet, or even with phallic necks, in rituals involving birth or puberty, that is, first menstruation. They insert the figurines into the vagina and remove them as part of the ceremony.

If the Stone Age Europeans used their "Venus" figurines in a similar way, it would open up a whole range of meanings. First of all, it would explain why so many of the statues lack feet. The legs needed to come to a tapering point for easy insertion. And it would give us a new understanding of the statues with phallic necks or other representations of male sexuality. By using these in a ritual for women the male organ becomes a part of the sacred female body, not just in an abstract symbolic sense but in actual practice.

Remember that these figurines were often painted with red ochre. Used in birth or menstruation rituals, they would have joined the individual woman's blood to the blood of the Goddess, so abundant in life and meaning. Consider too that the act imitates sexual intercourse. Done during a birth ritual, this penetration would make the Goddess the symbolic father as well as mother. Such an idea does not belittle the importance of the actual father. Instead, it joins him to the Goddess's body as well, through the similarity of the two actions, intercourse and ritual penetration. And notice that it indicates a knowledge of the necessity of intercourse for conception.

When we consider the idea of Goddess penetration of girls entering puberty, the possibilities become even more provocative. First of all, the ritual would join the young woman's newly flowing blood to the blood of the Goddess, and through the Goddess, to all the long river of women's life-blood. Secondly, it would claim her sexuality for womanhood before she would have given herself to men. It would make it much more difficult for any man ever to take her as his property, to be used solely for his own satisfaction. (Looked at in this light, the fantasy of cavemen clubbing women becomes more and more a projection of modern attitudes towards male–female relations.) And finally, penetration with a Goddess figurine would open the hymen, preparing the girl for intercourse. The sacredness of the ritual would help to raise the action beyond any level of brutality or fear. And of course it would remove the question, so obsessive in later cultures, of a woman's virginity.

The Cave as the Interior Body – Pêch-Mèrle

The sense of the cave as the inside of the Goddess's body strikes us as a provocative idea when we first read about it. It can become very intense when we visit actual caves. In the French cave of Pêch-Mèrle the chambers are large and irregular, the tunnels wide and winding, usually with a view of the vast halls. Stalactites and stalagmites in wondrous formations diminish the sense of bare rock walls. Moreover, a strong presence of ferrous oxide in the walls gives them a red color. Dripping limestone makes them wet as well as red. The effect is highly organic, so much so that my friend Leslie Hunt and I both felt like microbes inside a huge body. The sculptor Christina Biaggi created a "Mound" with an interior form modeled on the inside of a woman's body, after visiting Pêch-Mèrle.

Biaggi visited Pêch-Mèrle in winter after the tourist season, so that she received a private tour. The woman who guided her stressed that Pêch-Mèrle was a "woman cave," pointing out the carved vulvas in the walls. Others have also observed Pêch-Mèrle's female quality. The handprints on the walls match the size of hands from skeletal remains of Paleolithic women. As with the Teaching Rock in Canada, none of the images shows violence in any form. But then, violence appears hardly anywhere in Paleolithic art. Remember that Marshack and others have pointed out that while a few humans carry ceremonial objects, none holds a weapon – an odd situation for art supposedly meant as hunting magic. We will find the same lack of weapons in Cretan art, more than 10,000 years after the Paleolithic.

Alexander Marshack writes of Pêch-Mèrle, "female figures are associated in the cave also with symbols, handprints, series of colored dots, horseshoe arcs, and serpentine meanders," providing an indication that the supposedly abstract signs, here and elsewhere, may have belonged to a Goddess iconography. As mentioned earlier, these same signs show up on the later Goddess statues and vases of the New Stone Age. This does not guarantee that the signs meant the same thing in both time periods. However, in both cases, Pêch-Mèrle and the Neolithic, we see the symbolic forms associated with clear female symbols.

Pêch-Mèrle also contains some of the relatively rare engravings of human female forms. These include a figure with drooping breasts, pointed feet, pronounced buttocks, and a beak-like head which Buffie Johnson describes as the "first known bird deity."

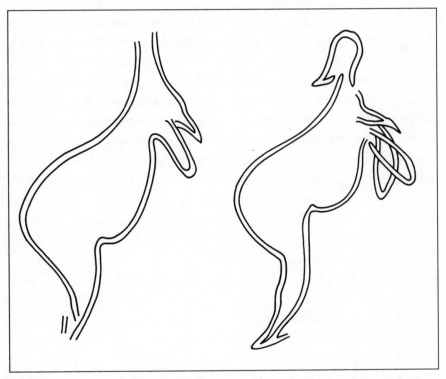

Figure 5 Drawing of headless and bird-headed dancing pregnant women, drawn in clay, from the cave of Pêch-Mèrle, France, c.20000 B.C.E. (after Vicki Noble).

Along with the Bird Goddess we find two headless women (see *Figure 5*). Monica Sjoo and Barbara Mor describe the three figures together as a Triple Goddess presiding over ecstatic dances. When my friend Leslie and I visited the cave the guide showed us a large stone disc by an open flat area. Experiments with stone clubs as drumsticks have demonstrated the possibility that the stone was a drum, and the space a dancing ground.

We should remember that in places such as Haiti and much of Africa people use dance as the primary means to enter a trance. Unlike the trances of shamans, in which the shamans themselves go on journeys, these dance-induced states usually involve possession. That is, a God or Goddess takes over the person's body. We might say that the dancer temporarily withdraws the *self* so that the Spirit can take a physical form.

The cave artists may have used sound to augment the intense power of the paintings. The same *U.S. News and World Report* article mentioned earlier describes provocative experiments with sound in a number of caves. People walked through various caves whistling and mapped where the sounds resonated most powerfully. Almost always these same places displayed paintings on the walls. Lascaux provided even more interesting results. In the areas showing the running bulls and horses, researchers found that clapping their hands caused the sound to echo back and forth, producing the effect of a stampede. Ultimately, the caves may have been places to celebrate the divine body in dance as well as in ecstatic journeys.

4

The Constructed Stone Body – Part 1

The body of the Goddess is the source incarnate.

Marija Gimbutas

*O*ur earliest ancestors were nomads, travelers in small groups who followed the seasonal plants and the herds of reindeer. Settled societies and urban cultures could not develop without a major technological discovery, possibly the most significant of all time – the development of agriculture. Whatever human society may have lost by abandoning the nomadic life, agriculture opened the way for new worlds of experience, including new ways of seeing, and creating, the divine body. The planting revolution bred other revolutions – stable houses, temples, cities – and a group of constructions so remarkable we still can stop and stare in amazement when we come upon them on a country road – megaliths, stone monuments.

Previously, people entered caves to join with the Goddess's body. Now they themselves created caves, and even entire hills, altering the very surface of the Earth. And if the megaliths expressed the Goddess's physical presence, many of them did something more. They encoded a deep and complex scientific knowledge of such things as the movement of the year through its different seasons and the way the Sun year intersected with the phases and cycles of the Moon.

We live by these great beings in the sky. Our food depends on the Sun. Women's fertility follows the Moon. Through the incredible daring and dedication of the megalith builders, the people of the New Stone Age united different aspects of the sacred body, the delicacy and openness of the sky, the mathematical cycles of the Sun and Moon, and the long-standing solidness of rock. In so many of these constructions, from the circles to the mounds to the interior passageways, a particular aesthetic seems to have inspired the builders – the rounded form and opulence of the female body.

The Beginnings of Agriculture

Writers on early human culture offer different times and places for the beginnings of deliberate planting and harvesting. According to Joseph Campbell agriculture begins at around the same time, 10000 B.C.E., in four distinct areas – the Americas, South-east Asia and the Pacific, South-west Asia, and Africa. Focusing on the Middle East, Merlin Stone has written that the earliest evidence of agriculture dates to about 8500 B.C.E., in Syria, Jordan, and Jericho. James Mellaart dates agricultural tools to 9000 B.C.E. Mellaart also writes that people first domesticated sheep at about 8900 B.C.E., and that evidence exists of trade (in obsidian) as early as 8300 B.C.E., between Anatolia, in Turkey, and the city of Jericho near the West Bank of the Jordan river.

In most of Europe these vast cultural changes did not come until some time later. The academic discipline of archaeology comes out of European culture, which is one reason why we know so much more about early European and Middle Eastern agricultural societies than we do about cultures in Asia, Africa, or the Americas.

Another reason is the megaliths themselves, the vast number of mounds, stone circles, barrows, dolmens, cairns, and other constructions stretching from Ireland and Britain across Western Europe to Scandinavia, Malta, Sicily, Crete, and beyond. The megaliths command our attention, inspiring us with awe and curiousity. Who actually built them? What purpose did they serve? Why did they appear at the same time as agriculture? And above all, what do they mean?

Megaliths Beyond Europe

There are megalithic and earthen remains in other places. We find stone circles, dolmens, standing stones, and other structures in New England, Alaska, Madagascar, Peru, the New Hebrides, and so on. The process of colonization, however, has hidden or even destroyed them. What is now the state of Ohio in the United States once contained thousands of burial mounds of a people extinct by the time the first Europeans arrived. The later Indians were not the mound builders, but neither did they destroy the mounds. European farmers, however, plowed almost all of them under, so that now only a tiny fraction remain, preserved in state and national parks. In their gently swelling shape they too invoke the image of a pregnant belly.

Most Americans have heard of Stonehenge and seen photos of it. Very few know of the Ohio mounds, or the quarter mile sculpture of a serpent in southern Ohio, or Cahokia Plain in Illinois, with its astronomically-aligned earth mound two and a half times the size of the Great Pyramid.

Knowing of the intimacy of serpents and Goddesses in so much of the world, can we guess that these elegant sculptures speak of a time and a culture when no angry God had "put enmity" between the woman and the serpent?

The Chaco Canyon Observatory

Americans may have heard that the sunrise on the winter solstice penetrates the chamber mound of Newgrange in Ireland, just as the first rays of the *summer* solstice touch the heelstone at Stonehenge. However, very few will have heard of Chaco Canyon in New Mexico. There the Anasazi people of 1,000 years ago created a solar calendar in stone, rediscovered in 1977 by Anna Sofaer, an artist. On top of a 430-foot-high butte the Anasazi incised two spiral petroglyphs (pictures carved in stone), sheltered by three leaning slabs of rock. (We will see in a moment that the spiral, along with its other symbolism, charts the apparent path of the Sun through the year.) At noon each day light passes through slits between the slabs. At the summer solstice, with the noon Sun at its highest point in the sky, a dagger of light pierces the center of the larger spiral. At the winter solstice two daggers touch the outsides of the spiral. At the equinoxes light pierces the center of the smaller spiral. Further, a shadow passes through the center of the large spiral every 19 years, on the day the sun rises at a position reached by the full Moon only that one time in a 19-year cycle. The shadow bisects the spiral's 19 rings (the Moon's path also forms spirals), and aligns with a pecked groove. The Moon itself casts a shadow tangential to the far left edge of the spiral.

Like most other Americans I knew nothing of this wonder of art and science in my own land. I am indebted for the above description of Chaco Canyon to Lucy Lippard, in her book *Overlay*. Lippard points out that the creation of this calendar involved detailed knowledge of astronomy, the physics of curved surfaces, and precise surveying to get the carvings in exactly the right place at exactly the right size. We can add that it also involved a desire to root the changing body of the sky in the permanence of rock.

Despite such wonders in my own country, this chapter will focus primarily on the Neolithic period in Europe. Having lived in Europe during the research for this book, I visited primarily European sites and, as mentioned above, the archaeological record for Europe is much more detailed than for anywhere else.

The Beauty of the Megaliths

The European megaliths range from the grandeur of Avebury Stone Circle (so large that a modern village actually sits in the center of it) to Stonehenge, to stone circles only a few feet across in the fields outside Sligo, Ireland. They range from the covered mounds of Newgrange and Knowth, each more than an acre, to small artificial hillocks in Scandinavia, to cairns in Ireland hardly big enough for someone to crawl inside. Even the individual stones can carry great mystery. Massive, weathered by thousands of years of wind and water, they evoke strange shapes, like images out of dreams (see *Plate 11*).

Visiting the megaliths, especially the circles, grounds us in the long and mysterious history of humanity. However much we can investigate or intuit about their meaning and purpose, their builders, like the cave painters before them, left no records other than the works themselves. The circles and mounds simply exist, by now joined to the landscape, part of the great body of ground and sky and water. Made of stones fitted together or of individual boulders, either bare or covered with dirt, they give off an image of simplicity, despite the complexity of their construction. They seem wholly to belong to where they are. If we enter them, go inside the mounds, or sit in the circles, we too become attached to this joining of human history with the cycles of life and death, the turning year, and the body of our Mother, the Earth.

Mysteries of the Megaliths

The European megaliths have inspired many theories as to their origins and purpose. British legend tells us that the Welsh magician/prophet Myrrdin, known in French as Merlin, magically constructed Stonehenge for King Arthur's father. For people of later cultures, who had lost the sophisticated technology of the Stone Age, it must have seemed as if only magic could transport and raise such huge stones to their proper places.

Later accounts held that the Druids made Stonehenge, where they supposedly practiced human sacrifice. When people realized that the megaliths pre-dated such cultures as the Celtic Druids, they then assumed that the builders constructed them under the influence of Egypt or other "advanced" Mediterranean cultures. Only recently, with radiocarbon and tree calibration dating have archaeologists found that there are, in fact, three Stonehenges, built over 1,500 years, with the oldest built about 3100 B.C.E., centuries before the pyramids.

The debates about megaliths continue. To paraphrase Wallace Stevens's poem, *Thirteen Ways of Looking at a Blackbird*, here are thirteen ways of looking at a megalith, each of them a contemporary theory to be found in one or more books.

A megalith forms a giant sculpture.
A megalith marks a place of sacred power in the Earth.
A megalith pins down fluid Earth energy.
A megalith generates "ultrasound" and electrical energy through quartz crystals activated by light.
A megalith is a computer, tracking eclipses, extreme alignments of Sun and Moon, appearances of planets and constellations, and other events in the sky.

A megalith marks territorial boundaries.

A megalith harmonizes aesthetic landscape elements.

A megalith is a festival site.

A megalith is a burial site.

A megalith is a rebirth site.

A megalith is a sacrifice site.

A megalith marks a convergence point of ley lines.

A megalith indicates an acupuncture point on the planetary body.

The proponents of these different views often compete with each other, as if the megalith builders could have had only one purpose in mind. The advocates of astronomy insist that the arcs and circles on Irish passage mounds or on the standing stones in Gavrinis, Brittany signify only Sun and Moon patterns. They scorn the suggestion that the images form anything anthropomorphic or religious. Others insist, just as strongly, that the arcs symbolize regeneration by water. And many (though not all) archaeologists consider the engraved arcs mere decoration, "doodles" (see *Plate 12*).

Astro-Archaeology

In recent years, attention has focused on "astro-archaeology," the discovery of extensive alignments between stone circles and celestial events such as the solstices and equinoxes. Gerald Hawkins, whose book *Stonehenge Decoded* first brought these ideas to the general public, describes Stonehenge as a giant computer for tracking eclipses, extreme positions of the Sun and Moon, and, of course, the famous midsummer sunrise.

For example, the full Moon does not rise and set in the same place each month, but moves in a cycle which takes, on average, 18.61 years to complete. Because the number includes a fraction (the .61), and because the time actually varies between one cycle and the next, Hawkins calculates that the best whole number to track the Moon's orbit over several decades is 56 years. The Stonehenge site contains a circle of 56 holes, known as Aubrey holes, after their 17th-century discoverer. Markers moved from hole to hole over 56 years could have charted the Moon's progress.

Hawkins writes that it took the invention of computers for modern science to process all the data required to determine Stonehenge's full range of alignments. We also might add that it took a giant leap of thought. The ideology of primitivism makes it hard for us to credit Stone Age people with such complex knowledge. Even today, the argument against astro-archaeology often runs along the theme that prehistoric people *couldn't* have done something so complicated.

Not all megaliths align with the sky. In his book *Beyond Stonehenge* Hawkins describes the testing needed before we can claim that a particular site tracks astronomical events. But even if we do accept the larger stone circles as computers, this does not really explain why people made them. Knowledge of the eclipses, or the Moon's cycles, or even the solstices and equinoxes, does not really serve any practical purposes. For instance, by the summer solstice on 21 June, the crops should be long since planted in the ground.

Scientific knowledge for its own sake is a possibility (just as art for art's sake is a possibility when considering cave art). Some of the largest scientific projects in modern society, such as the "super-colliders," do not serve any immediate purpose. Breaking apart nuclei helps us to understand the first moments of creation but does not help us to function in our daily lives. Did Stone Age people look on knowledge as a benefit in itself, worthy of the vast investment of resources and labor required to create a Stonehenge?

Let us try out an assumption. Let us assume that rituals took place at Stonehenge and other megalithic sites, that the events in the sky all fit into a religious as well as a scientific pattern. Some people might find it odd that people capable of precise astronomical observations, and complex surveying, and monumental feats of engineering would see the whole thing in terms of God/dess and ceremonies and mythic stories. But maybe our own culture is odd. We have split science and religion off from each other, as if religion lies only in books and emotions, and not in the physical world. As if a scientific search for the beginnings of the universe has nothing to do with religion.

The Newgrange Sun and the Lunatic Fringe

Many professional archaeologists disdain the suggestions – and serious research – of non-archaeologists, lumping them all together as "the lunatic fringe," of which P. R. Giot writes, "As they are a permanent nuisance to archaeologists it is often difficult to give them due credit for the few ideas one owes them." (Giot, "The Megaliths of France," in *The Megalithic Monuments of Western Europe*, ed. C. Renfrew.) But the archaeologists have their own prejudices. If amateurs too readily accept new ideas, perhaps professionals too readily dismiss them – and some old ideas as well.

Just as the first appearance of the midsummer Sun touches the heelstone of Stonehenge in England, so the midwinter sunrise sends a strong shaft of light down the central chamber of Newgrange passage mound in Ireland. The light travels slowly, moving down the floor until it reaches the back wall, where it rises up in a vertical beam, stays there for a time, then retreats back out the way it came, leaving the observer once more in the total darkness of this remarkable artificial cave. When the mound was built, 5,000 years ago, its makers aligned it so carefully that the light would enter on mornings before and after midwinter as well, each day touching a precise place on the wall, so that even if clouds should obscure the midwinter Sun, the people would still know the day by counting from the marks. Since that time, the Earth's tilt has shifted slightly, making the effect less perfect, but still clear and visible.

From 1849 Newgrange was excavated enough for anyone to witness this yearly event. In 1867 George Russell, who wrote as A. E., described a vision of the God Aengus appearing as light in "a lofty cross-shaped cave" which may have described Newgrange. By the turn of the century the beam of light had become a "legend," spread by the caretaker, Robert Hickey, who took local visitors to observe it, and told visitors about it. Moreover, in 1909 Sir Norman Lockyear, Director of the Solar Physics Observatory, wrote of Newgrange as orientated to the winter solstice in his book *Stonehenge and Other British Stone Monuments Astronomically Considered*. Around the same time, W. Y. Evans-Wentz, an anthropologist studying Irish folklore, described Newgrange and the mounds at Gavrinis as solar orientated. (According to Marija Gimbutas, Gavrinis primarily aligns with the Moon's extreme positions.) Lockyer and Evans-Wentz did not view the light, or write about it. But Hickey did, and showed others, year after year.

And yet, as late as 1960, Glyn Daniel, perhaps the most distinguished megalithic archaeologist of his time, wrote about this "legend:" "It is a strange wild-cat account which needs quoting almost *in toto* as an example of the jumble of nonsense and wishful thinking indulged in by those who prefer the pleasures of the irrational and the joys of unreason to the hard thinking that archaeology demands." The strange thing about this dismissal of Hickey's account is that all they had to do was look. Only in 1969 did an archaeologist named Michael J. O'Kelly enter Newgrange before dawn at midwinter and observe the light. When he published his observations he met with great resistance, including suggestions that the light was a chance occurence, and even accusations that O'Kelly had faked the evidence.

This account comes from Martin Brennan's book *The Stars and the Stones* (to give Professor Daniel due credit on this question, the paperback edition of Brennan's book includes a positive endorsement from Daniel). Brennan sometimes goes quite far in his claims, and his earlier writing puts forward some extreme ideas, but his work has included remarkable discoveries of complex solar and lunar alignments throughout Ireland. Most of these discoveries came from direct observations made by Brennan and Jack Roberts (both Brennan and Roberts are artists, putting them in the company of such people as Merlin Stone, Buffie Johnson, Vincent Scully, Monica Sjoo, Barbara Mor, Dorothy Cameron, Anna Sofaer, and Michael Dames). Not only did their findings meet tremendous resistance; they often had to sneak in to the various mounds to observe the effects of the different alignments ("archaeological espionage" Brennan calls it). And once again, those who tried to discredit Brennan's and Robert's work needed only to repeat the experiment – to see with their own eyes.

Body Forms

Brennan himself rejects the idea of any anthropomorphic representation in the mounds. And yet, the form is not strictly functional. The passages do need to be a certain length for the light to penetrate correctly, but it is not clear that they need to be cruciform, a shape which sacred architecture has always used to portray the human body. And the great size of the mounds, let alone their rounded shape, implies some symbolic significance, if not gynecomorphism (shaped like a woman). The full mound of Newgrange covers vastly more space than would be needed to cover over the interior. The passage reminds us of a cave in a hill – or a womb.

As well as large mounds, Ireland contains many "court cairns," so named for the semicircular entrance formed by two curved rows of large stones. These too contain that interior form like a body with the arms and legs out. We see it as well in West Kennet Long Barrow, the rectangular passage mound near Avebury Stone Circle in England. And we find it in Neolithic shrines as far away as Poland and what used to be Yugoslavia.

A Year Day

One of Brennan's discoveries concerns Dowth, the third in the series of giant mounds which includes Knowth and Newgrange. Unlike the other two sites, Dowth has not been restored, so that it appears as a small hill, green with trees and high grass. When we look closer we find that this natural looking hill contains a "cave" at its base, with an iron gate blocking the entrance. And if we examine the bare rock at the base of the grassy hill we discover carved spirals.

According to Brennan, the light that penetrates Dowth comes from the midwinter sunset, not the sunrise as at Newgrange. Perhaps the people who built it observed a ritual "day" over the course of the year. Such a year-long ceremony might have taken place at special intervals, say, every seventh year. (The importance of the number 7 in religion is neither arbitrary nor "archetypal" but derives from the seven "planets" – including the Sun and Moon – visible to ancient peoples without telescopes.)

The year day would have begun at Newgrange at dawn on the winter solstice, continued throughout the year at different sites (possibly uniting different communities throughout the island), with special events at Knowth for the equinoxes. Knowth, the largest and possibly most complex of the mounds, has two opposite passages, one opening east, the other west, to mark both the sunrise and sunset on the two equinoxes – or perhaps the sunrise on the vernal equinox and the sunset on the autumnal equinox as the "year day" approached its end. Finally, the ritual day would end once again at midwinter, but now at sunset, at Dowth.

We can never test such a speculation. I freely acknowledge it as fanciful, but it does, I think, give a symmetry to the great network of monuments. And it ties in with the way other cultures have viewed the world, and the great solar events of the year, as a single creation, alive and filled with sacred power.

The archaeologists prefer to avoid such fancies (as they should, since they need to deal with actual evidence). Contemporary archaeologists have chosen to ignore issues of religion (not to mention the evidence of folklore) in favor of concentrating on the economic and social conditions of ancient peoples. In the book *The Megalithic Monuments of Western Europe* edited by C. Renfrew, Michael J. O'Kelly quotes an article by A. Fleming published in 1969, the same year that O'Kelly himself confirmed the light in Newgrange: "The mother-goddess has detained us for too long; let us disengage ourselves from her embrace." To which those of us exploring the (re)emerging Goddess religion might respond simply: "Let us not."

Tombs and Archaeologists

Professional archaeology describes the megaliths throughout Europe as "tombs," sometimes describing Neolithic culture as death-obsessed, or centered around a cult of the dead. To a non-archaeologist the insistence on seeing every monument as a tomb may seem obsessive. Excavators have found skeletal and cremated remains in some megalithic structures, but by no means all. Writing of circular structures in Italy Ruth Whitehouse (in *The Megalithic Monuments of Western Europe*) cites Lilliu's observation that only 50 or so showed signs of burial use. "Indeed," Whitehouse writes, "only three tombs have actually yielded skeletal material." Whitehouse goes on to say, "Most of the dolmens ... have yielded neither skeletal remains nor artifacts ... We do not know whether the dolmens were intended for single or collective burial." She does not seem to consider the possibility that they were not intended for burial at all.

The society that built Newgrange presumably used it for hundreds of years. Excavations in 1967 revealed burnt and unburnt human bones – for a combined total of about five people. Five for a structure so complex and huge. In *A Concise Guide to Newgrange* Claire O'Kelly describes these remains as "sufficient to show that the tomb was used for burial and was not, as has been suggested, a cenotaph or a temple." Five in a vast hill built to catch precisely the winter sunrise over thousands of years

In many cases, no one has dated the human remains found at megalithic sites, leaving open the possibility that later cultures, or individual communities, used them as burial places. But even if the remains belong to people from the original culture why should this make them primarily tombs? Brennan points out that Westminster Cathedral contains far more bodies than Newgrange, from a much shorter period of use. Would we consider these remains "sufficient" to claim that Westminister is not used for religious purposes? Those who see all the monuments as tombs argue that grave robbers removed the evidence. But grave robbers usually seek gold and jewels. Why would they cart away bones? And even if it's *possible* that grave robbers did this, there is no actual evidence.

The tomb assumption has a long pedigree. Celtic legend described Newgrange as the burial site of the ancient kings of Tara. For centuries, people in Wiltshire, England considered Silbury Hill a giant tomb for an imagined King Sil. And even though people usually did not consider the stone circles or dolmens as cemeteries, many thought of them as places of human sacrifice. However, these beliefs came from the attitudes of later cultures who had nothing at all to do with the monuments themselves.

The term "cult of the dead" might refer more to our own culture than the Neolithic. What other society has ever buried each corpse in its own private plot of land, in ornamental metal and velvet coffins, embalmed, dressed, and made up to resemble life, and honored with a large slab of carved marble?

Questioning the tomb assumption for megaliths does not mean that people never thought of them as burial places. Obviously, some megalithic structures did serve primarily for burial. Of 76 "tombs" on the Orkney Islands only 26 contained human bones. However, two of these contained, respectively, 157 and 341 people, enough, Marija Gimbutas writes, "to represent all the dead of an entire community." We question the tomb assumption so that we might see a variety of possibilities, scientific as well as religious, which may have co-existed in the minds of the builders. If mounds *were* used as tombs, then the form chosen – and an alignment towards the sunrise on the equinoxes, or midwinter – suggests an idea of rebirth, with the circular mound as the womb, and the passage as the birth canal.

Marking Place

The archaeologist Colin Renfrew suggests that the monuments acted as "territorial markers," signifying that a particular group dominated an area of land. It is a little hard to see how this might work, how a stone circle, say, would indicate what portion of land it was "claiming," or why some places required several huge mounds or circles quite close to each other, and others nothing, or why a cairn would suffice in one place, a dolmen in another, and a giant passage mound in a third. Yet why should we dismiss the idea out of hand as some advocates of megalithic spirituality seem to do?

People often feel a need to mark their presence. In New England and eastern New York State, countless homes, churches, banks, and shopping centers display fairly large (and often beautiful) standing stones, or even whole lines or semicircles of stones, by their driveways, lawns, entrances, or parking lots. In the tiny village of North Salem, New York, one may view a huge boulder, some 90 tons, shaped somewhat like the head of a snake or a turtle, resting on several small limestone rocks, all conically shaped and arranged in an isosceles triangle. Advocates of North American megaliths consider this a dolmen (and some suggest that people passed under it for ritual rebirth). Official archaeology views it as the chance remains of a glacier. Dolmen or not, the boulder stands very close to the local church, and before the church stand two magnificent upright stones, like a gateway to the spiritual world.

Why couldn't the megaliths function both as markers and spiritual realities? Human beings appear to need to imprint themselves on the land. As with the handprints in rock art (handprints also appear on the walls of Çatal Hüyük, including the print of a child's hand on a statue of the

Goddess's body), the much larger stone constructions may have established a place as sacred territory. They may represent a need to make the invisible body of spiritual power visible in the world.

Handprints in a vast cave carry a tentative quality, a small gesture of presence. By the time of the Neolithic, human beings in Europe had gained in confidence, so that in England they could alter the landscape itself, through the construction of entire hills, such as Silbury, or by sculpting the side of an existing hill into a maze form, changing the natural land into something human-made, as at Glastonbury (*see* Chapter 5 for the Glastonbury "maze").

The idea of "wilderness" as something untouched and pure appears to be a relatively modern, European concept, in which we create a duality in our civilized world – that is, places inhabited by proper humans, and the wild, inhabited by animals and savages. With the urbanization of the world, we have become nostalgic for "wilderness," but this is really only the other side of that older belief in nature as dangerous, evil, alien – and female.

Many cultures have not set up a dichotomy of safe, human territory and the wilderness out there. *Seeing the whole world as the body, the whole world becomes sacred.* This may lead to a desire to understand the landscape and map it very precisely, in the way mystics will *Shiur Komah*, "measure the body" of God (*see* Chapter 1). This mapping is spiritual, but also practical, for people need to know the patterns of nature. They need to know how to find game, and water. They need to know where each group's territory begins and ends, not only so that they can avoid conflicts, but also so that they can take care of the land and be responsible for it. These practical needs do not exclude, but rather complement, the spiritual urge to join our own bodies to the bodies of the land. Or, to turn this around, we can say that perceiving the landscape as the divine body provides a powerful context for the practical value of mapping territory.

The Australian Aborigine Songlines

The Australian Aborigines consider every feature of the landscape as the body of a "Dreaming," a mythic ancestor who has gone into the land, and now appears as a waterhole, or a hill, or a bush. Every feature becomes

94

mapped. The people know the land intimately, and can travel, sometimes alone, over vast distances, by following these maps, which are both precise and spiritual at the same time.

In recent decades the elegant, abstracted paintings of the Aboriginal people have become famous around the world. The paintings portray the landscape in great symbolic detail. And yet the Aboriginal people do not use them for their maps. They do not map with pictures, but with songs. This may seem odd to people of European descent, to such an extent that we consider a journey by a songmap almost a psychic feat, a variety of magic or telepathy. But why should a diagram on a piece of paper work any better as a map than a song? Any map is a human creation, a metaphor for the world. Its value lies in how precisely and accurately the metaphor describes the territory. Dolores La Chapelle writes that Californian desert Indians followed trails which they mapped with songs. Evidence exists of commerce and migration across the Pacific Ocean in prehistoric times, all the way from New Guinea to the Americas. Some people believe that the sailors who crossed these vast distances, going from island to island, used songmaps to follow the stars and currents.

As well as guiding journeys, the "songlines," as the English writer Bruce Chatwin called them, define territory. Tribal groups or individuals will sit at boundaries and sing their songs, sharing these according to a complex system of personal and group responsibility. The system works practically and efficiently on many levels and has helped the people live for tens of thousands of years in a variety of environments, often harsh. It is also sacred. *The practical and the sacred do not contradict, but support each other*. The sacred power of the songs enables people to remember them, and gives them the authority which has lasted for so long. In contemporary Australia, the national government has accepted sacred art and songs as testimony in land rights cases.

The Australian Aborigines live in a land and a culture very far removed in time and place from the European megalith builders, and yet we can learn from them that seeing the land as the divine body enhances, rather than excludes, a practical relationship with the Earth.

Spirals of the Sun and Moon

In our time, science has labored to separate itself from religion and give a "pure" picture of physical realities. This situation arose partly because religion separated itself from science in the Middle Ages and the Renaissance, and the official doctrines of the Church became hardened, no longer concerned with reflecting what people actually knew of existence. This in turn derived from a religion based on a transcendent God, who is more important than the mere physical world, and knowledge of whom comes from a book rather than from observing nature. To free itself from such stultification, science took all religion as superstition. Only now have we begun to discover the great depths of observation coded into Neolithic and other "primitive" religious structures.

When scientific knowledge attaches itself to the divine body of nature, when it becomes an aspect of that body, it gains in power as well as meaning. Images taken from nature become sacred symbols and then those symbols in turn lead back to a more sophisticated understanding of the world. Knowledge moves not in a straight line but in a spiral, opening up from a central observation to wider and wider awareness. The image is appropriate, not only because we find spirals in sacred art all over the world, but also because the spiral itself is an example of the mixture of scientific knowledge and spiritual symbolism.

Earlier we saw how spiral images may have derived from snails and other natural forms, from sea shells to galaxies. Spiral imagery may also track the patterns of the Sun and Moon. The Sun rising and setting implies a circle (with the bottom half of the circle invisible), but this circle gets larger or smaller with the change in the Sun's position each day. As we move from winter solstice to summer solstice the circle begins at a wider point each day, so that the apparent motion actually forms a clockwise spiral (when facing south, the direction of the Sun). In the other half of the year the apparent spiral stays clockwise but shrinks rather than expands.

A more complex spiral develops if we chart the different position of the Sun at noon over the course of a year. Charles Ross – once again an artist – has mapped the Sun by using a lens on his New York studio roof to burn a mark on wood every day at noon. Arranging all the marks in order reveals a double spiral, reversing direction from winter to summer (see *Figure 6*). The double spiral form appears on Irish passage mounds. It also formed a migration symbol for Indigenous Americans in the south-west United States (that is, a marker along the path they would take through the course of the year, the same period of time the Sun takes to create that double spiral image).

The Moon's path is more subtle, for even though it rises in the east and sets in the west its path through the month forms, as Martin Brennan says, "a spiral whose successive loops cross the ecliptic in a westward, anti-clockwise motion opposed to the direction of the sun and planets" (Brennan, *The Stars and the Stone*).

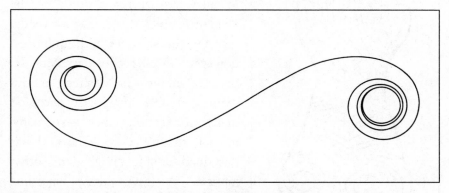

Figure 6 Drawing of the path of the Sun through the course of a year. Construction by Charles Ross, "Sunlight Convergence, Solar Burn: The Year Shape," 1972.

We can interpret opposed spirals as representations of the Sun and Moon. Various spirals, therefore, trace the patterns of our most important heavenly bodies. But the Sun and Moon are not simply objects in the sky giving off light and heat, they are also symbols. Sun and Moon signify the different qualities of day and night. They represent simplicity and complexity, rationality and intuition, and in some cultures, male and female. At a more complex psychological level, motion that spirals clockwise connects us to the Sun. Clockwise spirals evoke involvement with the world and with raising up energy. Counter-clockwise spirals can bring separation, disengagement with the outer world (a feeling of "turning inward") or a release of energy. And they do this on a subconscious level. We get this reaction in body movement, with spiraling dances. Spirals will often arise spontaneously in people's minds during meditation. This intuitive emotional response to spirals happens because of the Sun and Moon, and what they mean in our lives. These *symbols* – the Sun, the Moon, their movements and their spiraling paths – are not just intellectual. They affect our bodies in ways both conscious and unconscious.

Figure 7 Drawing of spirals on a figurine of the Goddess from the Cucuteni – a culture of Romania, c.4300 B.C.E. (after Gimbutas).

Double spiral images occur in many places, such as the temples of Malta, where there is little suggestion of astronomical alignments. (Paul I. Micallef has written a study of the Maltese Temple, Mnajdra, as a calendar marking the solstices and equinoxes; however, Micallef considers Mnajdra unique among the Maltese monuments.) Double spirals also occur on many Goddess figurines – so many, in fact, that O. G. S. Crawford has described double spirals (and other forms) as "the Eye Goddess," suggesting that where "oculi" forms occur by themselves they signify the Goddess through her power of sight.

On the Irish stones, by Newgrange and Knowth and lesser mounds and cairns, single and double spirals (and sometimes triple) appear without any surrounding imagery. In other places, however, they appear directly on the Goddess's body. A marvelous figure from Romania, in the Cucuteni A period of *c.* 4300 B.C.E., shows opposed spirals on the buttocks (see *Figure 7*).

When we think of mounds and the female body we think primarily of breasts or the pregnant belly. However, Paleolithic and Neolithic art often emphasized the buttocks, sometimes exaggerating them to a suggestion of hills or mountains. With most mammals the male mounts the female from behind. Early hominids may have done the same, with the practice continuing down to *Homo sapiens*. In sexual intercourse, then, the buttocks would rise up before the entrance to the mysterious darkness of the vagina, the source of life and the gateway to the invisible secrets of the female body. The opposed spirals on the Cucuteni Goddess's buttocks *might* have signified the most powerful presence of the visible light world, the Sun and Moon, at the very opening to the invisible place of creative darkness.

The Constructed Stone Body – Part 2

Our hearts are sore for the outrage done to the order of ancient goddesses.

Jane Ellen Harrison

*W*hen we think of the New Stone Age we think of the circles and the mounds, and maybe of Hollywood fantasies of people in long robes performing rituals under the Moon. But less obvious aspects of this distant world call to us as well. It was a time when the Paleolithic worship of animals and the female body merged, so that along with statues of the Goddess as a woman we find the Goddess worshipped as a bee, or a cow. And beyond the animal world we find Her embodied in certain trees, and even human-made objects, such as knots. It was an age in which humanity entered a revolutionary time of invention, developing both technologies and social structures that would make all later societies, including our own, possible. And, most startling of all, it was an age when people did not kill each other.

When we look at this time, and its astonishing record of non-violence, we find ourselves asking several questions. First and above all, did it really exist? Or are we creating a fantasy out of partial evidence and our own yearning? Could a culture of human beings worshipping a Goddess really get by without murder or war? And how did it all end? Did we move from a peaceful matrifocal world to a violent patriarchy because of some necessary step of evolution, or did it all somehow just go wrong, becoming lost in a tragedy we cannot even begin to measure?

The Age of Non-Violence

Neolithic culture has received a great deal of attention in contemporary Goddess religion. There are several reasons for this. Like the earlier Paleolithic period, the remains from the Neolithic period abound with female images, from paintings on the walls of shrines to great statues to small figurines. And then there are the megaliths, with their more abstracted evocation of the female in rounded forms and womblike interiors. Most striking of all, however, even revolutionary, this period of several thousand years shows virtually no evidence of war, aggression, or daily violence.

If these people really existed without violence, we can guess that they accomplished this through a religion centered around motherhood. We also can guess that such peacefulness would have come from a view of the world rooted in the Earth and our own bodies.

The lack of evidence of violence in the Neolithic period is so complete it becomes almost hard to believe. Wherever excavators have found mass burials, either of large communities or small groups over a long period of time, virtually none of the bodies shows any sign of violent death – not from war, not from raids, not even from fighting among neighbors. Possibly the people of that time considered violent death a defilement and did not bury victims of violence with everybody else. However, no one has found any evidence of this, and even if it were true, it would indicate a profound distaste for violence. Compare such an attitude with the glorification of heroic killing that comes with later cultures.

The evidence for non-violence goes beyond individual deaths. The Neolithic city excavated near Çatal Hüyük, in Anatolia, Turkey (usually called simply Çatal Hüyük), is one of the oldest cities in the world, dating from 7250–6150 B.C.E. Archaeologist James Mellaart found evidence of 800 years of continuous habitation. Not once does the archaeological record show signs of a sack or a massacre – not once in 800 years.

The builders of Neolithic Çatal Hüyük, like the builders of many other New Stone Age cities, did not even seem to think of defense as a criterion when they chose their site. High hill forts surrounded by walls do not appear until the Bronze Age, when Indo-European invaders overthrew the earlier civilization which had lasted for over 3,000 years. In some instances, the settlers of a town seem to have based their site primarily on aesthetics, the desire for pleasing surroundings. In Crete, which carried Neolithic social and religious structures into a later period of development, cities and palaces were built on sites in harmony with particular landscape formations. Often, this left them in very vulnerable positions militarily, and yet we do not find any walls or fortifications. Other considerations for siting Neolithic settlements included good water and soil, and convenient pasture land for newly domesticated animals.

Glastonbury Tor and Avebury

Where later societies put great resources into fortification the Neolithic people built monuments. Glastonbury Tor, in England, is a striking hill made famous through its association with the legend of King Arthur. At some point in the past, people accented the hill's natural beauty by shaping one side of it into a series of terraces. The terraces form a kind of maze that some people believe was used for processional dances. (Contemporary neo-pagans have staged joyous processions at Glastonbury, see *Plate 13*.) A pamphlet about Glastonbury Tor puts forward very interesting arguments that the Stone Age people must have done the carving. Firstly, the hill is not suitable for defense or agriculture and therefore must have served a religious purpose. Secondly, later cultures had to spend too much time, resources, and energy defending themselves against invaders. We might add that later cultures did not dedicate themselves to what we might call sacred aesthetics – transforming an entire hillside into a ceremonial dancing ground.

As the Cretans harmonized the landscape through the building of a palace, or the Australian Aborigines mapped every aspect of the land as a divine ancestor, or the Old Stone Age painters used the form of the cave wall to bring out images of animals, so the sculpting of the Glastonbury hillside implies seeing a divine power within the land and sensing the need for human action to bring that hidden body directly into reality.

The Neolithic builders created monuments to rival the hills themselves, an activity that required a massive dedication of resources. Avebury Stone

Circle forms one part of a group of monuments including Silbury Hill and a long rectangular mound called West Kennet Long Barrow. Archaeologists estimate that it must have taken 1.5 million work hours to construct the Avebury complex.

Non-violence and Art

In the Neolithic period we do not find the glorification of war and killing that is so prominent in later societies. At Çatal Hüyük 150 paintings have survived on the walls. Art clearly mattered in this very early city (Mellaart stresses that it was indeed a city, not a settlement), and, of those 150 paintings not one shows battle, war, or torture.

In Crete too, the elegant art found throughout the ruins shows no scenes of war. Archaeologists have found weapons from these places. James Mellaart reports evidence from Çatal Hüyük for the use of the slingshot, bow and arrow, lance, and spear. But all of these are hunting tools as well as weapons, so we cannot assume they represent evidence of warfare. More significantly, no weapons figure in the art. According to Stylianos Alexiou, in the book *Minoan Civilization*, Crete had a navy and fought sea battles. On Crete itself, however, fortifications remained unknown, and no sea battles appear in the art. The Cretans may have battled outsiders, but they lived peacefully with each other.

As well as showing no evidence of violence, Neolithic art shows no glorification of a chief or ruler, whether male or female. In Cretan wall frescoes and seals we mostly see groups of people acting together in such activities as bull dances or sacrifices. Single females are usually Goddesses, or possibly priestesses, rather than queens. Only one image of an individual male appears, and this figure, a graceful young man holding flowers, hardly suggests the all-powerful "King Minos" described by later patriarchal Greek legend.

Social Equality and the Question of Matriarchy

Along with the indications that there was an absence of violence we find signs of social equality. Neolithic remains show no indications of slavery, so common in later cultures. They do not show a structure of an all-powerful (and all-rich) God-king, or ruling class, and they do not seem to show large inequalities between men and women.

This is a difficult subject. In some cases we find clear signs of women in a superior position, so that we face the possibility that what we have seen for the past 5,000 years was a simple turnaround of what had gone before. When historians and anthropologists first began to investigate the issue of pre-patriarchal cultures they made two assumptions. First, they assumed that such cultures formed an early evolutionary stage in humanity's development, neccessary at a certain point, but just as necessary to be overthrown in favor of a more civilized, more dynamic patriarchy. In fact, as we shall see later in this chapter, the Neolithic period was possibly the most inventive period in human history.

The second assumption concerned the idea of "matriarchy." If men didn't rule and hold down women, then women must have ruled and held down men. Modern feminist scholarship has developed a different model for Neolithic culture, that of a "matrifocal" or "matristic" society. These two terms refer to the idea of a "woman-centered" rather than woman-ruled society. (Actually, to be more precise, "matrifocal" means "mother-centered", and "patriarchy" means literally "leadership by fathers.") In such a situation, spiritual thought and practices revolved around a Goddess, and name and property passed from mother to daughter.

In this model councils of women made decisions for the clan, but they neither enslaved men nor excluded them from power in society or decision-making. The model depends partly on the idea of the Mother Goddess loving Her female and male children equally, and partly on those images of males that do appear in Neolithic art, such as a painting in Çatal Hüyük of a man and woman embracing.

The Burial Record

Burial, and the honors given to individuals and groups can tell us a great deal about the relative positions of different members of society. The evidence of the burial record does not give a consistent picture with regard to the status of men and women in the European Neolithic period. In some places, we find very little distinction between male and female.

In others, we see evidence of females highly honored and males almost disregarded. Nowhere, however, do we find such extreme differences as those that came afterwards, in the era of warlords and kings.

The Sesklo, Starçevo, and Karanovo cultures of 7000–6000 B.C.E. in south-eastern Europe buried children and young people of both sexes as well as adult women under the floors of houses. Adult male graves do not appear. By contrast, graves from the Orkney Islands, Brittany, Normandy, and southern England show equal numbers of males and females. While in some places women and men were buried separately, in others females and males, children and adults are found in collective burials. Overall, we do not see any distinct pattern of extreme power differences between women and men.

Grave goods also give us clues to the different roles of men and women. Judging by the tools and objects buried with them, men often appear as craftsmen and women as potters. The women sometimes seem dedicated to beauty and art, both for personal adornment and spiritual symbolism. The Lengyel culture of the Danube river basin buried men with stone axes and antler hammer-axes, and women with jewelry and vases decorated with spirals and meanders. These symbols signify more than adornment. Spirals and meanders appear on Goddess art and figurines over thousands of years (for information about graves *see* Gimbutas, *Civilization of the Goddess*).

In Çatal Hüyük, women slept on large platforms facing east, towards the rising Sun. Men slept on small platforms that faced no particular direction. Does this mean that men didn't matter? Or does it mean that women's bodies carried a sacred power of fertility?

If women did receive more attention and respect than men in Neolithic culture it certainly occurred on a subtle level compared to the inequalities that came later. In patriarchal societies we find enslavement of women, women buried alive with a dead chieftain, women treated as property, and women confined by law to their husband's house, so that they could not even go out in the street. No evidence for a similar treatment of men exists anywhere in the Neolithic, whether in the burial record, the art, or the excavated remains.

In later cultures we find the king or chief buried with vast wealth and often with slaves. By contrast, the honored figures in Neolithic culture – old women and in some cases teenage girls ÷ receive offerings and beautiful objects, but nothing requiring exploitation of "lower" classes.

Individual Graves

Sometimes honor in burial involved symbolism more than riches. In Poland archaeologists found a grave with a 50–60-year-old woman. The grave contained a pot "filled to the brim," as Professor Gimbutas says, with red ochre. This may have meant more than honor or even symbolism. Red ochre implies sacred power, and a whole pot of it represents spiritual wealth (compare, however, the masses of gold buried with later warrior chiefs). If the woman had acted as an elder in life, the people might have sought her benevolence as an ancestor spirit after death.

In Neolithic cultures the community may have honored older women partly for their wisdom and life experience, but also because it was less common for people to live past middle age. Women particularly would have been honored because individual women embodied the Goddess's creative power, and because that power passed from mother to daughter by the most natural means possible, through the act of giving birth.

The embodiment of the Goddess in women gives women authority. Because that power comes so naturally, the elder women may not have felt the need to subjugate men. The power would have come to them from their bodies, not just from social controls. In some North American nations, notably the peoples of the Iroquois Confederacy, people worked out a balance in which the elder women's council made decisions, but also appointed males to positions of authority in the community. A few years ago the Mohawk nation staged an uprising against the Canadian and United States governments. Before going into battle, the Mohawk warriors told the news media that they needed to consult their grandmothers. "Grandmother" is an indigenous American term for an older woman of power.

If an older woman received honor as an elder, what do we make of the examples of adolescent girls buried with tributes? In the Çernica cemetery discovered at Bucharest the richest grave, with ten arm rings and a mass of shell beads, contained a girl of about 16. In a cemetery from the Late Cucuteni period in Moldavia excavators found two burials of girls about

9–10 years old. The Cucuteni graves contained vases, beads, spindle whorls, and three Goddess figurines in each one. No other grave contained three figurines. (Notice the still modest degree of wealth in these special graves.) The community may have honored the girls simply for the poignancy of their early death. Possibly they were daughters of a community leader, a priestess or elder.

The importance of both older women and adolescent girls may have derived from the power of menstruation and childbirth. In some cultures, people believe that crones – post-menopausal women – keep the power of their menstrual blood contained within their bodies. In general, when a woman in a Goddess-worshipping community passed the age of childbearing she grew in wisdom and often in healing power. By contrast, a girl dying before giving birth to the next generation may have taken her power into the grave as a blessing on the land, helping the plants to grow.

A Multitude of Goddesses

If Neolithic peoples truly lived without violence or mass inequality, did this necessarily derive from Goddess worship? Not everyone accepts the idea of the Neolithic period as woman-centered. Some scholars and reviewers have criticized Marija Gimbutas for seeing Goddesses in everything. Often, the critics assume that "Goddess" means "Mother Goddess," as if females fulfill only one function. If images do not appear as motherly they cannot be Goddesses. However, Professor Gimbutas suggests that the Goddess displayed different characteristics. She has described four categories of deity in Neolithic "Old Europe." These are: 1 – generative forces of nature, particularly birth and life maintenance, a category that would include the growing plants and the milk of the Goddess's breasts; 2 – death; 3 – regeneration, that is, life cycles; and 4 – male deities, who comprise 3–5 percent of religious images, and who usually appear with a female figure, as the Goddess's lover or son. Each of these sacred areas derives directly from the body, and its expression in birth, death, and sexuality.

Female images appear in many forms, in great abundance throughout the thousands of years of the New Stone Age, just as they did in the Old. They appear in greater variety as well. We find both realistic carvings and nearly geometric "stiff nudes," sometimes with long necks without heads. Carvings of figurines continue to be found, and also monumental statues. In Malta excavators found small carvings, easily held in the hands, of a birth-giving Goddess, a woman asleep on a couch, a Paleolithic-style figure with large breasts and hips, other figures with flat chests and wide hips, some naked, some wearing skirts, and so on, but they also discovered huge statues, including the bottom half of a large version of the skirted figures, the skirt and legs alone being a meter high.

When archaeologists excavated Jericho (a city thousands of years older than the Hebrew account of its destruction) they found Goddess statues in every room. The Biblical phrase "land flowing with milk and honey" probably derived from the Goddess religion, for the milk ran from her breasts, while bees, the makers of honey, remained sacred to the Goddess over millennia, down into Classical times.

Like Jericho, Nineveh (described in the book of Jonah as a wholly wicked town) was a prosperous and culturally developed Neolithic city. Excavators found headless Goddess figurines, squatting in birth postures. The Bible describes both cities as evil precisely because people there worshipped the Goddess.

Building models found in various places make explicit the connection between the Goddess and temples or dwellings. These models show a building surmounted by the head, or head and body, of a woman. Indeed, even in the world today, many people, such as the Dogon of Africa, look at houses as the body of a woman. (The Dogon balance this by laying out the whole village as the outline of a man.)

Mellaart comments that the structures seen in the remains of Çatal Hüyük changed over hundreds of years, but the position of certain things in the house remained constant. These were the ladder (the people entered through the roof), the hearth, and the oven. Each of these items suggests the Goddess's body. Descending by a ladder from the roof might have symbolized entering from the great world, the sky, into the womb of the Mother. The hearth gives off the heat of life itself, while the oven demonstrates the miracle of creation. As we saw in Chapter 1, Mellaart found Goddess figurines on top of the ovens.

The Lady of the Beasts

In the Paleolithic caves the relationship between Goddess images and the animal paintings implied the idea of the Goddess as mistress of the animals, or, as Buffie Johnson calls Her, Lady of the Beasts. In Neolithic times (and later periods) this becomes much more explicit and we see the Goddess with various animals. A painting in Çatal Hüyük shows Her calmly giving birth while seated on a throne-like chair, flanked by lions. Often She will appear with a bird head, or with snakes wound around Her body. Animals themselves often represent the Goddess. They include snakes, deer, fish, bears, hedgehogs, butterflies, pigs, toads and frogs.

These animals were not the deity, but rather embodiments of Her great and varied power. Mellaart found no evidence of actual animal worship at Çatal Hüyük. Instead, he says, the Goddess was portrayed in human form. At the same time, the qualities of particular animals embodied aspects of Her human body. For example, the toad and frog became important because their form resembles a woman squatting to give birth. The earliest known Egyptian deity, the Goddess Heket, took the form of a frog. Later, Heket appeared as midwife to the birth of the Sun.

The bull, and in particular the head and horns of the bull, became especially important in the Neolithic period. At Çatal Hüyük, bull heads, or *bucrania*, appear in a chamber apparently used for birthing. The remarkable resemblance between a bull's head and horns, and a woman's uterus and fallopian tubes was first noticed by Dorothy Cameron when she was working with James Mellaart. Large bull horns have been found in tombs in Sardinia. Possibly they symbolize regeneration. Some Neolithic communities buried children under the floor of the house, with *bucrania* and horns set alongside them.

The horns of cows and bulls resemble the waxing and waning Moon, showing one reason for their importance to the Goddess. Through the Moon, the horns become linked to the body power of menstruation. People may have considered the horn the focus of the bull's tremendous vitality. In Crete young men and women danced with bulls by grabbing the horns and flipping acrobatically over the animal's back. We know of the sport from a fresco in the palace of Knossos. In this fresco, the women and men appear almost identical, their bodies graceful and fluid, very different from the stiff matador of later centuries, who does not see the bull as a source of life, but as a means to test his own mastery of nature, through conquest and slaughter.

Interestingly, the pictures show the women bull dancers wearing codpieces to give the groin the image of male genitals. By contrast, pictures of men in religious ceremonies show them dressed in flounced skirts. The two types of picture tell us that the Cretans identified certain activities, such as sport and bull dancing, as male, while they considered others, including the sacrifice of the same bulls, female. We need to realize, however, that they saw "male" and "female" as *cultural ideas*, not biological facts. Both men and women could take part in each type of activity. In other words, worship derived from the female body, but men could take part by, in a sense, becoming female during the time of the ritual. Similarly, athletics apparently belonged to masculine vitality. To accommodate this, women simply became male in the bull dance. This fluidity of gender illustrates the idea we saw in Chapter 1, that male and female are ultimately offshoots of the same original body. Instead of a rigid structure, gender becomes an open house for men and women to enter and leave.

When Arthur Evans excavated and "restored" the Cretan palace of Knossos (beginning at the start of the 20th century), he found the remains of a large abstracted carving of horns, which have since become known as the "horns of consecration." They resemble the crown of the Egyptian Goddess Isis (see *Figure 8*).

Isis's crown symbolizes the Moon in its three phases, and we can guess that the Cretan horns also represented the Moon. The horns on the Egyptian crown also related Isis to the earlier Hathor, the Egyptian version of the universal Cow Goddess. It is very likely that the Cretan horns of consecration signified the cow or bull. Evans found them at the foot of the wall facing Mt Jouctas, the horned mountain with its cave sanctuary to the Goddess. The human sculpture of horns probably framed a view of the greater stone horns sculpted by nature. However, the form of the horns of consecration did not originate with Crete. We know of them from the Neolithic Vinça culture of south-eastern Europe, 3,000 years before their appearance in Crete.

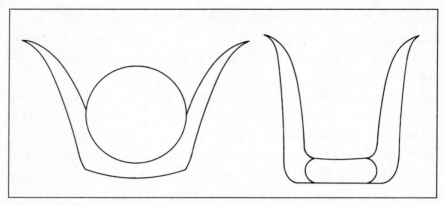

Figure 8 Drawing of the crown of Isis *(left)*, compared to the Cretan Horns of Consecration from the place of Knossos, Crete *(right,* after Alexiou).

Excarnation

Ancient peoples may have observed the conjunction of the bull's head and the uterus through excarnation, a funeral process by which a body is either exposed to nature before burial or disinterred for a second burial. Not only might people have seen the insides of the female body through this process, they also would have seen the uterus while the body was lying down, when the fallopian tubes fall most obviously into the shape of a bull's horns.

At Çatal Hüyük and other places people practiced excarnation through exposing the body to vultures who would remove the rotting flesh to reveal the bones. Bones signify the eternal being which does not decay. Shamans in their initiatory trances often experience their bodies torn to pieces or boiled alive, so that the skeleton becomes exposed and then filled with healing power. Shamans are said to receive the power to see a person's bones within the flesh. (For more on shamanic dismemberment, and its relation to later Greek myth, in particular Dionysos, *see* Chapter 7.)

The agents of excarnation, vultures, appear very dramatically in wall paintings found in Çatal Hüyük. One painting, covering several walls, shows stylized vultures, with huge broom-like wings and human feet. The feet indicate that they embody the Goddess rather than literal birds.

In Çatal Hüyük the images of life and death mingle in a way that may strike us as bizarre. Mellaart's team discovered the skulls of vultures, foxes, or weasels embedded in representations of breasts. Sometimes the jaws of the animals, or of wild boars, protrude from the nipples. Mellaart describes a shrine with a bull's head, and then double breasts with open nipples from which the beaks of vultures emerge. There was one building, decorated with a series of boar heads, that had burnt. When the people replastered it, they transformed each boar's jaw into a woman's breast.

From our modern viewpoint we tend to view the sacredness of nature as either naïve or philosophical. That is, since we have learned to see God as apart from nature we assume people directly worshipped animals or else saw them as symbols of something else. I have used the term "embodiment" to indicate an alternative, one that credits ancient peoples with intellectual subtlety while not removing them (or ourselves) from directly encountering the sacred in living creatures. To see the Goddess embodied in a vulture or a bull (and there is no reason why the Goddess cannot embody Herself in a male animal as well as a female, in men as well as women), recognizes that these creatures contain the living power of the divine.

Trees, Mountains, and Other Embodiments

It was not just animals that were thought to embody the Goddess. Trees, water, and even stones and mountains expressed Her power. We have seen how many of the Neolithic monuments, such as Silbury Hill, were built over underground streams. Standing stones, whatever their other functions and meanings, embody the strength of the Earth rising up before us. Mountains, especially, contain the Goddess's power. In Crete Vincent Scully found a repeating pattern of palaces and towns built in line with horned mountains. Possibly that reverence for horned mountains extends back to the Neolithic period. James Mellaart, in his description of the site of Çatal Hüyük, mentions a twin-peaked volcano 84 miles to the east and there is some evidence that indicates that people from the Anatolian region of Çatal Hüyük, settled Crete.

Trees embodied the Goddess throughout the Neolithic period and later. According to Gertrude Rachel Levy, the Egyptians considered the sycamore the "living body" of Hathor, the Cow Goddess, possibly because the fruit gives a white liquid. As a sycamore, Hathor suckled the infant pharaohs. Egyptian texts describe the murdered Vegetation God Osiris as enclosed in a sycamore tree. Levy also describes the Hebrew seven-branched candle-stick as derived from the Neolithic Tree Goddess. The Biblical book of Deuteronomy denounces planting an "Asherah," that is, a tree or a pillar representing the Goddess, beside the altars of Yahweh.

I could cite many more examples of the tree as the Goddess, especially her Tree of Life. In Donna Read's film *The Goddess Remembered* a temple caretaker in Malta, referring to the Tree of Life image in the Hypogeum (an underground temple), tells the film-makers "The tree was the medium between Mother Earth and man." In a much later period than the Neolithic, the alchemist Paracelsus wrote of woman, "She is the tree which grows from the earth, and the child is like the fruit that is born of the tree."

Shrines in Crete and other places included a pillar in the center of a room. These pillars may have represented stone columns or stalagmites, but they also may have represented trees. Vincent Scully describes cylindrical wooden columns in Cretan palaces as the Goddess's person enclosed in a "female state of being." He writes, "Thus the whole palace became her body as the earth itself had been in the stone age."

A tree connects Heaven, Earth, and the Underworld. It also represents life itself. Where a tree grows, life can exist and this is especially recognized in a hot country. The palace is female because it shelters, encloses, nurtures – as does a valley. Therefore, a tree (wooden column) in a palace in a valley becomes a multi-layered image of life growing within the protective love of the Goddess.

A tree embodies the Goddess in more than symbolic terms. A tree contains the energy of the Earth and the Sun concentrated into living form. Every tree is unique, with shapes that evoke a person standing upright with raised arms. Olive trees especially may embody the Goddess, for they live a very long time. As they grow older they become gnarled, and densely packed with energy, sometimes taking on suggestively female forms, like a bent old woman.

By their shape, pillars signified trees, but also stone columns. Throughout the Old and New Stone Ages people decorated stalactites and stalagmites to bring out resemblances to clusters of breasts. Mellaart writes of finding stalactites with sacred figurines "on almost every occasion." The Temple of Artemis at Ephesus, Turkey, one of the seven wonders of the ancient world, contained a famous statue of the Goddess. The sculpture portrayed Her as an upright column, like a tree, with her torso covered in round globes like eggs or breasts.

In later periods people worshipped the Goddess as a stone, often black and/or conical. Cybele, the Great Mother of the Gods, entered Rome ceremoniously each year as a conical meteorite carried in a chariot pulled by lions. Cybele was originally the Goddess of Phrygia, another name for western Anatolia. According to Monica Sjoo and Barbara Mor the people of Canaan worshipped the Goddess Astarte on Mt Sinai as a stone. The name "Sinai" means "mountain of the Moon." The Ka'aba, the huge black stone enshrined in Mecca, and the focal point of the Moslem Haj (pilgrimage), originally embodied the Goddess. Sjoo and Mor tell us that the ancient Arabs imprinted vulvas on its surface. When priests took over from priestesses they received the title "Beni Shaybah," that is "sons of the old woman."

Knots

It was not just aspects of the natural world that were considered to embody the Goddess's being. In many places, knots signified her power, and images of knots appear on the sacred pillars of underground crypts. Often, drawings or carvings of knots show the rope leaving a loop; curiously, the form of the knot itself resembles the modern necktie (see *Figure 9*).

A knot would seem to symbolize Levy's concept of religion as an abiding relationship. She describes the knot as an emblem of the Goddess in Crete, and adds that the Egyptian ankh sign was a "knotted sign of life," described in the *Book of the Dead* as set before "the horned gate of the cloven mountain." We already know the significance of horns and a double-peaked mountain. The Egyptian Goddess Isis also displayed a knot as Her emblem. A lead coffin excavated in Palestine was decorated with knots and vines and when archaeologists opened it they found that the skeleton's mouth contained knots made of gold leaf.

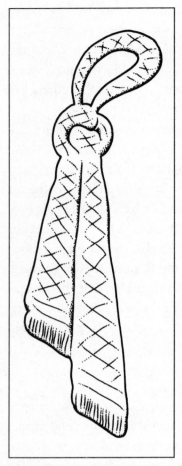

Figure 9 Drawing of the sacred knot from Knossos, Crete, c.1700 B.C.E. (after Alexiou).

If knots signify the bonds between the Goddess and the world, they also represent restraints, in particular sexual restraints. We untie them to release our desires. In many cultures married women unknot their hair and loosen their clothes only when making love or giving birth. By contrast, unmarried virgins walk in public with their hair unknotted. In modern Western culture, we still refer to marriage as "tying the knot," and speak of "letting our hair down" when we want to have a good time.

But knots symbolize more than repression. As a human construction, they represent culture, the ideas and images which bind us together. The importance of the knot survived into later centuries in folklore and magical practices. Barbara Walker, in *The Woman's Encyclopedia of Myths and Secrets*, describes various magical knots, including special knots tied in umbilical cords by midwives. The knot symbolizes both our origin in our mothers, and our separation as individual beings. A knot binds the magical forces of life. By tying knots we demonstrate our knowledge and ability to deal with the powers of the world.

The Gordian Knot

Knots also symbolize tradition. Many of us have learned the legend of Alexander the Great and the Gordian Knot. This vastly complex knot had stymied various would-be conquerors of Asia, and a prophecy declared that whoever untied the knot would become ruler of all Asia. Alexander, we learn admiringly, simply took his sword and sliced the knot in half. (It is not clear

Plate 1
The kerbstone at Newgrange, Ireland, c.3300–3200 B.C.E. The triple spiral appears on the left side of the stone.

Plate 2
The Serpent Mound in southern Ohio, date unknown, possibly c.1000 B.C.E.
Reproduced by permission of Courtney Milne.

Plate 3 The Nana Goddess created by Niki de St. Phalle for a Swedish fair.
Photo by Hans Hammerskiold; by permission of Niki de St. Phalle.

Plate 4 The "Artemis" hill formation near the temple of Artemis at Brauron, Greece.

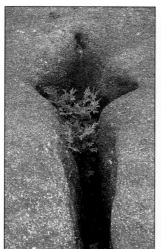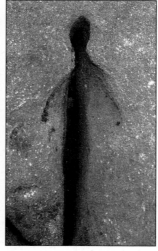

Plate 5
Naturally "carved" fissures in rocks near the Teaching Rock at Peterborough, Canada.

Plate 6
Carved spirals at the temple of Tarxien, Malta, c.3000 B.C.E.

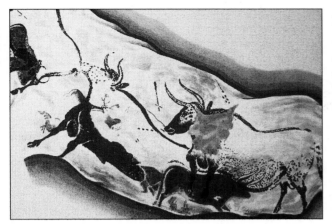

Plate 7
Paintings of bulls in the Lascaux
cave, France, c.15000 B.C.E.
*Reproduced by permission of Aras
Archives, Jungian Institute,
San Francisco.*

Plate 8 (*left*)
The "Venus of Willendorf,"
Austria, c.30000 B.C.E.
*Reproduced by permission of Aras
Archives, Jungian Institute,
San Francisco.*

Plate 9 (*right*)
The "Venus of Laussel," France,
c.15000 B.C.E.
*Reproduced by permission of Aras
Archives, Jungian Institute,
San Francisco.*

Plate 10
Moonrise over Stonehenge,
England, built c.2800 B.C.E.
*Reproduced by permission of
Courtney Milne.*

Plate 13 Glastonbury Tor, England, at sunset. *Reproduced by permission of Marilyn Bridges.*

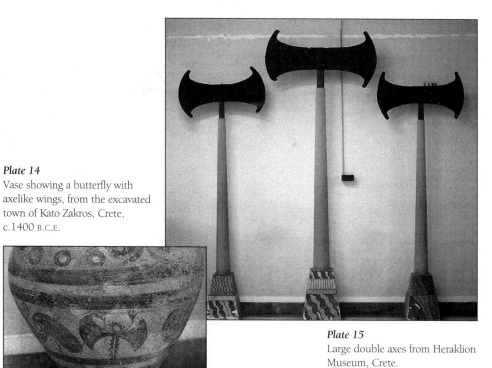

Plate 17 The remains of the ancient town of Gournia, Crete, c.1500 B.C.E.

Plate 18 Mt. Ida seen from the court of the palace of Phaestos, Crete, c.1700 B.C.E.

Plate 20 The large standing stone in the Old Temple of Athena Pronaia, Marmaria, Greece, c.700 B.C.E.

Plate 21
The Lion Gate, Mycenae, Greece,
c.1350 B.C.E.

Plate 22 The sacred precinct of Eleusis, Greece, c.400 B.C.E. The cleft peak of Mt Kerata
can be seen in the background.

Plate 23
The remarkable stone mound
that I found in the woods near
my house in New York State.

exactly what lesson our teachers wanted us to take from this – to smash through our problems rather than try to solve them?) This little fable gains a greater depth when we discover that Gordium was the main city of Phrygia, homeland of Cybele, the Great Mother (as well as of Aphrodite, who in the Fifth Homeric Hymn, describes Herself as a daughter of Phrygia). Barbara Walker tells us that the knot represented the binding in mystical marriage of the Mother and Her son/consort/king. (Compare the modern – negative – image of a man tied to his mother's apron strings.) To slice through that knot represented a kind of infanticide, the killing of the Goddess's children, as well as the attempted murder of the Goddess Herself. And indeed, Alexander's conquest brought death, as well as rape and slavery, to vast numbers of people.

The complexities of the knot symbolized the thousands of years of Goddess tradition, science, and sacred knowledge. The rising patriarchy, symbolized by Alexander, did not try to understand this great civilization, or even to change its beliefs and structures by working through its various traditions. Instead, it simply conquered it through the power of the sword, and has continued to do so ever since – in the Americas, Australia, Africa, and, most recently, in the depths of rainforests, where the genocide known as "development" wipes out entire cultures of human beings, and renders species of plants and animals extinct at the rate of *three every hour*.

And yet, the knot remains. Alexander's heirs have no choice, really, but to keep on cutting it, over and over, for the knot is the umbilical cord that connects us to nature and the divine, and it reappears – over and over – retied with every baby, every cycle of life.

The Age of Invention

The evidence that Neolithic culture in Europe was Goddess-centered, egalitarian, and without violence appears very strong. This is radical information, for it tells us that human nature does not automatically embrace violence. War – and inequality – are not inevitable. Many people resist this idea, saying they would like to believe it, but doubt that humans could act differently. In fact, they probably would *not* like to believe it. We accept war and violence by assuring ourselves that we have no choice, that human beings cannot behave any other way.

Genetically we are no different from our ancestors. Instead, our culture has changed, and has taught us that nothing different ever existed. This, too, is the Alexandrian method of conquest, to obliterate the past. As we have seen, it is no accident that the Bible tells us that God created the world, intact, 6,000 years ago, or that our history books start with the first patriarchal cultures and call that the beginning of civilization.

Some people who accept the peacefulness of the Neolithic period as fact will acknowledge the benefits of such a "stage" in human culture, but insist that humanity had to "progress" to patriarchy. Mother-centered culture, they maintain, becomes too static, too placid, and lacks creativity. Patriarchy may bring war and violence, and slavery, and inequality, and the confinement of women, but it also (supposedly) brings dynamism.

Now, this is part of the ideology and fallacy of primitivism. Matrifocal society was good in its time, the argument runs, but had to give way to "true" civilization. Mother love stifles. Human culture cannot grow under a Mother Goddess. So imbued have we become with the doctrine of "progress" it becomes difficult to think in other terms.

In fact, the Neolithic was possibly the most dynamic period in human history. It saw the development of agriculture, the domestication of animals, the growth of trade and commerce, the creation of writing and mathematics, the invention of pottery, house and temple construction, monument building, astronomy, and, no doubt, conceptual systems for which we have no records. Moreover, the change to patriarchy weakened civilization rather than enhanced it, for this change came through war and conquest. When people from the Mycenaean culture of Greece invaded Crete they adapted much of Cretan culture and religion, including the worship of the Goddess. However, by putting so much of their resources into war, and into great wealth for a single chief, they achieved nothing like the quality of life previously enjoyed by the Cretans. When the later Dorians invaded Greece, bringing their pantheon of war Gods, they began what historians of ancient Greece call "the Dark Ages," a period of 400 years during which (according to Vincent Scully) the Greeks did not build anything lasting or substantial.

(The creation of large buildings is, however, not the only measure of civilization. It has been almost exactly 400 years since barbarian invaders from Europe first began their conquest of North America, a conquest which continues to this day. Despite the dynamism – and large buildings – which have resulted from this invasion it is most likely that the indigenous peoples of the continent would consider these past 400 years the Dark Ages.)

Assumptions about Creativity

The idea that society needs masculine energy for creativity, rather than the combined energy of women and men, calls up a very old prejudice, perhaps as old as patriarchy itself. Women create out of their bodies. Somehow, we have learned that this does not represent "true" creativity, that truly to create one must do so out of the head, out of abstract thought. And we have learned that males excel in this by virtue of being male. It is as if we consider that the world must somehow balance itself by giving women the power to create babies, and men the power to create ideas – and that ideas are better than babies.

After all, the prejudice tells us, any woman can grow a baby. It doesn't require any special talent. *Thinking* requires talent. And men supposedly think better than women. Supposedly, women are bound to their bodies just because they can grow other bodies inside of them, while men, like the male transcendent God, exist on an abstract level apart from their bodies.

This ancient distortion sets up false dichotomies. We consider women who think or create art or simply work outside the home to be imitating men. Some people consider them superior to women who have babies, whom we call "cows," not knowing that the cow once symbolized God to people all over the world. Others consider women with babies superior to thinking women by virtue of following their "true" nature.

No evidence exists of any real split between creativity of the body and creativity of the mind, or between feminine and masculine creativity. We might guess that many of the Neolithic innovations came from women. For instance, if women gathered the plants in the Paleolithic (as they do in most hunter-gatherer societies we know of from historical times), then it would make sense for women to observe the processes of seeding and growth which would lead to agriculture. By the same logic, male hunters, through their intimate knowledge of animals, may have led the way to the early domestication of sheep and other species.

The activity of hunting requires men to stay silent and to communicate with signs (a language of the body). As food gatherers and child minders, women would have communicated with words. As a result, women may have invented writing, as well as scientific knowledge and other intellectual systems that involved sharing complex information. We cannot prove this. There is no reason to assume women created human culture all alone any more than there is to accept the common assumption (still found in most books on prehistory) that men invented everything while women just had babies. We cannot even assume that only men hunted and only women gathered plants. Rock art at the edge of the Sahara Desert in Africa depicts groups of women hunters.

Just as our society teaches us that "men think and women do," so it teaches us that thinking does not connect to bodies. "I think, therefore I am." (Vicki Noble describes an ancient inscription which translates as "I have breasts, therefore I am.") In our age, we have seen how weapons scientists and engineers will excitedly "create" systems designed to kill vast numbers of people, and never seem to connect this intellectual work with the death of actual human beings. And yet, the body intrudes itself. Pentagon slang describes advanced missiles and bombs as "sexy." When scientists at Los Alamos exploded the first atomic bomb, they passed around cigars and announced "It's a boy."

The valorization of abstract thinking and the assignment of such creativity to males may have arisen with the need to contradict the most obvious fact about our world, that women create out of their bodies. To envision God as female presents few problems. The female gives birth and so does the Goddess. A problem only develops if males wish, first, to separate themselves from women, and second, to establish dominion over women and the world. To do this they need to separate creativity from nature. Only then can they envision a male God creating the universe.

Some myths of male creation describe the creator God as cutting Himself open to bring the world out of His body. We can imagine men rejecting this image. It involves such an obvious imitation of what women do naturally. How much more satisfactory to suppose a God who creates from "pure" (disembodied) thought, who creates the cosmos and life simply by speaking or still better, from a book, since the men did not allow women to learn how to read. (In September 1996, fundamentalist Moslem rebels seized control of Afghanistan. Almost as their first act, they stopped education for girls.) In the past 150 years we have begun to emerge from this particular aspect of our own dark ages. And yet, the old assumptions still hold a lot of power, for our culture has built them into us over 50 centuries. The discovery of Goddess-centered cultures in the Neolithic period, and their great achievements, can help free us from such limited views of creativity in both women and men.

How Did It All Vanish?

Where did the world of the Neolithic people go? How and why did human culture change from a peaceful, dynamic society based on nature and the Goddess to one based on war, class structure, inequalities between men and women, and an all-male God demanding fear and obedience? If indeed a matrifocal culture existed for tens of thousands of years, and that period saw the development of science and structured civilization, including cities and agriculture, why did humans abandon it? If we do not view patriarchy as a necessary and inevitable step in human cultural evolution, how did it come about?

A number of writers have put forward detailed accounts of patriarchal takeover, especially in Europe and the Middle East. Merlin Stone, in *When God Was a Woman*, traces the changes that occurred in Palestine. Marija Gimbutas gives a detailed chronology of the changeover in the area she calls Old Europe. She describes the Indo-European invasions from what she terms the "fringe areas" of civilization, and shows how they distorted or replaced the older symbols of Goddess culture. The bull, for example, changed from a symbol of vitality and the uterus to a symbol of the Sky God Thunderer.

Feminist accounts of the fall of matristic culture in Europe usually attribute the change to tribal groups worshipping a male warrior God. But this begs the question. How did those particular groups develop their war-based ideology?

The Discovery of Paternity

Many people assume patriarchy developed when men discovered their importance in human reproduction. According to this argument, early, "primitive," people did not comprehend the connection between sex and pregnancy. After all, women do not get pregnant every time they have sex, nor is pregnancy immediately noticeable. Women were held in reverence, and fear, for their magical ability to produce babies, but when men found out their own place in this process they became arrogant and insisted on male supremacy.

This argument seems to me to be based on several questionable assumptions. Why should the discovery of paternity automatically lead to a male seizure of power? The idea apparently stems from that old belief in matriarchy as the only alternative to patriarchy. In other words, when people did not know of men's importance, they gave all power to women who suppressed men. When men discovered their value they then suppressed women. What inherent reason would require humans to behave in this way?

The discovery of paternity does not sweep away the significance of women becoming pregnant. Men contribute the essential sperm but the baby still must grow inside the woman. To give all power to men requires an extreme distortion of the most obvious realities. Some patriarchal cultures have done exactly that. The Greeks developed the idea that the human exists entirely within the sperm and that the woman serves simply as a vessel, an incubator, for the baby to grow until it can emerge into life. It is precisely such twisting of reality that leads to the separation of thought from observation, of religious (and scientific) ideology from nature. But we cannot assume that humans would naturally or inevitably develop such distorted ideas.

More fundamentally, why should we assume that Stone Age people did not know of the male contribution to procreation? We can guess that people who domesticated animals, and raised herds of different species over several thousand years, would understand very well the mechanics of sexual reproduction. And even in the Old Stone Age, the intense observation of animals, the mingling of phallic imagery with images of vulvas and of the Goddess's body, and the use of red ochre, possibly to symbolize menstruation and birth, suggest the possibility that these people too understood reproduction. The engraved marks on bones and other objects may have counted the months of pregnancy, suggesting a knowledge that conception begins with intercourse. The concept of male supremacy does not come from any observations of nature, but just the opposite – an ideology that deliberately turns reality upside down in order to justify itself.

A slightly revised theory of the ignorance of paternity involves the idea that women and men led largely separate lives. Those who support this idea point out that women probably developed the agriculture and ran the towns, so that women did not need men except for procreation. The theory then suggests that women knew the mechanics of reproduction but deliberately kept this information from men, pushing them to the periphery of society. Having little to do but test their strength, men developed into marauding gangs who began to discover the power of violence. When they then found out about their own significance in procreation they seized power entirely. This argument assumes the marginality of men in a matrifocal culture, but the burial record and the art dispute this.

Laws Suppressing Women

Much of what we think of as natural or basic to human beings may have derived from patriarchy's need to suppress women in order to maintain its own structures. In many ways our sexual morality stems largely from the institution of patrilineal descent, that is, property passing from father to son, instead of the older matrilineal pattern by which property passed from mother to daughter. When property moves from the mother, few problems result, since all children, sons as well as daughters, can know with certainty who gave birth to them. However, when property passes through the male side, how does a man assure that a male child is actually his son? Controlling paternity means controlling women and the products of their bodies. Laws must establish that a woman sleeps with one man and one man only. She must remain a virgin until marriage and must never take any lovers other than her husband. To make sure this system works women must be convinced that they desire "modesty," and that monogamy comes naturally to women. It requires extreme punishments for women who "stray," or even suffer rape. This explains why patriarchal legal codes sometimes ostracize and punish the victim of rape as much as the rapist.

Are women naturally monogamous? Do women instinctively want to find a mate and never stray? Five thousand years into patriarchy it becomes hard to tell how much of our behavior, even our desires, come from our own nature and how much from cultural patterns.

In our schools we learn that civilizations started with the great lawgivers – Moses, Hammurabi, Confucius, Solon, Zoroaster, Mohammed – who lifted humanity from ignorance and superstition through the institution of moral codes. We now know that human culture had developed to a very high degree of organization and technology long before these figures instituted their patriarchal systems. And when we look at these legal codes we discover that in every case they involve the systematic restriction of women's power, women's property rights, women's knowledge, and women's freedom of movement. The Mosaic laws make women the property of first their fathers and then their husbands, so that a man literally buys his bride from the woman's father. Women may not take part in religious services, and women's sexuality becomes extremely restricted. "Solon the Lawgiver," as he was called in Greece, instituted the confinement of women in ancient Athens, making it unlawful for women even to leave their husbands' courtyards and walk in the street. Confinement not only kept women from power and property, it also prevented them from communicating with each other and sharing their thoughts, desires, and experiences.

The Demonization of Women

The Zoroastrian myth of creation, as recorded in the late text, the Bundahish, gives us an idea of the image of women projected by the great patriarchal lawgivers. The Bundahish describes how the evil principle, Angra Mainyu, slept after creating Evil Mind and the Lie. A female demon named

Jahi came and woke him, promising to cause misery in the world, to poison "the righteous man," and the animals, the water, plants, even fire, and all creation. According to Joseph Campbell, the name "Jahi" means "menstruation." A separate text tells of a visit to the Zoroastrian after-life, where, as in Dante's *Divine Comedy*, the visitor views souls suffering individual torment. He sees a woman's soul forced to drink cupfuls of "the impurity and filth of men." When he asks what crime prompted this punishment, he learns that the woman "approached water and fire during menstruation." (Quotations from Joseph Campbell, *Occidental Mythology*.)

The pattern of "advances" in civilization at the expense of women continued into modern times. We have learned to think of the Renaissance as a great awakening of culture, a time of rebirth from ignorance and fear. Only recently have feminist historians demonstrated that women in the Middle Ages wielded a certain amount of power and influence, with economic and legal rights, and that the Renaissance systematically stripped away these rights, leaving women much more at the economic mercy of their husbands. Similarly, the rise of modern medicine developed at the expense of midwives and village healers, most of whom were women. The witch burnings, which caused the deaths of vast numbers of women, possibly millions, did not occur in the Middle Ages, as most people think, but in the Renaissance, when medicine was becoming a "profession," requiring a formal education open only to men. In order to take the power of healing away from women, society branded the healers as worshippers of Satan, supposedly using their bodies in ritual sex with demons.

World-Wide Patterns

The problem of change from matristic to patriarchal society becomes more complicated when we discover that peoples all over the world, in many different kinds of cultures, including non-technological hunter-gatherers, show signs of having passed through a transition from woman-centered to male-centered power.

Much of this evidence exists in the myths. The common pattern describes an archaic Goddess conquered, demonized, and often dismembered by a male God who now emerges as all-powerful. Other stories tell of a time when women possessed great power, simply by virtue of their women's bodies, and how men rose up and took the power away. Still others teach a "moral" lesson of proper male dominance, but with an underlying tone of changing an older order.

We will look at some of these myths in a moment, but here we need to consider what they tell us overall. The myths and the archaeological record seem to imply a world-wide pattern of power taken from women. Many writers on this subject, including many feminists, doubt that, historically, there was a point when males seized power. They argue that myths of matrifocal societies and women's power actually derive from male anxieties and fear of women. Some feminists see myths of one-time female power as men's justification for exploiting and suppressing women. Peggy Sanday, in her book *Female Power and Male Dominance: On the Origins of Sexual Inequality*, argues that stories of former female control indicate women had wielded "considerable informal power" within the existing society, a power that makes the ruling men uncomfortable.

But why should we discount what the myths actually say? If the men of a particular culture say in effect, "Women once held power but we took it from them," (and some tribal accounts say exactly that) why should we assume they only made this up – especially when the archaeological record, at least in Europe, shows such strong indications of societies focused around women's (sacred and creative) power? And there is something else. If the myths reflect male anxieties about women's "informal power" that anxiety might come from something deeper than, say, women's commercial power in the marketplace. Female power can never go away, whatever the social structure, for it rests ultimately in the miraculous female body, that body which bleeds with the Moon and which gives new life – to boys as well as girls.

Lilith

The method of using myth and religion to control women involved moral lessons as well as demonization. In a typical story a woman or Goddess takes a certain action and disaster results. Another female figure then acts in a "proper" manner and the world rights itself. These myths justify male control as necessary to prevent the supposed chaos that results when women take control. At the same time, they often are the stories that hint at earlier societies when women wielded more power, and very often these stories involve sexuality or some other aspect of the body.

The ancient Israelites developed many of their mythological and legendary themes during their exile in Babylon. For instance, the Tower of Babel may have referred to the ziggurat temples of Babylon, worked on by slave labor from many different lands. (Feminist scholars consider Mesopotamia, or Babylon, a transition land, with an older Goddess culture still present but heavily distorted under patriarchy.) One Babylonian Goddess, Lilith, became transformed in a way that says something about the Israelites themselves.

Lilith, whose name means "screech owl," became the center of a series of Hebrew legends which described her as Adam's first wife. According to these stories, God created Adam and Lilith at the same time, from the same dirt. (The name Adam derives from the Hebrew *adama*, meaning "ground"; similarly, the Latin *humanus* derives from *humus*, "dirt.") Another version of the story contains the extreme detail that while God created Adam out of dirt, He created Lilith from filth and excrement. When they went to have sex, Lilith refused to allow Adam to go on top, saying God had created them equal. For this sin, God banished her and created Eve. Since Eve came out of Adam she would show proper subservience.

Comic-book writer Neil Gaiman has found another midrash story, describing a female creation between Lilith and Eve. God built this nameless woman's body piece by piece, from the inside out, with Adam watching. Adam refused to have sex with her, because, according to the midrash text, "he saw her full of secretions and blood."

We can see the story of Lilith and Eve (and their nameless sister) as simply a fable to keep women in their place – or we can see it as a hint of a time when women and men enjoyed equality. To take away that equality and make sure women accepted an inferior position as "natural" the rabbis constructed this moral lesson.

In addition to their political meanings, the myths of Adam's other wives tell us something about anxieties concerning the body. Lilith, a woman close to nature, comes out of excrement. Adam could not bear his second wife because he saw the inner workings of her body. By contrast, the magical Eve grows out of Adam, and not the natural processes of the physical world.

An Esoteric Interpretation

The later Jewish system of esoteric ideas known as Kabbalah, which flourished from the 12th century to the 16th century, revived the idea of equality between male and female, even describing God as androgynous. Following an earlier Talmudic interpretation, the Kabbalists maintained that the phrase in Genesis, "Male and female, He created them" describes *God* as both male and female. They then went on to revise the story of Eve's creation from Adam's rib, the tale which most fundamentalist Christians and Jews point to to demonstrate that women are lesser beings. According to this later version, God created Adam as an androgynous being, a man and woman together, joined at the rib cage. (*See also* the description of "Adam Kadmon" and the androgynous God in Chapter 1.) However, this being had no companion with whom to share experience. Therefore, God separated the two parts. The story of taking a rib from Adam and making a woman becomes a metaphor for the separation (some versions describe Lilith, not Eve, as the other part of hermaphroditic Adam).

Though this story comes to us from the medieval Kabbalists, it recalls much older tales. Zoroastrian myth includes the idea that Ahura Mazda separated an androgynous first being. Plato tells a story of God – Zeus – breaking apart a formerly complete human being. In *The Symposium* Plato has Aristophanes describe Prometheus creating humans as half man half woman. Angry at this godlike completion, Zeus splits them with lightning. Plato tells us that some of the original beings were double men, or double women, accounting for homosexual love.

These various stories may reflect the mystery of two sexes and the way people long for a partner – or they may hint at an earlier society which recognized female and male as both part of a greater physical reality.

A Japanese Brother and Sister

A Japanese myth teaches a similar lesson to that of Lilith. The story tells how various beings of creation came into existence through the actions of a brother and sister God and Goddess, Izanagi and Izanami, the Male-who-invites and the Female-who-invites. When they meet they circle round an "August Heavenly Pillar," an indication of an older ritual dance which may remind us of the Goddess worshipped as a pillar in faraway Crete. Izanami praises Izanagi, and he returns with praises for her, though it worries him that the woman spoke first. Nevertheless, they mate and produce Leech and Foam Island, two beings considered failures.

So they consult an oracle, and as we might guess, they learn that creation has gone wrong because the woman usurped the man's right to speak first. Repeating their actions in the "proper" way produces a proper creation.

Creation continues after Izanami's death, for when Izanagi goes to bring her back he becomes terrified by her decaying body and runs from her. As she and her servants chase him, various aspects of all their bodies become transformed into aspects of creation. The story suggests a male terror of both the female body and the realities of death.

Again, this story may serve only as propaganda, or it may indicate an earlier culture in which women held power. The Japanese emperors trace their mythological lineage not to a male God, but to the Sun Goddess and creatrix, Amaterasu Omikami. Whether or not we assume an earlier matristic culture, we are still left with the fascinating similarity between the stories of Lilith and Izanami. And just as with the tale of Adam's reaction to his nameless second wife, the Japanese myth expresses the terror of the physical reality of bodies.

Twisted Myths

Myths which seem bizarre or strange to us sometimes derive from a patriarchal need to twist, or turn upside down, an earlier myth of the Goddess. The Greek Goddess Athena was originally a figure of great power and many aspects, whose animals included the owl and the snake, symbols of different levels of consciousness. (*See* Chapter 1 for further comments on the connections of birds and serpents.) To bring Her under the control of

129

Zeus, the Greeks developed the story that Zeus swallowed his first wife, Metis, to prevent her bearing a child who might overthrow him. When a terrible headache siezed Zeus, the God Hephaestus split open Zeus's skull with an axe. Athena burst forth, armed as a warrior. From the perspective of an earlier Goddess religion we can decode this myth as a tale of the patriarchy conquering – swallowing – the Goddess culture. That culture refused to die, giving the patriarchy a headache. And indeed the head *should* hurt, for they had elevated thinking above creation out of the body.

When the Dorians invaded Greece they encountered the powerful Goddess Athena. Since Athena would not go away, they recast Her in their own image, as a warrior. And they described their version of Her as bursting forth from Zeus's head fully grown – as if the patriarchy had made Her up complete, as if She had never existed before Zeus "created" Her. At the same time, we might notice that when Hephaestus splits open Zeus's skull, the God's head becomes transformed into a vagina. Did Hephaestus use a double axe, a labrys, taken from Crete?

A similar turnabout occurs with the story of Pandora and her box of evils and torments. The name *Pan-dora* literally means "All-giving," an indication that she originally signified a Mother Goddess rather than a foolish child. A further clue emerges from a comment by Nor Hall, in *Those Women*, that the Greek word *kista*, which means "basket" or "box" was seen in ancient Greece as a pun on *kustus*, or "cunt."

Eve and the Apple

The story of Adam and Eve and the apple may strike us as strange until we learn its earlier versions. As a child, I never could make sense of this tale, which, of course, I learned as historical fact. ("The world is full of origin myths," writes Joseph Campbell, "and all are actually false.") Why, I wondered, would God make these two trees if He didn't want Adam and Eve to eat from them? Why bother? And why make this entire garden for them and then throw them out just for one mistake? My teachers explained that God gave man free will, and set the two trees there as a test, but that seemed like a nasty trick, especially since these two trees represented the glory of the garden – and especially since an omnipotent God must have known the outcome ahead of time. It simply made no sense. Only when I read Merlin Stone's *When God was a Woman* and Joseph Campbell's *The Masks of God: Occidental Mythology* did I begin to understand what was going on in that confusing tale.

We have seen how the Neolithic and early Bronze Age people worshipped the Goddess as a tree, setting temples in groves of trees. And we have seen how all over the world the snake embodies the Goddess's life energy. There is a curious passage in Genesis, where God curses the snake by saying "I will create enmity between you and the woman." This statement also makes no sense, until we learn about the snakes wound about the Goddess's arms and through her hair. Statues of the Cretan Goddess show Her holding snakes in each hand. The oldest images of Athena show Her, not as a warrior, but as a Snake Goddess. In Greece, too, the God puts enmity between the woman and the serpent, for in classical Greek myth the serpent Goddess becomes Medousa. Athena helps Perseus to kill Medousa and cut off Her head – but Medousa was originally Athena Herself.

The apple too embodies the Goddess. Cut an apple across the middle and the center will reveal a perfect pentagram. The planet Venus, seen from Earth, follows a path like a pentagram, or a five-petaled flower, over a period of eight years (for more on this pattern, and its relation to plants, *see* William Irwin Thompson, *Imaginary Landscapes*). Thus the apple forms an earthly connection with the heavenly path of the planet Venus, identified with Ishtar, Astarte, Aphrodite, Roman Venus, and other Goddesses.

Much simpler than the Biblical Eden myth, the Goddess version does not involve prohibitions, or a "jealous" God, or disobedience and banishment. Instead, it begins with the reality of our lives and offers to us a promise. The Goddess has grown a Tree of Life within Her garden of joy, where She waits with Her serpent. She holds out Her apple to us, and while it is the apple of "immortality," it also is the apple of knowledge, for only through *knowing* that the Goddess lives in all things can we release our fear of personal extinction in death.

The Biblical story does more than turn the older myth on its head. It encodes the overthrow of the Goddess-centered world. The knowledge that

Eve gains from the serpent signifies the awareness of sacred reality – but it also symbolizes knowledge of history itself. For the garden is the Neolithic world of the Great Goddess, and when the warrior tribes overthrew it they banished it even from memory, so that until the great discoveries of modern archaeology it existed only in folklore and confused tales of a lost paradise.

An Explicit Myth

Possibly the most specific male takeover story comes from the Ona people of Tierra del Fuego, a people of whom there is no question of evolution from "primitive" to "higher" stages of civilization. In *Primitive Mythology* Joseph Campbell recounts how the Ona explained the origin of the *Hain*, the lodge of the men's secret society. In the early time of the world, the Ona told a certain Lucas Bridges, the women wielded all the power, and the men "lived in abject fear and subjection." So the men killed all the women, leaving only the little girls who had not yet learned about female power. To make sure that future generations of women never banded together to rediscover their magical strength, the men created an all-male lodge. They then invented various spirit beings who would terrify the women and keep them away from the lodge and from knowledge. The men themselves would impersonate these beings. What astonishes about this story is not just its open brutality, but its clear description of institutionalized religion as a fraud set up to confuse and subjugate women.

The Ona men impersonate Gods in order to suppress women. Impersonations and masquerades become a strategy for men in other cultures as well. Judith Gleason writes that among the Yoruba "The feminine is primary," and yet, also dangerous, so that the men must contain it by "male structures of thought and language." An aspect of this containment consists of elaborate costumes, part abstract design, part supernatural images, and part imitations of women, or rather female qualities (for example, extremely exaggerated breasts and hips). In most places, these *egungun*, or masquerade, rituals belong only to men. However, various West African myths describe them as originally women's art, used to terrify and dominate men until the men wrested it away from them.

Killing a Dragon

Many patriarchal myths tell of the world order established out of chaos through the killing of a dragon, giant snake, or sea serpent. We find this especially in Greek and Near Eastern mythologies. The Hebrew God kills Leviathan, Apollo kills Python, by which he establishes control over the Delphic Oracle, Zeus kills Typhoeus (or Typhon) who is the last child of Gaia, the Earth, and so on. Many of these tales explicitly identify the serpent/monster as female, or associate it with an archaic Goddess, or with the site of female power.

The most famous of these stories tells of the Babylonian hero Marduk, who kills Tiamat, the original serpent Mother Goddess, who is also Marduk's great-great-great-grandmother. Tiamat, so the *Enuma Elish* tells us, had turned evil and was giving birth to monsters.

To defend creation the Gods enthrone Marduk, telling him, "We give thee sovereignty over the whole world. Thy weapon shall never lose its power," a phrase that suggests phallus worship, and the anxiety that results when male power resides in an organ that by its very nature must fall as well as rise. (The adulation, and even worship, of swords and other weapons may develop from the fact that swords will never become limp.) The Gods give Marduk the thunderbolt and other weapons and he goes forth to destroy Tiamat. He not only kills her, he crushes her skull and splits her body like a shellfish.

Anne Baring and Jules Cashford, in their book *The Myth of the Goddess*, analyze the story as a political message. Not only does it symbolize the rise of patriarchy, it also coincides with the Babylonian conquest of Sumeria. In Sumer, the story goes, the Goddess brought forth the world out of Her body, forming a heavenly mountain. Now Marduk, having split open his great-great-great-grandmother, "creates creation again," as Baring and Cashford put it. He heaps a mountain over Tiamat's head, more mountains over Her breasts, pierces the breasts and eyes to make rivers, uses Her crotch to support the sky, and so on. He also establishes the 12 months of the year, sets the Sun and Moon on their paths, and in general makes the world an orderly place. Finally, He creates man as a lowly creature to serve the Gods so that "they might be at ease."

Everything in this tale works to validate the "dominator" political system, in which men rule women, and the king, the God on Earth, lives by the labor of his slaves, just as the Gods receive the sacrifices and prayers of humanity. But we also might detect another layer in this tale, and all the other serpent/dragon slayings. A number of modern researchers and writers on the Goddess, such as Luisa Francia, author of *Dragon Time*, and Mary K. Greer, a leader of women's menstrual mysteries, have suggested that the "dragon" is menstruation, and that the destruction of this dragon means the breaking of the magical/religious power that comes to women through their blood. A dragon is a mythic snake, a snake of consciousness. Snakes ripple across the ground like liquid, like a stream incarnate – or like blood. And there is another association: in menstruation the uterus sheds its lining the way a snake sheds its skin to be "reborn."

We have seen (in Chapter 1) that human culture might have begun through women experiencing the power of "menstrual synchrony," that is, menstruating together during the new or full Moon. Most of the Western "dragons" are, in fact, sea serpents, such as Tiamat and Leviathan living in that salt water which is similar to blood. Others, such as the Delphic Python, live in dark moist caves.

Many cultures have demonized menstruation. Zoroaster named menstruation itself as the source of all evil. Medousa, the terror twin of Athena, may have received her monstrous image, with her snake hair and her eyes capable of turning men into stone, from male fear of menstruation. Freud described Medousa as a masculine projection of the female genitals.

Male Appropriation

In some places, an emerging patriarchy may have taken over the power associated with menstruation. In an article titled "Menstrual Synchrony and the Australian Rainbow Snake" in the book *Blood Magic* (edited by Buckley and Gottlieb), Chris Knight tells us that kings in ancient European cultures were not allowed to see the Sun or touch the ground – the same taboos that were placed on menstruating girls. Chinese myths describe the emperors as born out of copulation with a dragon, whom the myths described as "wet," "dangerous" – and female.

Knight traces the links between menstruation and the Rainbow Serpent, who acts as creator in many Australian myths. Fearful of this female power, men sought to gain control of it through establishing their own blood rituals. In some places in Australia, initiation for young men involves cutting and scarring the penis through sub-incision. During the initiation boys experience rebirth out of collective womb-pits. The older men then describe the (original) female womb as a pit of devouring *snakes*, and female power (which Knight equates with menstrual synchrony) as a "cannibalistic monster" from which humanity had to be rescued. (By comparison, men in Western countries have commonly believed that a vagina can have teeth, a concept known to folklorists as *vagina dentata*.) Knight tells us how the men will open the sub-incision wounds in ritual together at the time of the new Moon. As in Tierra del Fuego, some Australian men's secret societies describe power as all "women's business," saying that the men tricked them and stole their magic.

The Ona men tell of killing all the females old enough to know about women's power. This implies menstruation. But future generations will menstruate. The magic does not come from menstruation alone, it comes from *understanding what menstruation means*. Knowledge of the body and its power is as important as the body itself.

A Different View of Menstrual Taboos

Most people have heard of the complicated taboos placed on menstruating women in cultures as far apart as the Middle East and North America. We know of women confined to dark huts, not allowed to touch food, and so on. Many of these taboos derive from patriarchal societies taking the power of women and turning it on its head. For instance, the nutrients in menstrual blood help plants grow. To turn this around, early Judaism taught that menstruating women must keep away from plants for fear of destroying them. This superstition persists even today. A few years ago my sister told me that her rabbi had insisted that one drop of menstrual blood would kill a plant. With such ideas in the world it becomes possible to imagine men who believed that "Medousa" (menstrual blood) would turn them into stone.

At the same time, some anthropologists have begun to question the whole concept of "menstrual taboos," at least in tribal society. The editors of *Blood Magic*, Thomas Buckley and Alma Gottlieb, point out that most anthropologists have been male, and have therefore talked to male informants from the culture under observation. From this point of view, menstruation may seem fearsome and dangerous, with the actions taken around it seen as a protection from women's magical energy. However, when anthropologists seek the women's point of view, they often find the same actions seen in a more positive light. The men may see the "women's lodge" as a place to confine women and keep them from endangering the community. The women, on the other hand, may see the women's lodge as a place of power and celebration. In a similar way, some Orthodox Jewish women have begun to look at the positive side of the prohibition against sexual intercourse during and after menstruation. Rather than see it only as "unclean" they consider their menstrual periods a time apart, when they can enter into a different relationship with their partners, and especially with their own bodies.

A Religion Based on the Reality of Life, Not Power

People critical of the modern Goddess movement sometimes ask, if the Goddess is so all powerful why did women lose their place? How did men seize control everywhere and suppress women, keeping them ignorant and enslaved? Those who believe in the Goddess may also find these issues troubling. Some develop mythical ideas that the Goddess deserted Her children, or punished us for some lack of proper worship, or some broken taboo. Others fall back on the assumption of progress, saying that the Goddess allowed men to take over as a necessary stage in human development.

To some extent, these questions themselves arise from a patriarchal model of deity. We picture God(dess) as Almighty, controlling and directing everything that happens with deliberation, purpose, and unstoppable power. This is God made in the image of man (or rather, man's fantasies of omnipotence), particularly the master-slave "dominator" model of the world, as Riane Eisler calls it. In such a religion, God stands apart from the world and stage-manages it, commanding us above all else to fear Him ("Fear of the Lord is the beginning of wisdom," the Bible tells us).

The religion of the Goddess is not an "abiding relationship" with an all-powerful controlling being who exists apart from the world. Instead, we might term it a relationship with the world as it really is, with its cycles, its abundant life and ever-present death, its joy and pain. The abiding relationship emerges out of the body of the world and our own bodies. The Goddess is not in charge of history. The Goddess *is* history, with all its pain and horror as well as its beauties and discoveries.

The evidence from the Neolithic period teaches us that the Goddess does not require a split between nature, science, and the sacred. The beauty of such places as Stonehenge, Newgrange, or Chaco Canyon lies in their evocation of the sacred through channeling light into stone – giving form to the shifting body of the natural world. When we recognize creation as female we do not need to posit a God who creates out of thought alone, and who therefore determines everything that happens. We do not need to look for religion in something "higher" than the world right in front of us.

A religion based on the world as it is liberates men as well as women. I mentioned above that basing power and control on the phallus necessarily produces anxiety, because the penis falls as well as rises. In cultures where the Goddess embodies life, the phallus becomes an instrument of life, and therefore of liberation, but not conquest. The philosopher historian Michel Foucault suggested that St. Augustine's concept of "rising up against God" derived from Augustine's own inability to control his sexual urges. Following a transcendent God of thought alone, Augustine believed his mind should conquer his sexuality. The fact that his penis would rise without his bidding seemed to him a primal disobedience, leading to his concept of original sin, of each generation infected with Adam's crime, of the sperm itself infected (Augustine followed Aristotle, who taught that the baby existed wholly in the sperm), so that our creation through sexuality ensures our damnation. However, if we base our religion on the world as it is, then the phallus does exactly what it should do – and no more.

We do not need to fight great battles, or kill, or suffer martyrdom, to "restore" the Goddess, for She has never gone away. We only need to *look*, to acknowledge the reality of nature and of ourselves. In a way, we are all living out the myth of the Ona people of Tierra del Fuego. A distorted religion has turned the world upside down, denying that anything ever existed before itself. Through the recovery of knowledge – through science, through archaeology, through the acts of women, minorities, and indigenous peoples searching out their histories – we have begun to recover ourselves.

The Body in the Land

All wandering is from the Mother, to the Mother, in the Mother.

Nor Hall

*T*he European Neolithic age did not just vanish all at once. While some areas fell to invaders others continued to develop and flourish. This "civilization of the Goddess," as Marija Gimbutas called it, reached its height on the island of Crete 4,500 years ago. Until their world fell under a combination of earthquakes and successive invasions from the mainland, the Cretans enjoyed a society both complex and graceful, with large and complex palaces set in harmony with the Goddess's physical presence in the landscape. The Cretans celebrated the sensuality of life, in their horned mountains and cave sanctuaries, in their elegant frescoes showing such things as lush flowers and leaping dolphins, in their bull dances, even in their animal sacrifices, which they depicted in their art as joyous processions. The Greeks who came after them distorted these things, in particular creating nightmare stories of a half man, half bull *minotaur* devouring helpless young Athenians. Through archaeology and the insights of art historians and Goddess worshippers we have awakened from this nightmare to discover a veneration of life.

Like the later Greeks, the Cretans honored the body and its beauty. Unlike the Greeks, who sought balanced perfection, the Cretans expressed the body's vitality. We see this in the figurines of the Goddess Herself, bare breasted, filled with energy, holding snakes in each hand. And we can experience a distant echo of it ourselves, as we follow the ancient processional pathways around and within the palaces, set against the eternal presence of the horned mountains.

A Culture Older than Greece

From the point of view of Goddess history the island of Crete represents a culture distinct from the rest of Greece. Though Crete has belonged to the nation of Greece for thousands of years, ever since the mainland Mycenaeans colonized it and joined their own Gods with the Cretan Goddess, the original culture, with its great palaces, its elegant art, and its reverence for horned mountains, was pre-Greek, an extension of the Neolithic culture.

Much of what we know of this civilization comes down to us distorted through the myth-making of the later Greek culture. Though the names and stories about Crete do come from the island itself they actually reflect the later, patriarchal religion rather than the Goddess-centered myth revealed in the Cretan frescoes, seals, and other remnants uncovered by archaeology. Zeus himself, the chief of the Olympian Gods, probably began his mythic existence as a Cretan Vegetation or Bull God. Folklore describes one of the horned mountains dominating the landscape near the major Cretan palaces, Mt. Ida, as Zeus's birthplace, while another, Mt. Dikte, supposedly contains his grave. Since the Greek myths emphasize Zeus's immortality, it seems strange to speak of his *grave*. Still another myth describes Mt. Dikte as the site of Zeus's "marriage" to Europa; but the standard story tells of Zeus taking the form of a bull and *raping* Europa. Elinor Gadon, in *The Once and Future Goddess*, tells us that *Europa* means "full Moon" and that the character of Europa embodied the Goddess as a "Moon cow." Piecing these clues together, we can guess that at one time Zeus may have been the bull consort of the Goddess on Crete, married to the land and sacrificed to ensure the land's renewal each year from winter or from the lifeless drought of summer. The many depictions of bulls in Cretan art include images of bulls sacrificed to the Goddess in joyous processions.

Greek myth describes bees feeding the infant Zeus in his Mt. Ida cave. Once again, when we go back to the Cretan seals and jewelry we discover

140

bees with the Goddess. Bees embody the Goddess throughout southern Europe and the Middle East. The ancient writer Porphyry calls the grain Goddess Demeter a bee, and Greek myth tells us that Demeter came from Crete. Tablets from Knossos, on Crete itself, written in the Mycenaean script known as Linear B, describe offerings of honey given to the birth Goddess, Eileithyia.

Another Greek bull God, Dionysos, the God of Wine, also may have originated on Crete. Greek vases show Europa holding vines laden with grapes. In Classical myth Dionysos marries Ariadne, princess, but maybe originally Goddess, of Crete. In the story Ariadne's marriage to Dionysos raises her to the level of divine. Originally it might have worked the other way around, with the bull becoming a God through his marriage to Ariadne. The name Ariadne means "most holy," an epithet applied as well to Aphrodite. We will see more of Dionysos, this enigmatic God of Ecstasy, in the next two chapters.

Greek Myth as a Puzzle

So many of our images of Crete came to us through that confusing lens of Greek mythology. The vividness of Greek myth derives partly from its conjunction of clear and lucid thought – exemplified in the elegant columns of Greek temples – and wild violence, including murder, cannibalism, incest, rape, mutilation, and dismemberment. Through it all runs a sense of deeper layers, of other stories and meanings disguised and twisted, some elements brought together, others torn apart, so that as you read the myths, you feel you almost can grasp a simpler truth – but not quite. It is as if a particularly neurotic genius has shaped these stories, filling them with their own brilliance, and their own overwhelming anxiety. In a moment, we will look at the possibility that this anxiety derives from overthrowing the religion of the Goddess, a religion the Greeks themselves recognized as older, and more deeply wedded to the land and to the natural facts of existence, than that of their brutal warrior Gods. Here, however, we might look, all too briefly, at how this genius twists the facts of that prehistoric civilization Arthur Evans called "Minoan."

We can start with the term "Minoan" itself, coined by Evans when he excavated the palace of Knossos at the beginning of the 20th century. The title derives from a King Minos, son of Zeus and Europa, who supposedly ruled Crete before its downfall. This assumption still affects discussion of Crete. Archaeologists have designated certain rooms in the various palaces "the king's megaron," and assigned other, smaller, rooms to the "queen." Evans and his professional descendants described a stone chair found in such a room at Knossos as the king's throne. The chair is simple and elegant, with wall paintings behind it flanking it with griffins, but nothing about it necessarily indicates that it is a throne for a king. It might have served for a priestess or priest, or someone receiving honor at a particular time, or some purpose unique to the culture and unknown to us. The one clue comes from frescoes and vases that depict griffins protecting a seated Goddess. Maybe the Cretans meant the chair and the wall paintings behind it to bring the pictures to life, with a woman sitting majestically in the role of the Goddess.

Marija Gimbutas has questioned the very term "palace" for the large complex ruins uncovered by Evans. She writes in *The Civilization of the Goddess*, "The palaces were not administering centers for a ruler, but were palace temples, where elaborate religious rituals took place within a theacratic system."

Written texts found in Crete give a picture of complex bureaucracy. The script of these texts, Linear B, is actually Greek, from the Mycenaean invaders who gradually took control of Crete. The earlier, strictly Cretan script, known archaeologically as "Linear A," has never been deciphered. When we look at Cretan art, we find no images of all-powerful rulers, male or female, but only a Goddess receiving the praise and delight of Her worshippers.

Pasiphae and the Bull

According to Greek myth, Minos married a woman named Pasiphae, daughter of Helios and Perseis. *Pasiphae* means "all-illuminating," while Helios and Perseis are the Sun and the Moon. The names reveal the mortal woman as the Goddess of the Sky. Did the Greeks take the name of a Cretan

Sky Goddess and give Her a minor role as King Minos's wife? The myth tells us how Poseidon, the Greek Sea God, sent a white bull out of the sea to Minos, so that Minos might sacrifice the animal back to the God. (Other versions say Zeus sent the bull, which makes sense since Zeus took the form of a bull to rape Europa. Zeus, God of the Sky, Poseidon, God of the Sea, and Hades, God of the Dead, were brothers in the myth, but may have been one figure split into three functions.)

Sacrifice of bulls, which appears in Cretan art as such a powerful aspect of the religion, may have derived from the domestication of animals. In the time of hunting and gathering, humans stood in awe of beasts. Intense images of bulls, huge, painted in great detail as well as in wild movement, dominate Lascaux. To tame and control such creatures as bulls might have produced an anxiety, or guilt. Paradoxically, the ritual slaughter, and offering of the animal to the Goddess, may have relieved the sense that domestication had reduced, or trivialized, the power of beasts. On a more practical level, more than one bull in a herd produces a danger of violence as the males compete for dominance. The farmer may castrate the excess bulls, creating steers, or slaughter them. And why not give the slaughter of this young magnificent creature a sacred meaning equal to the experience of giving it death?

In the Classical myth, Minos could not bear to part with this great bull, and so killed another in its place. It was as if he thought Poseidon somehow would not notice. The angry Poseidon inspired Pasiphae with a passion for the bull itself. She turned to Daedalus, a master craftsman, and ordered him to fashion a wooden cow, which she might enter in order to entice the bull. Thus the world-wide cow Goddess becomes reduced in Greek myth to a dirty joke.

The Minotaur

From the union of woman and bull, Pasiphae bears a child, the "minotaur" or "bull of Minos," as if Minos himself somehow has fathered, or even given birth to the monster. Now Daedalus constructs a giant maze in which to hide this emblem of Minos's shame, this half man, half bull, who, in fact, like Zeus or Dionysos, really represents the Goddess's male consort. To the patriarchal mind, the worship of nature and the land as the Goddess, the female body, is terrifying, and anything that results from this "surrender" to the female can only be monstrous. And so Daedalus builds his "labyrinth" to hide the minotaur, and King Minos demands that Athens send seven youths and seven maidens as sacrifices to the minotaur every nine years. Just as seven calls forth the visible planets, so nine is the supreme number of the Goddess, for the nine Moons of pregnancy, and the magic of three times three, that is, the lunar Triple Goddess tripled. Thus, both numbers hint at celestial movements. The minotaur, in fact, bears a name, Asterios, Greek for "(King) of the Stars," yet another clue that he originally represented the partner to the cow whose udders gave forth the Milky Way.

The story of Daedalus himself, the master craftsman, may have arisen from the Greek warriors encountering the complex technological civilization of Crete, with its cities, multi-storied palaces, indoor plumbing, network of roads, and developed harbors. The pirate Greeks would probably never have seen anything remotely like it. Similarly, the idea of the labyrinth may have originated in the complexity and splendor of the palaces, for the word *labyrinth* means "house of the double axe," and the double axe forms the ubiquitous symbol of the Goddess throughout Crete.

The Double Axe

As mentioned in Chapter 3, the double axe did not serve as a weapon, and the image never appears in art with male figures, but only alone, on pillars sacred to the Goddess, or else in scenes of the Goddess and her female worshippers, sometimes alongside the Tree of Life in the garden of paradise. (A tourist guide to Crete describes the double axe as a symbol of Zeus, an example of the way patriarchal distortion continues into modern culture.)

Professor Gimbutas has suggested that the *labrys* derived from the butterfly, and indeed, engraved butterflies appear on some of the earlier axes, while some of the more ornate axes appear almost identical to drawings of butterflies. In the museum in the Cretan capital of Heraklion, a vase from the excavated town of Kato Zakros shows a butterfly with axelike wings (see *Plate 14*). The Greek word *psyche* means both "soul" and "butterfly," a conjunction that may go back to the earlier Cretan culture.

The soul as butterfly implies a view of human life as a stage to a more fulfilling existence.

The butterfly's wings and the curved axe blades signify the waxing and waning Moon, and also the labia of the human vulva. *Labrys* and *labia* are related etymologically. Other images may come to us from the double axe. The handle resembles a stem, or a tree trunk, extending down towards the power of the Earth. The blade itself forms an endless loop, like the infinity sign in modern mathematics. Because of the opposition in the curves – concave in the horizontal, convex in the vertical – there is a sense of reaching the apex of a wave and then swinging down the other way. (Try tracing the double blade pattern in the air with an extended arm, letting your hand sweep completely through the air in each direction. The motion can produce an intense raising and releasing of energy.)

The double axe can appear very plain or can be decorated, sometimes with garlands of leaves or with lions or griffins. The axes that have been found range in size from a few centimeters to some that are taller than a human (see *Plate 15*).

The double axe appears in other places as well, including Çatal Hüyük, in Anatolia, and I have mentioned the theory that Anatolians settled Crete. The name *Cybele*, the Great Goddess of Phrygia (Anatolia) and Rome, is cognate with *cybella*, or cave, and *cybellis* – double axe. In Africa the Yoruba God, Shango, carries a double axe which he uses as a weapon (like the hammer of Thor, Shango's Scandinavian equivalent). Shango himself is the consort of Oya, whom Judith Gleason describes as "Buffalo Woman," connecting Her to a Saharan Neolithic rock painting of a dancing Goddess with horn breasts. An image like a double axe appears in the Paleolithic cave of Niaux, France, and in the Neolithic culture of Tel Halaf, in Iraq. Christina Biaggi argues that the double axe may have originated in the exaggerated buttocks of Paleolithic Goddess carvings (compare the spirals on the buttocks of the Cucuteni Goddess p.98). In Crete, we also find the double axe engraved on stalactite columns in caves.

In the 1970s many radical feminists took to wearing replicas of the labrys as jewelry. As an interesting reflection of our warrior culture, most of these women did not consider that the axe might *not* be a weapon. Taking the image as a tool of Amazon resisters of the patriarchy, they wore the labrys as a sign of militancy. When I visited the palace of Knossos, I noticed, in a room called a shrine of the double axe, a modern wood frame where someone with a pen knife had carved the labrys image alongside a double female (or Venus) sign, the contemporary symbol for feminist lesbians.

Human Sacrifice

The Greek story of the seven youths and seven maidens sacrificed to the minotaur raises the possibility of human as well as bull sacrifice in Crete. Both the Greeks and the Hebrews cited supposed human sacrifice as justifications for their overthrow of the ancient Goddess religion. In fact, we find evidence in Crete of one, and only one, human sacrifice. This was at the very end of the Minoan period, during a time of earthquakes. No one knows for certain the reason for the fall of Cretan culture and the destruction of the palaces, particularly Knossos, around 1400 B.C.E. However, most archaeologists guess that the fall came through a series of earthquakes, the most powerful occurring in 1450 B.C.E. The earthquake was centred on the nearby island of Thera, but the shock waves brought down Cretan towns and palaces. An earlier earthquake, in 1700 B.C.E., destroyed the first version of the palaces. The fact that they did not rebuild after the second great quake implies a fatal weakening in the social structure during the 250 years between the disasters.

According to Vincent Scully, the Cretans built Knossos on a site of maximum seismic disturbance, as if they wanted to feel the power of the Earth making the walls come alive. They might not have realized the danger before the first quake and then afterward rebuilt the palace in the same place because they believed it belonged there. Or, like contemporary Los Angelenos, they may have decided to stay and risk "the big one."

Smaller earthquakes leading up to the one on Thera threatened the palace culture over a period of time, during which the people could see what was happening, and seek through prayer to avert this catastrophe which they could not hope to control by their own efforts. This took place during a period when the proto-Greek Mycenaeans had established rulership in Knossos, bringing in warrior chieftains while adapting much of the Goddess religion.

Archaeological evidence shows that towards the very end of the earthquake period a priest took a young man to an altar at a crude site in the hills and drove a knife into his back. Archaeologists uncovered this singular site only recently. The small ruin stands high in rough hill country. In contrast to the harbor area or the wide interior plains, the land there appears neither gentle nor enfolding. Instead, hard peaks and jagged rocks thrust up from the ground like knives. The sacrifice structure (much too crude and makeshift to be called a temple) stands on a north-south axis, with the mountains behind it, and the sea before it. I visited the site in late September, at the end of the summer drought, with the land grey and lifeless. In contrast to much more "developed" ruins, such as the palaces, the site is very carefully fenced in, without signs, and protected by barbed wire.

We know of what happened in this place because another earthquake struck at exactly the moment of the sacrifice. Rubble buried the killer on the floor alongside his victim, the knife still buried in the corpse's back. If indeed the people imagined that a human death would appease the Goddess they obviously got it wrong. The message says, "No, no, this wasn't what I meant at all."

The Bull Dance

From the archaeological evidence it would seem that the single killing stands in contrast to all previous practice. So why did the Athenians imagine a bull-headed "King of the Stars" devouring Athenian children? Besides the obvious value of propaganda they might have been distorting the famous Cretan bull dance, in which young men and women took hold of the bull horns and leaped gracefully over its back – a truly powerful distortion of something so positive and joyous.

The art showing the bull dance not only celebrates the youthful body, it also helps demonstrate the equality of women and men in Cretan society. Thousands of years before our Western "unisex" styles, the Cretans practiced that loose mingling of cross-gender imagery discussed in

Chapter 5. The bull dancing women in their codpieces and the men in rituals – another kind of dance – in their flounced skirts blend together gracefully. The art shows both sexes with slim waists and much jewelry. Women and men were also shown hunting together. Yet they were not asexual, or unmindful of the differences for other images show bare-breasted women, or men with erect penises.

The bull dance, like religious dances everywhere, expresses the power and beauty of the sacred body. We have seen the possibility of dancing grounds in at least one Paleolithic cave, Pêch-Mèrle. Dance is as instinctive as sex, as giving birth. Nor Hall comments that dance and midwifery both grow out of instinctual rhythms. A Greek hymn describes Artemis – ruler of women in childbirth, mother of the mountains, protector of the animals – putting aside Her bow to dance with the nine muses before the dwelling of Her brother, Apollo (for more on Artemis and Her *dancing* partners, *see* Chapter 7).

Through dance we experience our own bodies as alive, and we experience the life that flows rhythmically through all creation. In the wonderful words of a song of the Gabon Pygmies (collected in Jerome Rothenberg's anthology *Technicians of the Sacred*), "All lives, all dances, and all is loud."

Cells dance, electrons dance, galaxies dance in their spiral swirl. Religious dance takes us outside ourselves, to a state of ecstasy (literally "standing outside oneself"). But it also contributes to a communal good, for by joining in a ritual dance we offer our isolated selves, we "sacrifice" our individual egos and surrender our bodies, to evoke the Goddess's power.

Dance appears as a theme in much of Cretan art. Stylianos Alexiou describes pictures on a sarcophagus that show music being played at a bull sacrifice. He further describes a fruit stand showing women dancers on each side of a Goddess holding flowers, a similar scene on a bowl, clay figures showing four men dancing in a ring with their arms on each other's shoulders, a ring with bare-breasted women dancing, and a painting from Knossos of priestesses dancing in a sacred olive grove. On the day I wrote this passage I received information about "The First International Minoan Celebration of Partnership." The cover for the pamphlet shows a museum photo of three clay figures performing a ring dance around a central figure playing a lyre.

Theseus and the Labyrinth

The spiritual is political. All religion carries a social message. Much of patriarchal Greek mythology bolstered the current regime at the same time that it denigrated the earlier culture. In the Athenian myth, Daedalus – an isolated male genius – builds the "labyrinth," a supposedly impenetrable maze, so intricate that no one can escape it. The Athenian hero Theseus kills the minotaur and then retreats from the labyrinth via a thread, given to him by Ariadne. He unravels it as he penetrates the maze, so that he only has to follow it back to escape.

Again we find a mystery of distortions, both of the psyche, and of the historical facts of Cretan religious practice. The design known today as the labyrinth is not a puzzle maze at all, but a pathway to a center, with the special quality of doubling back on itself without crossing any lines. The path leads only to the center, and one can only go back by retracing one's steps (see *Figure 10*).

The labyrinth symbolizes the Goddess's uterus, through which we travel in an ecstatic dance, back to the source of our existence, then once more return to the outer world of our daily lives. The distortion of this clear pattern, a kind of dance, into a puzzle where one may get lost for ever, demonstrates the mysteries and confusions of Greek mythology itself. It also represents the fear of losing the ego in processional dances to the heart of the Goddess. The thread in the story originally may have meant the umbilical cord and the eternal connection to the Mother of life, another version of that knot we saw binding our lives to the Goddess. In the story of Theseus, however, the thread becomes the connection to rationality and control.

There are many suggestions regarding the origin of the labyrinth pattern. It may have derived from an erotic dance performed in spring. In the *Iliad*, one of the scenes on Achilles' shield depicts a dancing floor supposedly designed by Daedalus for Ariadne. G. R. Levy writes of a Cretan seal depicting "Ariadne" watching an ecstatic dance (the identification of the

Figure 10 The pattern of the Cretan labyrinth.

unnamed figure with "Ariadne" presumably derives from the Greek myth). Nor Hall suggests that the labyrinth dance may have copied the weaving patterns cranes make during mating, while Robert Graves writes that the labyrinth design comes from a trap set for partridges, who perform a hobbling dance in the mating season.

Though the labyrinth pattern has received the title "the Cretan labyrinth" it does not appear very widely in Minoan art. We know of its existence on Crete mostly from the design on coins. Strangely, the exact same image appears on rock art in the American South-west. Unlike such symbols as the cross or spiral, the labyrinth seems too complicated to appear independently in different cultures. Did the Cretans travel to North America 3,500 years before the Vikings?

The idea of a winding dance may signal an essential element of Cretan religion, that of a processional way beginning outside a palace and moving in a winding or spiraling pattern to the hidden mystery of the pillar crypt at the palace center.

The Power of the Land

The ideas of Vincent Scully about sacred landscapes have received very little attention from Classical archaeologists, although Donald Preziosi, in his book *Minoan Architectural Design*, comments that Scully deserves more consideration than most have given him. While critical of some of Scully's details, Preziosi acknowledges the overall plausibility of Scully's two main points, that the Cretans deliberately orientated their palaces on a north-south axis, and that they aligned them with particular landscape features.

Scully himself, in the preface to the 1979 edition of *The Earth, the Temple, and the Gods*, expresses his exasperation that for most writers on Greek sacred sites "the landscape still does not exist." He comments that human beings "see selectively, not empirically," their sight conditioned by "the conceptual structure of their culture."

If professional archaeologists have not warmed to Scully's landscape aesthetics, the movement to reawaken the religion of the Goddess has taken great inspiration from his work. This has come in part through the dissemination of Scully's ideas in other writings, such as Mimi Lobell's article in *Heresies*, or Elinor Gadon's book *The Once and Future Goddess*, or Dolores La Chapelle's *Earth Wisdom*. Like the work of Marija Gimbutas, Professor Scully's writing does more than provide information. It conveys a sense of the power and beauty of the Goddess, whose body in the land only emerges fully into being through the symbiotic actions of human beings.

Scully describes the ancient architecture as "a miracle of reconciliation" between human needs and nature. On the Greek mainland this delicate balance tilted towards the human, so that the temple forms an image of "victory." In the earlier Cretan culture, the palaces sought the harmony of the landscape as the Goddess's body. There were no temples, partly because the Cretans, like the Paleolithic painters, worshipped the Goddess in her cave-womb. The building of temples signifies a religion in which the Gods have begun to separate from the land. With the construction of temples for their worship, the Gods take on personalities distinct from nature. Though the Greek temples still settle into the landscape, their elegant columns and their statues evoke a deity more inspired by human culture than by the cycles of the Earth. The shrines in the Cretan palaces, however, did not prevent the Cretans from keeping their attention on the mountains and the caves.

Nature and Politics

Scully argues that the quality of the land itself helps create the sense of the sacred that is special to a particular society. Though Crete has some rough areas, the mountains are generally soft, the hills rounded. Scully observes that the "horror" sometimes found in other cultures' view of the Mother Goddess – what Erich Neumann called "the Terrible Mother" – does not exist in Crete. Unlike, say, the ferocious Hindu Goddess Kali, the Cretan Goddess does not devour, but inspires delight. The archaeologist Nicholas Platon writes of Crete, "a hymn to Nature as a Goddess seems to be heard from everywhere, a hymn of joy and life." The art of Crete is never static but filled with graceful movement.

If we posit a religion growing from the realities of nature, then certainly the special aspects of a place would help condition religious experience. At the same time, religion also grows out of political conditions. To the extent that the Terrible Mother exists in myth and is not an invention of modern psychologists She may reflect patriarchal anxieties about displacing an earlier culture. In India we find, as well as Kali, other cannibal blood-drinking Goddesses. Modern interpreters have given subtle analyses of these images. However, we should recognize that India, like Greece and Old Europe, suffered invasion and conquest by Indo-Europeans who brought their warrior Sky Gods to overcome the Earth-based Goddesses of the Dravidians. To this day, the Goddess remains revered in many villages, and the figure of Kali, that very image of the Devouring Mother, retains her honored place on household altars.

Actually, Professor Scully does not discount the significance of political, and indeed, military needs. He points out that the Mycenaeans accepted the Cretan principles but adapted them to their warrior situation (especially

152

at Mycenae itself), while the Dorians refused to accept the "conditions" of Cretan harmony, "including the hidden promise of immortality," and set Zeus above the Mother.

The Specific Landscape Forms

From 2000 B.C.E., Vincent Scully tells us, every Cretan palace shared the same landscape elements. These involve an enclosed valley in which the palace rests; a gently rounded, or else conical, hill on an axis with the palace to north or south; and on the same axis, "a higher, double-peaked, or cleft mountain." This mountain may possess other features, but the double peak or notched cleft remains constant. This shape gives the mountain a profile of horns, though it also may suggest raised arms, or wings, or breasts, depending somewhat on the size and shape of the double peak. As the landscape's most striking quality the mountain, and the cone before it, draw the observer's eye. The palace enhances this quality through its long flat courtyard, which leads us directly to the rising horns. Scully describes the cone as "the earth's motherly form," and the horned mountain as "the symbol of its active power."

It is worth repeating here Mimi Lobell's description of the landscape as the body. "The valley was her encircling arms; the conical hill her breast ... the horned mountain her 'lap' or cleft vulva ... and the cave sanctuary, her birth-giving womb."

At the most famous Cretan palace, Knossos, Mt. Jouctas appears very strikingly over the wall (see *Plate 16*).

Jouctas is also clearly seen, to due south, from the ancient harbor of Knossos. Indeed, it stands very clearly, also due south, from the shore line of the modern capital of Heraklion, a fact which I discovered while walking towards a cone-shaped mountain due west from the modern harbor.

Jouctas, like Ida and Dikte, contains cave sanctuaries where the Cretans worshipped the Goddess. Later, the same caves became places of Zeus, including the immortal God's "burial" site. All through the Middle East, religion focused on the sacred mountain. In flat countries, such as Mesopotamia, the people built ziggurats and pyramids to mimic the Goddess's mountain body. In *Earth Wisdom* Dolores La Chapelle describes mountains as a natural place of revelation, citing her own experience of seeing a "glory," a magnificent optical play of light and shadow visible only at high altitudes.

Subtle Differences

In fact, only the palace of Phaestos stands on a precise north-south axis with its mountain, Mt. Ida. At Mallia, a palace on the northern coast, Mt. Dikte actually appears over the south-east corner, while at Knossos we see Mt. Jouctas a few degrees off north-south. Since the builders were dealing with a conjunction of principles, such as the directional alignments and the practicality of fitting their palace in line with the contours of the ground, we would have to expect some variation.

Façades two or three stories high surrounded the palaces. Standing in the courtyard inside the walls, only the peaks of the mountains could be seen. This would in fact emphasize the horned mountain. Worshippers still would have viewed the lower hills during religious processions outside the walls, and they would have known of the other features even if they could see them only outside the palace. Donald Preziosi points out that mosques around the world have certain features pointing to Mecca, even though that city will be invisible from virtually all locations.

At all three major palaces people could see the mountain summit from the center of the court, directly opposite the principal shrines on the west side. The shrines might have commemorated the creation of the palaces themselves. Turning away from the natural mountain and towards the human-created shrine, the worshippers would have acted out the symbolic beginnings of human culture.

The Horns of Consecration

Knossos, Preziosi tells us, had a large doorway interrupting the southern façade. This doorway did not stand in the center of the wall, which seems unusual. However, it opened directly to a view of Mt. Jouctas. The early excavators of Knossos found the large Horns of Consecration lying precisely in front of this doorway. If set on the roofline above the door, they would have framed the cleft mountain.

At certain times of the year, the Horns would also have framed the Sun in their graceful curve. This combination would have echoed Egyptian images of the disc of the Sun between two peaks. Similarly, when the full Moon appeared between the Horns the sight would have duplicated the Egyptian crown of Isis.

Did Crete and Egypt influence each other, or draw inspiration from a common source? Mimi Lobell has described the yearly procession of boats traveling down the Nile between two peaks, one on each side of the river. The pharaoh in his barge embodied Amon-Ra, the Sun God, traveling to mate with the Goddess Nut. In a lecture, Lobell linked the journey to Crete. She showed a slide of a Cretan Goddess with upraised arms, horns on Her head, and a cone standing behind Her and seen between Her arms. If we stand in this posture, with our feet together, and our arms upright and curved, like horns, we will experience an openness in the body, an opening to the universe. This is especially true if we stand this way facing the Sun – and even more so if we stand facing the upraised peaks of a horned mountain.

Other Alignments

The alignment with horned or cleft peaks appears in places other than the three major palaces. At the town of Gournia, set into a hillside along the northern coast (see *Plate 17*), we can discover a sense of the Earth protecting us, with the nearby double mountain more like breasts than horns.

Both Gournia and Kato Zakros, a palace on the eastern tip of the island, contain courtyards orientated towards the mountains. Excavating a one-room shrine at the top of the hill in Gournia, archaeologists found a tripod altar, pedestals, a model of the Horns of Consecration, and a clay Snake Goddess.

Walking ashore at Gournia and entering the town compares to entering the Goddess's body in the temples of Malta. Gournia was roughly contemporary with the Maltese temples at Mnajdra, the only group of temples facing the sea (and the only ones aligned with solar events). In fact, the Mnajdra temples look out to the small island of Filfla, which has a double-peaked profile.

Gournia seems to have been a thriving town in its time. Today, the ruins possess a gentle quiet (due partly, no doubt, to the lack of great numbers of tourists). Set into a steep hill green with trees, they look out upon the sea. At the same time, the site sets up rhythmic contrasts of hard and soft landscape. A ridge seems to enclose the town, and beyond that rise the jagged mountains of Crete's rough interior. The rounded breastlike hills rise up due south, but harsh rocks stand in front of them. The sea appears as the only opening.

Even private dwellings follow the same pattern. Near the beach of Amnissos, outside the capital, Heraklion, stands the ruin of a villa, on a north-south axis, with a double peak behind it, more a hill than a mountain, as befits a house instead of a "palace."

Amnissos, near Heraklion, has become a popular tourist beach. Classical mythology, however, links the beach to Artemis. Zeus asks three-year-old Artemis what gifts She would like to claim for Her attributes. (Part of the program to give Zeus supremacy included turning the archaic Artemis into a child of the younger generation of Olympians.) Laughing, the Goddess says She would like freedom from marriage, a bow and the right to hunt, the rule of mountains, and the companionship of nymphs from Amnissos.

The name Artemis is of uncertain origin and is not Greek. It first appears in Linear B tablets from Pylos. Thus, She goes back at least to the Mycenaean period, and possibly to Minoan Crete or even the Stone Age. Three Cretan Goddesses became linked to Artemis – Diktynna, "She of the Net," Britomartis, or "Sweet Virgin," and Eileithyia, the Goddess of Childbirth. According to Anne Baring and Jules Cashford, the spring festivals at Artemis's great temple in Ephesus in Anatolia included a bullfight and sacrifice.

Processions

The idea of a processional way at the Cretan palaces derives from several sources. First of all, clear pathways, often lined with frescoes, suggest ritual movement. Images from seals and from the frescoes themselves show people moving majestically in ceremonial costumes to places of sacrifice. Later Greek mythology tells of the Kouretes, guardians of the infant Zeus, banging on shields to cover the concealed God's cries as he lay in his Cretan cave, nourished by bees. This image may have originated in Cretan processions that included banging on shields shaped like the number 8. Evans found such shields, plus paintings of them, in his excavation of Knossos. The figure 8 brings to mind the rounded breasts and hips of the female body and recalls the Old Stone Age "Venuses" and the floor plan of the Maltese temples.

Cretan images show a Goddess traveling in a boat with Her worshippers. We know also of journeys to cave sanctuaries and of bull dances held in the courtyard, in sight of the horned peak. Finally, we can assume processional rituals by looking at later practices in Greece, where the worship of Goddesses often involved processions, such as that of the *arktoi*, or "she-bears," – girls of around nine years old who traveled from Athens to Artemis's temple at Brauron.

Crete and the Mysteries of Eleusis

The most famous Greek procession was that of the *mystae*, the initiates who journeyed from Athens along the coast of Attica to Eleusis, where they celebrated the Greater Mysteries of Demeter and Persephone (*see* Chapter 8). Many observers of the Mysteries, ancient as well as modern, have claimed that the Mysteries at Eleusis, and the later Hellenistic Mysteries, represented the survival and even the return of the Cretan religion of the Great Goddess. And in fact, the site of the Mysteries looks across to a horned peak on the island of Salamis, while the processional way itself passes in and out of view of a cone-shaped hill. G. R. Levy describes a funeral image from Crete showing the Goddess in a boat, and portrays this as a link between the burgeoning of the Earth and the rebirth of the dead, the concept that became the basic idea of the Mysteries.

Anne Baring and Jules Cashford point to a number of Cretan paintings that suggest a Cretan origin for the myth of Demeter and Persephone, the story at the center of the Mysteries. In particular, they cite a simple line drawing on a cup from *c.*2000 B.C.E. The picture shows two women leaning downwards, as if in mourning, towards a third who may be plucking a narcissus flower. In the Eleusinian myth, a narcissus lures Persephone to the place where Hades, the God of the Underworld, kidnaps Her. A second drawing, in the same style, shows the trio rising upwards, with the middle figure now holding two flowers.

The Processional Way: From the Sea to the Inner Palace

The Knossos processional way may have begun in the harbor. Scully describes the path to the palace as winding "serpentine" through the lower hills, until the hills rise up to define the valley. The ceremonial entrance would seem to have been on the north wall, where we find double stairs leading to an area sometimes called a "theater" (though drama did not develop until much later, on the Greek mainland). The stairs are approached along a raised pavement so narrow the people must have walked along it in single file. Professor Scully sees this as looking back to the Paleolithic caves, like Lascaux, in which people passed in single file through the entrance corridor to the wider chamber of the paintings, with their thundering bulls. If the palace and the landscape *together* signify the body of the Mother, then entering one at a time would have reminded worshippers that all of us have passed alone from our mother's bodies into the world.

Now the path diverges into two. One way moves to the east, entering a pillared hall, then turns south and mounts a ramp to come out into the open court at the north end. Here the line of sight travels down the open courtyard to the mounded hill "closing" the valley. Beyond that stands Mt Jouctas. Already we get a sense of a labyrinthine movement, the path turning back on itself as it mounts to the place of vision. Following such a path, through the valley and now the palace, a procession of human bodies forms the single body of a snake. Together with the landscape and building, the procession brings to life the Cretan Goddess with Her snakes wound around Her body. Here, as in Michael Dames's vision of Avebury, human bodies must join with the landscape and with human constructions to form a living sculpture of the Goddess and Her serpent companion.

The second path follows an even more labyrinth-like way, derived from that fact that the court does not sit precisely on an axis with the mountain.

This path, again narrow, moves south from the "theater" to the west side of the palace, where we see again the hill and the mountain. At an open space, the "west court," where a new path from the west joins in, we find an altar, and beyond that the west porch of the building, with a single column between its walls. We have seen how a column, or pillar, embodied the Goddess as a symbol of Her Earth power, recalling the stalagmites of the caves as well as Her eternal Tree of Life.

Now the way takes us through a corridor, again very narrow, and lined with processional frescoes (reminiscent again of the cave paintings), into "a dark place" (Scully) and then out again, to the light beyond the south terrace, where once again the soft hill and the more austere horns of the mountain come dramatically into view.

The path continues to turn, moving through light and dark, until we emerge into the bright light of the court. Here the bull dances took place, with the graceful young men and women leaping over the horns of the bull, while the equally graceful Horns of Consecration stood proudly on the walls above them.

The processional movement not only winds continually, giving views of Mt. Jouctas and then turning away from it, it also moves between narrow and open spaces, contracting and expanding, a replica of the breath, as well as of the contractions of women in labor. It moves as well between stairs and ramps and flat ground, and between dark and light. The whole effect becomes sinuous, like a striped snake, with a sense of change that is spiritual as well as physical.

The procession does not end in the courtyard. Professor Scully's reconstruction now takes us to the right from the open court down into the "low, dark, cavelike shrine of the goddess." This is a room known today as the "pillar crypt," containing dark pillars, offering pits for sacrifices, and a carved sign of the double axe. Having emerged in the joyful light of the bull court, where the dancers celebrated their exuberance, the way has brought us now to the darkness of the inner mysteries, the place most intimate with the Goddess, where the solemnity of the bull *sacrifice* may have balanced out the life-centered culture of the daily society. Professor Scully writes

159

The processional movement from light to dark to light and dark again – culminating as it does in the innermost cavern shrine where were found at once the hollow earth of the goddess and the pillar which both enters and supports the earth and is thus also hers – makes of the Minoan palace as a whole that ceremonial labyrinth around the secret place which the Greeks remembered in their myths.

Remembered – and distorted, turning it into a place of monsters and murder, of terror instead of sanctity. Was it simply propaganda that led the Greeks to tell of their hero, Theseus, defeating a savage killer inside a maze? Or did they carry with them their own fear of something deep inside themselves, something unacknowledged – *a fear of the dark, moist, interior of the female body*.

In the Paleolithic cave art and other rock art, the vulva often appears as a cleft like the letter V. We find this basic image, in gigantic form, in the horned mountain. Mt. Jouctas is conical as well as cleft, so that the Cretans may have seen it as the *mons veneris* (mount of Venus) of the Goddess in the land. To enter a cave in such a mountain produces a deep sense of entering the body. The palace may have duplicated this quality in a far more subtle fashion.

The Beauty of Phaestos

My own sense of the Goddess forms in the landscape and the palaces came not so much from Knossos (perpetually crowded with guided tours) but from the palace of Phaestos. Phaestos stands on a hill in the south of Crete, in an area more rugged than Knossos. From the stream at the bottom of the palace hill Mt. Ida is eclipsed by another hill, but from Phaestos itself Ida rises magnificently into view, seemingly closer and more intimate than Jouctas at Knossos.

Vincent Scully describes Mt. Ida as "embracingly female," descending from its wide, symmetrical horns "in rounded, spreading slopes, which are cut by dark horns" (see *Plate 18*).

Another Mt. Ida, in Phrygia, was the home of Cybele, the "Great Mother of the Gods." Cybele may reach back all the way to Çatal Hüyük, for some of Cybele's imagery strongly resembles that found in the 8,000-year-old city. The first Homeric hymn to Aphrodite describes the Phrygian Ida as sacred to the Goddess of Love. According to the myth, She lay there with Anchises, and later gave birth to Aeneas, hero of Virgil's *Aeneid*.

Because Phaestos sits on a hill, we get a wide sense of the valley and the surrounding mountains. A short distance away stands another "palace," more of a large villa really, called Agia Triada (the name, which means "Holy Trinity," derives from a nearby Christian chapel). Despite the closeness of the two buildings, the difference is remarkable. Agia Triada rests against a curving hill, with a feeling of quiet and restfulness despite the views of Ida and a pair of cone-shaped hills.

Scholars often refer to Phaestos as a "summer palace" for the Minoan rulers to escape the commerce and bustle of Knossos. Professor Scully remarks that the term "does not adequately describe its haunting power," and goes on to comment that Phaestos "seems purposefully stretched out as an act of worship for all the land ... possessed by the invincible mystery of the earth, praising the valley's breadth, the mountain's terror." For my part, I would add that walking through the ruins of Phaestos, standing in the open court or "theater," resting and looking out across the hills and to Mt. Ida, all of this brings a sense of attachment to that Earth mystery, with no need to solve it, or seek miraculous revelations. Phaestos, like Delphi on the mainland, is a place to belong to the Earth. As with Delphi, I can give Phaestos no greater tribute than to say that simply thinking and writing about the palace and its landscape awakens a deep longing to return.

As described in Chapter 2 I observed the sacred landscape forms and knew I had arrived before I actually found myself at the palace. Travelling along the road to Phaestos a cone-shaped mountain in a winged setting appears, surrounded by low hills, while a horned mountain becomes visible on the horizon. At the moment the two formations come clear of the lower hills, the modern road curves round and there stands the sign announcing Phaestos.

Cone and Mountain

As I found when I traced what might have been the processional way, the cone fulfills an important role in bringing out the connection to the land.

161

Ida stands due north of the Phaestos court, the most precise alignment of all the palaces. The cone rises to the north-west. The processional way begins at the north-west entrance, with the cone placed squarely behind you. The way moves west to the open theater, where it goes down the stairs and cuts diagonally south-east across the theater, the cone behind you. At the end of the theater the path turns so that you suddenly find yourself facing the powerful image of the horned mountain with the cone to the left. The way moves east, and then doubles back, labyrinth-like, to head north and up the stairs.

The way continues upwards to a room with the remains of a pillar. From there it seems to turn back on itself again and goes up a ramp, once more facing Mt. Ida. The propylon from the theater leads into a dark narrow stair which turns down towards the light and into the main court. Looking northward from the south of the court, Ida rises both above the wall and above a doorway into the northern apartments of the palace. At the same time, the southern end of the court opens to the valley, giving a view of soft hills.

Standing outside of the palace, the cone appears behind you. When you actually enter the building, the cone disappears, blocked by the wall. At the same time a smaller, more intimate and rounded cone-shaped hill comes into view due west of the open theater.

Similarly, when Ida looms behind you, unseen, a gentle double-peaked hill rises before you to the left, in the south-east, more or less on an axis with the sharper, more rugged cone. This hill even has a low mound in front of it, so that it appears as a smaller, and more accessible version of the sacred mountain.

The two horned peaks, the mountain and the hill, are both visible from the court, for while Ida rises above the palace, the court stands open to the gentler hills. At the top of the theater steps, the highest point, all four forms appear. As you move within the palace grounds, however, the gentler forms take over. The effect becomes a human softening of nature. The rugged peaks dominate as you enter the palace, only to give way visually to their more accessible counterparts. These low hills still contain the Goddess's body, but on a more human scale, in a form more susceptible to agriculture and development. Here, as in so many ways, the culture of ancient Crete somehow brings together – like the two halves of the double axe, or the two snakes held by the bare-breasted Goddess in Her long skirt – the human and the divine, neither overpowering the other, but blending together in graceful joy and elegance.

The Body in Song

Farewell
children of Zeus and Leto,
she of the beautiful hair,
Now
and in another song
I will remember you.

Hymn to Artemis,
translated by Jules Cashford

*O*f all the Gods and Goddesses we know the Greek Gods and Goddesses the best. We have seen the graceful statues and the temples with their mathematical proportions, we have read the stories of the love affairs and the battles, the manipulations of helpless mortals, the transformations of humans into trees or stars or rivers. And yet, the closer we look at the Greek myths, the more mysterious they become, filled with a strange mixture of violence and beauty, intelligence and fear. We begin to get a clearer sense of them when we see the way they enact the conquest of an older order, one built around the many Great Goddesses, each one from a different local area overrun by the invaders. This is not just a modern interpretation. The ancient Greeks themselves praised their Olympian Sky Gods for wresting the world from the "chthonic" deities, beings they described as dark, dangerous, earthly, monstrous – and female.

Part of this conquest involved reducing the complex and archaic Goddesses to emblems of particular qualities. Artemis becomes a kind of girl scout roughing it in the woods. Aphrodite gets caught up in endless love affairs while Hera broods furiously over Zeus's philandering. Athena, once an all powerful Goddess of the snake and the owl, now leaps from Zeus's head, as if He Himself has created Her. Despite this seeming triviality, the Goddesses also become exalted in Greek myth, for indeed that very individuality does allow them to show us mirrors of ourselves. These are mirrors with infinite depth, for the more we look into those mirrors the more we see a double image: the figures we know from the stories, and their much older counterparts, those Goddesses of land and sky and water, of birds and snakes and human passion, as old as stone, connected to us, through all the years of distortion, by the eternal truth of the body.

The Immortal Gods

Vincent Scully describes the temple architecture of mainland Greece as an image of "victory," in which the balance tilts to the human domination of the cosmos. Certainly few cultures have ever perceived the Gods in quite such human terms as did the Greeks. We need only think, on one side, of the graceful realism of the statues, or, on the other, of the domestic squabbling in the stories of Zeus and Hera.

At the same time, as the Gods become more human, humans themselves become lessened. The Cretan palaces served as homes, workplaces, and probably seats of government for the people, as well as focal points to perceive the Goddess in the land. The Greek temples house statues, not people.

In Crete, we find the idea of Zeus as the dying and regenerating God, embodying the miracle of plant life, who dies and goes down to the underground of the Goddess of Death, only to return as a new child with the coming of spring. The Dorians, however, perceived their Gods as immortal, without bodies, free from the cycles of nature. They may have characterized their Gods in very human terms, but they also described them as pure energy.

The concept of immortality derives from the fear and pain of death. More subtly, it may rise out of the need to separate the idea of *God* from the *Goddess*, that is, separate divinity from the essentially female body of the natural world. (Even our monotheistic culture refers to "Mother Earth" or "Mother Nature".) The Goddess's body involves us in the constant cycles of death and rebirth. Separation from the Goddess allows the possibility of immortal perfection.

But even though this view of God may satisfy the patriarchal desire to see the ultimate being as male and separate from (female) nature, it also creates a gulf between the Gods and humanity. Like the rest of nature, humans grow weak and die. The very act of imagining Gods exempt from suffering ensures that humans take no part in the deity. In the Greek cosmos, humans exist only at the mercy of the Gods, who can reach out and crush them at any moment.

Longing for immortality may have arisen in proud chieftains who hated the idea of death while fearing its arrival at any moment, during their many battles. And so they may have fantasized what it would be like to live forever, never to die or even feel pain, to expect tribute from all the world, to kill anyone who opposed or even annoyed them, and to possess any woman they desired. These are the attributes of Zeus, chief of the Gods.

The religion of the Goddess was a religion of *place* and *bodies*, with the two joined in the landscape and palace. The Gods divorce themselves from the land, and even though they take the form of idealized humans and can join in such human activities as sex and war, they are really bodiless. Whereas the Cretans and Mycenaeans pictured the Goddess receiving worshippers in Her garden, by Her Tree of Life, later Greek myth portrays the Gods as unapproachable, terrifying, liable to strike down or tear to pieces any mortal who happens to come across them. The Gods roam the world and mingle in human affairs, but they do so at their own whim. They do not belong to the world. They live forever in their splendor on Mt. Olympus, removed from the mud and labor of human life.

Greek religion does join with nature in all the origin stories of such things as star constellations or particular kinds of trees (significantly, many of these stories involve rape or killing). Almost like the Australian Aborigines, the Greeks imagined every tree and river inhabited by a nymph or dryad. The main objects of religion, however, the Olympian Pantheon, separated themselves from nature.

When humans die they are not reborn, but exist only as cold empty shadows. In *The Odyssey*, dead Achilles tells Odysseus that he would rather till the fields as a live slave than rule over all the dead. Only in the Greater Mysteries of Eleusis does this change, with the promise of rebirth bringing joy to all who take part in them – and the Mysteries may have descended directly from the celebrations of the Goddess in Minoan Crete.

Layers of Meaning: Psyche

Part of the fascination of Greek myth lies in that teasing quality of stories which seem to mask deeper layers of meaning. So often in Greek myth we get a sense that some great inner truth lies exposed yet hidden at the same time. The puzzle becomes a little clearer when we consider that many of the myths either distort some earlier myth, or act as justification for the patriarchal takeover of Goddess religion. And yet, the genius of Greek religon gives us a feeling that a genuine spiritual mystery has emerged from this wrenching conflict between the Mother Goddess and the Warrior God.

As with some of the Hebrew myths, such as the story of the Garden of Eden, we need to explore aspects of the stories which seem to make no sense. One such aspect occurs in a tale of a woman and the God of Love.

Our modern word *psyche* derives from the Greek word for "soul." But Psyche is also a character in a story. The story of Psyche tells of her love for Eros, the God of Love and the son of Aphrodite. To achieve union with her beloved, to become able to see His face and stand beside Him, Psyche must complete tasks for Aphrodite, including a journey to Persephone, the Queen of the Dead and the Goddess whose rape and kidnapping begins the myth underpinning the Eleusinian Mysteries.

In the beginning of the story, Psyche encounters her mysterious lover only at night, for Eros knows she could not withstand the full force of His beauty. Her sisters become jealous of her, and taunt her that there must be something wrong with her husband if she can never look at him in the light. So far this all seems straightforward. But then we learn that Psyche's sisters suggest to her that her lover is not a man at all – but a snake. Why would they say such an odd thing? And why would Psyche pay any attention to this peculiar idea?

Only when we learn of the great intimacy between the Goddess and snakes do we begin to get a sense of something deeper in this tale. Statues of the Minoan Goddess portray Her with snakes wound around Her arms and body. Athena was originally a Goddess of snakes as well as the owl. The people who made these images of divine beings and snakes did not do so arbitrarily. The myths and statues express that deep and mysterious fascination with serpents and their power to stir some hidden place in the psyche. Among other qualities, snakes evoke the fundamental energy of sexuality. In some older stratum of the story, the soul – Psyche – was indeed the lover of the snake – Eros. And if the snake becomes the lover of both the woman and the Goddess, then the soul, the individual self, and the greater Self of the divine become intermingled.

Psyche becomes a figure of the ancient female power who has lost Her knowledge of Herself, who has become reduced to a frightened girl afraid of the dark. As in the Genesis account of the condemned serpent, the God has put enmity between the woman and the snake. Psyche's sisters, the symbols of society, tell the *psyche*, beware, do not let your passion and your desire overwhelm you, for you may find it leads you away from the rational, the safely human, to something much deeper – to the snake, the ancient buried power of the body. Her surrender to love will lead Psyche to the Underworld, where she must go to recover the power of life in the Land of the Dead.

We can look at our brains as structured in layers built up over the course of evolution. The youngest, the neocortex, governs our rational thinking processes. The oldest, the limbic system, directs our deep automatic responses. In evolutionary terms, the limbic system belongs to snakes. Some people interpret this to mean that the neocortex makes us human and we must suppress the limbic serpent in ourselves. But so much of our power and our strength comes from our deep instinctive passions. If we deny them, we deny our selves, our humanity.

A Sea Journey

The above passage, concerning Psyche and the snake, comes from notes first written down on the ferryboat crossing the Aegean Sea at night from mainland Greece to the island of Crete, a journey back in time as well as through darkness and over the waters of our most ancient Mother. This journey, and the writing, took place on the fifth night of the Eleusinian Mysteries, which last nine days, so that the fifth becomes the mid-point of the journey in and out of the Underworld. On that fifth night, the *mystae*, the initiates, bathed in the sea and then marched with torches, acting out the search for Persephone, the Goddess whom Death stole away, taking her down into the darkness.

In the movement towards her own divinity, Psyche visits Persephone, for Aphrodite has given her a *pyxis*, a small box, and commanded her to fill it with cream containing Persephone's beauty. But the word *pyxis*, like the word for Pandora's *box* (see p.130), was slang for the female genitals (if we make the connection on a literal level, the cream becomes vaginal secretions), so that the real beauty of the Goddess belongs to the power of the womb – life out of death; sexuality out of darkness.

In Greek myth the dead travel in ferryboats across the River Styx. The modern ferryboat to Crete, a huge many-decked liner with restaurants, lounges and private cabins, still performs the ancient journey, a trip across the sea, whose dark surging waters match the salt blood within our own bodies. And that particular trip, to Crete, formed for me a journey of return to the Snake Goddess, Persephone's ancestor, whose arms reach out in both directions, as if to embody the flowing movement of life and death.

The Conquest of Delphi

Greek myth seemed to allow all the layers of meaning to exist at once, the prehistoric religion of the body just beneath the surface of the sunlit religion of abstraction and rationality. But this was no easy co-existence. The Olympians replaced the older religion through conquest. The fact that they could not simply banish it provided a source of tension and anxiety. We find this even at Delphi, maybe most of all at Delphi, the chief shrine of Apollo, Lord of Sunlight and measured reason. For Delphi was a place of prophecy, the major center of divination in the ancient world, a place where even Greece's enemies went to uncover the future and discover the will of the Gods. But we cannot perform prophecy as a rational act. We need to reach into those dark layers of the mind where our bodies merge with the body of the Earth and the flowing body of time.

Apollo's conquest of Delphi was a daring stroke of genius for the Olympian religion. It imposed the rule of rationality in exactly that place most likely to resist it. At the same time, however, it could not simply banish the old religion. For without the *women* and their connection to the Earth, who would bring forth the prophecies?

Apollo's temple in Delphi displayed the slogan, "Know yourself." And yet, we might describe the Apollonian religion as a movement *away* from self-knowledge, as a defense against the power of the body, the body of the Goddess. Vincent Scully writes that the Greeks invoked rational Sun-lit Apollo "wherever the most awesome characteristics of the old goddess of the earth were made manifest." Originally Delphi manifested the Goddess of Prophecy in a vaporous cave where fumes induced visionary trances. To build a geometric temple over that hole in the Earth, that dark archaic place of prophecy that embodies the source of our being, is precisely *not* to know ourselves, but to hide from self-knowledge of our origins, our reality.

A large part of the anxiety that runs through so much of Greek myth seems to spring from a suppressed awareness of having covered up (literally) the Goddess's body and hidden it from sight. The same aggression against the female took place in the body politic, for the Greeks confined women, hiding them in their houses, denying women citizenship, and taking away their ancient property rights even as they enshrined rape as a divine act. The sexual and reproductive power of the female became suppressed as well, with women despised for having babies, and Aristotle describing the female orgasm as an abomination, prescribing removal of the clitoris as a cure.

The Terror of the Conqueror

Wherever one group of people oppress another a rage builds up, not just in the oppressed group, but in the oppressors as well. This latter rage comes as a reflex out of denial of what the oppressors have done. Their victims stand as a constant reminder, both of their crimes, and of the reality they have tried to overturn. And so they hate and fear the people they have conquered. Where men oppress women, women's bodies become a place of terror. Menstruation changes from something magical to something evil or disgusting. Vaginas grow teeth to bite off a man's sexuality.

Greek myth carries a sense of the patriarchal religion wrenching itself away from the Mother. When the Sun God Apollo kills the python (described as the "Daughter of Hera") he tells her, "Now rot here upon the soil that feeds man." The Earth, and the Goddess, become fearful as well as despised. The name of the hero Heracles meant "Glory of Hera." In the Classical myths, however, he becomes yet another bastard son of Zeus, so that Hera becomes his tormentor, driving him mad out of jealousy. Oedipus follows the Apollonian charge to know himself, and discovers that he has killed his partner and married his mother. However in doing this he has only acted out an archaic ritual, in which the queen embodied the eternal life-giving power in the land, and the old king the vegetation that needs to die in winter so that the young plants, embodied in the son, can take their place in spring. Not wanting to know these things, not wanting to see himself, Oedipus rips out his eyes.

The Earth itself becomes a place of terror – wet, oozing, alive, and monstrous – with the Sky a refuge, a place all clean and shiny compared to the dark mud of the ground beneath us. Greek myth describes the pre-Olympian deities as "chthonic," of the Earth, at the same time as it pictures them as demonic, insane, bloodthirsty – and female. Apollo the Sun God, all bright and clean, strides forth to conquer and bury under his ritual temple those messy Goddesses of the dirt.

As the symbol of the Goddess, and the expression of Her intense energy, prophetic as well as sexual, the snake becomes the enemy, just as it does in Genesis. Against the instinctive snake, Apollo establishes the "light" of rationality, supposedly conquering the dangerous passions of the older Earth Goddesses. But if we see the Earth as the body, as *our* collective body, then Apollo takes us away from our bodies to that detached transcendence of the Olympian sky. He does this precisely by killing the python and building his calm, abstract temple, with all its columns and mathematical proportions, over the moist Delphic cave – the Earth's vulva – where the sibyls prophesied out of the mist and smoke. Writing about Apollo's killing of the python, Buffie Johnson in *The Lady of the Beasts* quotes Jane Ellen

Harrison's ironic comment "What need does the glorious shining Apollo have for a snake?"

Coming to Delphi

The ancient pilgrims to the oracle could travel to Delphi either overland or by sea. Apollo Himself came from the water, bringing Cretan sailors to be his priests. Crete remained the land of religious authority, even, or maybe especially, for those who overthrew her prehistoric traditions. Both Zeus and Demeter came from Crete. To increase his authority Apollo took over the sacred palm tree and grove from the Cretan Goddess. The God lured the sailors by disguising Himself as a dolphin. In the palace of Knossos, buried centuries before the building of Apollo's temple at Delphi, playful, leaping dolphins can be seen on the wall frescoes. The name Delphi relates to two Greek words, *delphis*, or dolphin, and *delphys*, womb.

For those travelling to Delphi on foot the way was rough and mountainous. Today, however, modern roads and the electric lights of towns tame the journey. Nothing, however, can dim the stark beauty of the hills. The site of Delphi lies under the deep cleft of Parnassus, the mountain of poetic inspiration, home of the nine muses (nine again, that magic three times three). Above the cluster of temples, above the sacred Castalian spring, rises a cliff "splendidly crowned by tremendous horns that open thunderously to the sky" (Scully). These are the Phaedriades, the Brilliant Ones (see *Plate 19*). The spring, where seekers poured water over their heads to purify themselves, falls from the cliff below the horns. Having trained ourselves to see, we recognize this spring, even if we have never seen it. It is the same water that emerges from Silbury Hill, or Glastonbury, or passes under the fissures of the Teaching Rock in Canada. The spring that gushes from a cleft mountain is the Goddess's blood.

The entire site looks across the valley to a further cleft in the mountains. A cleft embodies the Goddess's vulva, whether as a narrow line in the wall of a cave, or a fissure in the ground, or huge horns of a mountain. And with the run of spring water, and the original cave of the oracle, we get a series of images of the vulva, becoming more intimate as one approaches the shrine, from the mountain form against the sky, to the emergent water, to the dark mists now covered by the temple. The mists alone, rising from the hidden places in the Earth, inspired prophecy.

In Classical times the temple did not actually cover over the chasm of mists but surrounded it. Though Apollo had killed the snake, women still gave the oracle, as if the new religion could not banish the authority (and reality) of the old. Called *Pythia*, after the python, the prophetess washed herself in the spring, chewed a laurel leaf (the laurel grew from the body of a nymph who fled Apollo's attempts to sexually assault her), and then sat on a tripod over the chasm, where she inhaled the mists and called out her "prediction." Often the prophecy came out as wordless sounds, which a (male) poet then interpreted into coherent verse.

At the height of Delphi's fame, there were three pythia, that number invoking the Triple Goddess of the Moon and women's three stages of life. (Plutarch described the voice of the Sibyl – the Pythia – as carried about on the face of the Moon.) The three legged tripod triples this again, once more giving us the sacred number nine, the months of pregnancy. Rather than maiden, mother, and crone, however, the pythia were all women over 50, post-menopausal crones. Peasant women as well, they retained the connection to Earth, Gaia.

Some accounts of Delphi describe the oracle as available to all pilgrims who came and purified themselves. In fact, Apollo's rules forbade women from seeking counsel. His priests may have needed the power of the female body, but that did not mean they would tolerate women receiving any benefit.

Delphi's stunning site led its worshippers to see it as the center of the world. Even after Apollo's conquest of the shrine, the *omphalos*, or navel, remained the most sacred object. The omphalos was embodied in a conical stone, carved with a snake coiled round it, as if to protect it. From Crete we know that a conical stone (or mountain) projects the Goddess's power. The omphalos stone gained extra significance by being a gift from the Sky – a meteorite. As with Cybele and her conical black meteorite, or the huge Ka'aba meteorite in Mecca, the omphalos, with its snake, demonstrates the unity of Earth and Sky, two aspects of the same body.

The Rocks of Gaia

The Greeks sometimes called the cave at Delphi the entrance to the Land of the Dead. This Underworld aspect, along with the landscape forms and the snake and the meteorite, remind us that the shrine originally belonged to the Earth Goddess, Gaia, also called Themis. Gaia's original sanctuary was a circle of rocks, reminiscent of those of the Stone Age, surrounding the open chasm. Today, one still can see the large Rock of the Sibyl, where ancient tradition described the oracle as sitting to deliver her prophecies. Surrounded by all the Classical buildings, the huge unadorned rock brings us back to the power of the land.

An even larger rock evokes the Earth at a temple site a short distance down the hill from Delphi, at a place called Marmaria. Here stand the remains of the Old and New Temples of Athena Pronaia, whose title means "before (or guardian of) the shrine." Where Delphi rises up along the hillside, looking out at the sky, Marmaria rests in a low area below the path, giving the visitor a sense of closeness to the ground. Set at the back of the Old Temple (excavations have revealed a Mycenaean settlement at this spot), a huge standing stone, suggesting a human form, reaches far back in time, reminding us that Athena, Goddess of wisdom, of owls and snakes, was far more, and far older, than that armed warrior who supposedly leapt full-grown from Zeus's head (see *Plate 20*).

Though I cannot say I received any direct oracular messages at Delphi, I found it a place of great beauty and personal healing. Maria Fernandez and I traveled to Delphi with some trepidation, fearing we would find it, like the Parthenon in Athens, overrun with tourists. In fact, one sometimes sees as many as 20 tour buses parked along the roadside. And yet, the power of the land resists any trivializing. The visitor may spend days, weeks, studying the architecture of the different monuments – or simply sit and look out across the hills.

The Goddesses Individually and Together

The separation of the Great Goddess – wild, ancient, many-sided, strong as stone and water, as intimate as our own mothers and as unfathomable as death – into a host of characters, each with Her own narrow range, forms

175

part of that "outrage" Jane Ellen Harrison described as having been done "to the ancient order of Goddesses." And yet, that very fragmentation calls forth the brilliance of Greek myth. By narrowing the scope of each figure, the Greek stories allow us to look closely at such attributes as freedom (Artemis), wisdom and dedication (Athena), motherhood (Demeter), rebirth (Persephone), and sexual passion (Aphrodite). As the Goddesses become individual they stand in danger of losing their grandeur and mystery. But they also become people, characters in stories, and through knowing them we may discover mirrors (or maybe enlargements) of ourselves.

But we also gain so much from recovering the connections between them. We do this when we start to look closely at their attributes and the practices and symbols associated with them. While keeping their individuality the Goddesses begin to move together, drawing us back in time to the many-sided Goddess of the Stone Age. Of all the Olympian Goddesses, the one closest to the prehistoric Goddess of wild nature turns out to be the least likely figure of all – Artemis, Apollo's twin sister.

Artemis and Motherhood

Goddess of the Moon, dweller in mountain forests far from the world of men, attended by nymphs, hunter but also protector of wild beasts, Artemis certainly points back beyond even the New Stone Age to the Old. But it is only when we learn of another of Her attributes that the image of the Great Goddess begins to emerge from the girl scout of Classical mythology. Tough, virgin, Artemis was the Goddess of women in childbirth.

Classical myth gives its own justification for this anomaly. It describes Artemis and Apollo as twins, the children of Leto and (of course) Zeus. The story tells how Artemis emerged first, without difficulty, and then tended Her mother over nine days of labor to bring forth Apollo. As a result, mortal women called on this unlikely figure during their own labor. For some Artemis eased the pain. For those not destined to survive, however, Her arrows promised a swift and merciful death.

It would seem once again that the story distorts older traditions, in which the Mother of the mountains and the wild beasts naturally came to human mothers in their labor. Some stories of Leto tell how Zeus transformed her into a wolf for 12 days, while others describe wolves escorting the mother and her twin children.

The Classical account reads almost like a rationalization. Powerful, ancient, beloved by the common people who preferred the old ways, Artemis of the Mountains would have threatened the new religion of Zeus and Apollo. By making Her Zeus's daughter and Apollo's sister they not only brought Her into line with the Olympians, they also would have borrowed Her authority with the people. But women still would have revered Her and sought Her aid in childbirth the way they have done since time immemorial. To accommodate this special quality – and still make Apollo the center of the story – the Greek myth came up with the tale of Artemis tending to Leto.

Artemis and Modern Women

Artemis has become very important to many contemporary women, despite general books on Greek mythology treating Her as something of a minor deity. As a Goddess of the New Moon, Artemis (or Diana, as the Romans called Her) evokes the spiritual power of the menstrual cycle. Current worshippers and writers concerned with Artemis have stressed Her ancient roots, linking Her to the Old Stone Age Goddess. In doing so, they rescue Artemis from the Classical picture of Her as a tomboy version of Apollo.

At the same time, the character of Artemis in the Classical myths attracts many women. She is independent, strong, devoted to women, animals, and nature, skillful as well as wild. She turns Her back on cities and man-made civilization, choosing instead the woods and mountains. Above all, She remains free. Virtually alone of the Greek Goddesses, Artemis does not attach Herself to men, either through marriage or liaisons, as with most of the Goddesses, or through patronage of heroes and cities, as with Athena. And yet, She attends women in childbirth.

Many writers on Greek myth have commented on the seeming paradox of the virgin Goddess assisting mothers during their labor. To me, this has never been a problem, for I have known women just like Her. In the 1970s an entire movement of radical lesbians decided to turn away from men altogether. And not just individual men, but the whole structure of urban technological society. They went to live with other women on communes where they grew their own food and tended animals. They dressed simply, in rough clothes, and tried to follow the patterns and rhythms of nature. They studied herbal medicine as an alternative to the drugs of the medical profession. Many of them became pagans, worshippers of Diana, as they created women's rituals based on the Moon, the seasons, and their own bodies. At the same time, many of them committed themselves to women's health care, not just for themselves or other lesbians, but all women. Some of these "back-to-the-land separatist lesbians" became midwives. Worshippers of Diana/Artemis, they themselves imitated Her.

Solitude and Sexuality

Some writers, such as Ginette Paris, describe Artemis as a Goddess (or "archetype") of solitude, living eternally alone in the wild, a sort of virtuous campfire girl, uninterested in sex. What these writers seem to mean is that Artemis did not involve Herself with *men*. For how can we describe Her as solitary when the myths tell of Her 20 river nymphs from Amnissos, or the *arktoi* ("she-bears"), the nine-year-old girls who joined Her service, or the companions who attended Her and bathed with Her?

As for sex – Arthur Evans (in *The God of Ecstasy*) puts it very well. "In reality," he writes, "Artemis was quite famous for her sexual exploits – with other women." Evans describes the women who "held wild orgiastic dances in her honor, sometimes wearing masks." Marija Gimbutas tells us of vase paintings showing dancing Artemis-worshippers in animal masks, as if they join with those wild beasts so beloved of the Goddess. Gimbutas further describes the women of Lakedemonia performing "orgiastic dances to glorify Artemis." According to Evans, the sexual dance cult of Artemis's women spread so widely it gave rise to a saying, "Where has not Artemis danced?" The expression is clearly a euphemism for the scandalous sex practices of the Goddess's worshippers. Here too the Classical myths attempt to drain the Goddess's power, with the story of Artemis setting down Her bow to join the muses in dancing before Her brother Apollo, as if to entertain Him.

An interesting myth hints at Artemis's sexual involvement with Her band of followers. The story describes Artemis's rage when Her companion Callisto becomes pregnant. In some versions, Artemis kills her instantly and then relents and sets Callisto in the sky as the constellation the Bear, for Callisto had taken the form of a bear when Zeus (who else?) was pursuing her. In another version, however, before Callisto dies, she tells Artemis that she did not realize it was Zeus who came to her, for the God had disguised Himself – as Artemis, implying that Artemis and Callisto were lovers. Because of Callisto's innocence, Artemis raises her to the heavens. As with so many myths, many things happen simultaneously in this story. Artemis Herself often appears as a bear, evoking once again those Goddesses who reach all the way back to the Old Stone Age, and even to the beginnings of humanity, when the Neanderthals performed rituals with the skeletons of bears.

Anne Baring and Jules Cashford refer to Artemis's epithet, *Keladeine*, or "the Sounding One," and describe the Goddess as "evolving" out of the sounds of wild nature. They also consider it "inevitable" that virgin Artemis should preside over childbirth, for She embodies the animal drives within us as well as the instincts of a mother towards her baby. During childbirth women must surrender to this instinct, must give up their "cultural identity and allow the deeper wisdom of the body to lead."

Part of this surrender seems to have included the giving up of clothes, as emblems of culture, and the taking on of other clothes. The clothes of women who died in childbirth were offered to Artemis at Brauron, the same temple where the young girls dressed in bearskins to serve Artemis as wild animals. Girls planning marriage would dance at Her festivals and then consecrate their tunics to Artemis before their wedding, as if acknowledging they were giving Her up to join the patriarchal system.

Moon Goddesses

In Greek myth three Goddesses symbolized the Moon – Artemis, Selene (sometimes associated with Demeter), and Hecate. They form the trio of Maiden (waxing Moon), Mother (full Moon), and Crone (waning Moon). Again, they may have been one Goddess whose different sides became assigned to different personalities. Both Artemis and Hecate are often depicted with dogs. In the myth of Persephone, Artemis (and Athena) are gathering flowers with Persephone when Hades rises out of the ground and kidnaps Her. The Homeric hymn then tells us that only Hecate witnessed what took place, and only Hecate will tell Demeter what has happened to Her daughter. With Artemis, Demeter, and Hecate, all three aspects of the Moon appear in Persephone's story.

The characters of the three Goddesses evoke the different qualities symbolized by the shifting Moon. The young crescent Moon, in shape so like Artemis's taut bow, brings out the many possibilities of youth, when all things open before us and we yearn to run wild and free, testing our strength and courage. The full Moon stirs up powerful emotions but also shows us an image of completeness. The face looks down gently on us like a mother gazing at her children. The old Moon, moving into darkness, demands surrender even as it offers us the wisdom of having passed through the cycle of life.

Artemis and Apollo

In the ancient Greek world, the temples of the Sun God Apollo gradually took over the places associated with lunar Artemis. As described above, the Greeks may have joined Apollo to Artemis in order to borrow (steal) some of Her authority. On Delos, the oldest and largest temple belongs to Artemis, with the shrine to Apollo being much smaller, and on the periphery. Delos also contained a horned altar, supposedly set up by Theseus after he had killed the minotaur and then abandoned Ariadne on the island of Naxos (where she entered a divine marriage with Dionysos, the God whom Kerenyi considers the secret husband of Persephone). According to the Greek story, Theseus set up the Cretan-style horns and then taught a labyrinth dance to the young men and women of the island. We can probably regard this as another appropriation, for the horns symbolize the Goddess through their association with the Moon and with the horned mountains. And of course, they do indeed reach back to Crete.

By contrast with Delos, at Delphi we find no temple to Artemis at all. And yet, the forms of the hills and mountains speak of Her ancient power.

If it is true that horned peaks and clefts, and triple mountain formations, refer us to Artemis and Gaia together, then the oldest Goddess surrounds us at Delphi, the site most dedicated to Artemis's victorious younger brother. At the site itself one sees the Phaedriades as well as the deep clefts across the valleys, but even in the nearby towns one can suddenly come across that natural landscape form of winged Artemis in the hills.

Lions and Bees

Many of the early plaques and paintings of Artemis show Her with animals, often lions, an association found throughout southern Europe and the Near East. Inanna and Ishtar from Sumeria and Babylon, Isis and Sekhmet in Egypt, and the Cretan Goddess all appear with lions. Lions drew Cybele's chariot through Rome. From Çatal Hüyük, in Cybele's home region of Anatolia, came that statue of the Stone Age Goddess giving birth while seated calmly on rock, her hands resting on the heads of two lions. Thousands of years later, a statue of the Virgin Mary depicts Her sitting on a throne with lion heads on the arms.

The Mycenaeans invoked the Goddess in different forms at their great fortress of Mycenae on mainland Greece, a site traditionally associated with Artemis. We see lions on the famous gate entering the site at the bottom of the hill (see *Plate 21*).

The lions stand upright, a proud expression of the Mycenaean warriors. And yet, the pillar which supports them returns us to the Goddess, for we know from the "pillar crypts" in the Cretan palaces that such posts evoked Her presence, both as trees, and as stone columns or stalagmites in the cave sanctuaries. At Mycenae, the lions and pillars together form a cone, a Goddess shape as important as the horned mountain. Dolores La Chapelle describes how the "Cone of Mukli" appears centered between the horns of a gorge, across from Artemis's temple at Mt. Artemision.

The cone form on the lion gate also suggests the form of a beehive. Both the Minoan Goddess and Artemis were pictured as bees. A Mycenaean gemwork from 1500 B.C.E. shows two rampant lions dressed in beeskins, while a gold plaque from Rhodos, some 700 years later, shows a Goddess with Artemis-like wings and a beehive for Her lower body. The association with bees came from the queen bee as a goddess to her hive. Swarming bees symbolized abundant life, so that the Mycenaeans shaped their *tholos* tombs like beehives.

The early plaques and paintings of Artemis with Her wild beasts show Her with wings that stretch out from Her shoulders and then curl upwards at the ends. The landscape at Mycenae brings this image to life, for the hills on each side of the fortress sweep out widely before curling upwards to their sharp peaks.

Links Between the Goddesses

Through the heritage of Classical Greek mythology we have become used to thinking of the Greek Goddesses as distinct individuals, wholly separate from each other. Some contemporary books even give charts of the Goddesses and their attributes so that readers may choose the Goddess who best suits their own personality. In reality, we cannot isolate them so neatly.

Almost everywhere we look the Goddesses overlap each other. Think of dancing, for example. Through shouts and music and dancing we worship the Goddess with joyous bodies. Artemis's worshippers called Her the Sounding One and celebrated Her with loud noises. The worshippers of both Cybele and Demeter clashed cymbals in their honor just as the Cretans may have banged on shields in their processions and rituals. And we can recall the stone drum found in Pêch-Mèrle by an open area that may have served as a dancing ground. The image of dances returns us full circle to Artemis and Her animal-masked women dancing in wild sexual abandon.

Flowers express the Goddess's beauty and richness of life. The Romans adorned both Cybele and Venus (Aphrodite) with roses. In Greece too, Aphrodite's followers honored Her with roses, one reason why today, thousands of years later, we give roses to express passionate devotion. In Christian times, the rose became associated with Mary, coming to Her both from Cybele, the Mother of the Gods, and Aphrodite, the Queen of Love. Dante's vision of Paradise (borrowed from the earlier French poem *Le Roman de la Rose*) portrayed Mary at the center of a great rose created by the angels floating in adoration around Her.

Indeed, many of Mary's attributes borrow from the earlier Goddesses, particularly Cybele, Aphrodite, and Ephesian Artemis. The name Mary (in Hebrew Miryam) means "the sea." Aphrodite means "foam-born," for the Goddess of Love rose out of the salt water to step onto the shore of Cyprus, where the spirits known as the Hours adorned Her with roses.

Great Mother Cybele gives birth primarily to Attis, who, like Jesus, dies and comes back to life. Just as with the later Mary, Cybele does not need a male to impregnate Her. The early Christian Council that established Mary as officially the Mother of God took place in Ephesus, site of Artemis's great temple, with Her many-breasted tree statue. Like Artemis, Mary became the patron protector of women in childbirth.

Cybele

Pomegranates, as well as roses, belonged to Cybele. An early statue of the Goddess portrays Her holding pomegranates. The statue comes from Syria, the eastern end of the Hittite empire, which conquered Anatolia/Phrygia around 1740 B.C.E. A thousand years later, in Rome, statues of Cybele still showed Her with pomegranates. The pomegranate links Cybele most obviously with Persephone, who must return each year to the Land of the Dead because of eating two pomegranate seeds given to her by Hades, the God of Death. But Roman art sometimes depicted Cybele side-by-side with Demeter, Persephone's mother. Demeter gave knowledge of agriculture to humans as an expression of Her joy when Her daughter came back to Her. By comparison, the Roman writer Lucretius named the Phrygians as the first people to cultivate grain. Cybele's son Attis, who died and was resurrected each year, symbolized the grain, just as Zeus had done in Crete, or Osiris in Egypt. (Osiris began as a Vegetation God but over time His role changed. Having died and been resurrected, He became the ruler and comforter of the dead, promising them rebirth in much the same way that Persephone, and later Jesus, did.) At the end of the Mysteries of Demeter and Persephone, the Hierophant ceremoniously held up an ear of grain before the mystae.

In the Hittite empire, Cybele bore the name Kubaba. This name possibly means "cube" referring to a cube-shaped meteorite worshipped as the Goddess's Sky body in Anatolia. Archaeologists have found a cube-shaped black stone at Petra, a Hellenistic city in what is now Jordan, and to this day, the Ka'aba, a giant meteorite in Mecca, remains the focus of Moslem worship. In Rome, Cybele's lion-drawn chariot carried a conical black stone into the city during Her great spring festival in March-April.

As well as the black stone, other objects embodied Kubaba. These included a door and a gate, symbols of the vagina opening to the mysteries of the body. They also included a dove, the bird most sacred to Aphrodite (and associated by the Jews with Noah, and by the Christians with the Holy Spirit who impregnated Mary), and the double-bladed axe, that crescent Moon butterfly symbol of the Goddess that extends back through Crete, and in fact Anatolia, to the Stone Age.

Genital Sacrifice and Sex Changing

The strongest and most unusual connection between Artemis, Cybele, and Aphrodite comes through the myths and practices involving sacrifice of male genitals and a kind of ritual changing of sex. Such images and actions break down the assumed wall between the sexes. They remind us that we all belong to Her body and even the most fixed categories can become mutable under Her power and influence. Almost always the crossing of boundaries between the sexes occurred during ecstatic rites involving loud music and wild dancing processions.

While we find gender-changing rituals and sacrifices primarily among Cybele's Phrygian worshippers and in the myth of Aphrodite's origin, the same links appear in stories of Artemis. The women who danced so wildly in Her rites sometimes wore stag horns, and other aspects of male impersonation, including large phalluses. Marija Gimbutas tells us in *The Goddesses and Gods of Old Europe* "Offerings to Artemis include phalli and all species of animals and fruits ... Mutilated beasts, from which 'a member was cut off' were sacrificed to Artemis in Boeotia, Euboea and Attica."

The fullest expression of genital sacrifice comes with the *gallae*, who followed Cybele from Phrygia to Rome. (Many writers on this subject use the masculine form of the word, that is, *galli*. Like the Roman poet Catullus, a major source of information on the rites, I have used the feminine ending as a recognition that the gallae's self-emasculation involved a deliberate movement from a masculine to a feminine state. Similarly, most texts on this subject use the term "self-castration" for the gallae's actions. Castration, however, means the removal of the testicles only. The gallae emasculated themselves entirely, as if to remove all maleness from their bodies.)

The gallae made their offering as part of the long rites of Cybele and Attis, on 24 March, the "Day of Blood." Once again, music and dancing formed part of the ritual, as the elder gallae helped the initiates attain a state of ecstasy. Roses belonged there as well – according to Randy P. Conner, in *Blossom of Bone*, "devotees of Cybele and Attis showered the *galli* [sic] with coins and white roses." The gallae may have emasculated themselves or the elders may have done it for them. Either way, the removed organs became objects of magical power. Some accounts say the gallae stored them in underground chambers to be used in mystery rites.

After their self-emasculation the gallae ceremoniously received female clothes. Sir James Frazer described them as wearing bridal dresses for their initiation into the service of their Goddess.

A Widespread Practice

The cult of the gallae began in Phrygia, probably as far back as the Stone Age. It spread from there to Rome, and also to Athens and as far as London under Roman rule. But we also know of it from other cultures, including North Africa, India, Arabia, Canaan, and elsewhere. We find a clue to its widespread practice in Chapter 23 of Deuteronomy where we read "No man ... whose organ has been severed shall become a member of the assembly of the Lord." Commenting on this passage, Rabbi J. H. Hertz wrote "The first to be excluded are the self-mutilated or unsexed in the service of some heathen cult."

Today in India we still find the equivalent of the gallae, with people known as *hijras*. According to Anne Ogborn, an American transsexual woman (male to female) who has become an initiated hijra, the hijras remove their male organs in surgery performed by a *dai ma*, usually a leader in the local hijra community. Before the British officially outlawed the practice in 1888 the surgery took place in temples of the Goddess Bahuchera, a variant of the more well known Goddess Durga. The hijras, like the gallae, dress as women, and will often refer to themselves, especially amongst themselves, as women (though most Indians refer to them as neuter, "neither man nor woman"). Among their ritual functions, they dance at weddings and bless male babies. In the time of the moghuls the hijras performed a ritual known as *solah shringar* to prepare courtesans to meet their lovers.

Self Chosen, Goddess Chosen

The gallae, and the hijras today, never compelled anyone to join their cult. Roman law, in fact, restricted the practices to Phrygians and forbade any Roman citizen from becoming a galla. Both the Greeks and the Romans abhorred the gallae, recognizing their very existence as a threat to the rule of the phallus.

Prospective gallae came forward themselves, asking to join the Goddess's service. And yet, though they clearly offered themselves, they also may have felt the Goddess had touched or summoned them. While the gallae may have included a few men who had abused women and sought to atone, the great majority felt something in them push them to this extreme action of altering their bodies.

The gallae resemble contemporary "transsexuals," a word that means "cross-sexed." Touched by a strong sense of belonging to the "opposite" sex, transsexual people seek out surgery and other means to change their bodies. The body thus becomes an expression, or a medium, for a deep and passionate desire. Many transsexual women have identified themselves with the gallae, even establishing modern temples to Cybele and celebrating Her festivals. Others, like Anne Ogborn, see a connection with the hijras. While most do not link themselves directly to these cultures, a great many have viewed the crossing of gender and sex as a spiritual journey. Davina Anne Gabriel, editor of *TransSisters: the Journal of Transsexual Feminism*, has written that we cannot understand transsexuality without the idea of "transcendence." And Dallas Denny, writing about the lessons learned since Christine Jorgensen's 1952 surgery (the first modern "sex change" operation announced to the world), began with the statement "Transsexualism is a religious/spiritual experience."

The Myth of Cybele and Attis

While the gallae took their extreme action to express an inner drive, they also did so in imitation of both Cybele and Attis. In some versions of the myth, Cybele begins as Agdisthus, a double-sexed hermaphroditic God/dess. The arrogant Agdisthus represented a danger to the Gods. To tame Him/Her, Dionysos steals upon the sleeping Agdisthus and ties the male organ to a tree. When Agdisthus awakes, the phallus engorges and a sudden movement severs it. This gruesome act does not lead to Agdisthus becoming crippled, or withdrawn, or enraged. Instead, She/He changes to Cybele, the Great Mother of the Gods. (Another version of the story speaks of Agdisthus and Cybele as rivals for the love of Attis.)

According to Randy Conner, a pomegranate tree grows from Agdisthus's blood; we will see in the next chapter that other accounts describe the pomegranate as the heart of a dismembered Dionysos. Eating the fruit, a river nymph named Nana becomes pregnant and gives birth to Attis, who then becomes Cybele's lover. Other versions of the myth describe Attis as Cybele's son. The confusion may derive from the earlier myths of the Goddess taking Her son as Her consort.

Anne Baring and Jules Cashford tell us that in the oldest version of Attis's story the severed male genitals of androgynous Cybele give rise to an almond tree rather than a pomegranate tree, and that Nana becomes pregnant from eating the almonds.

Attis dies emasculating himself in imitation of Agdisthus. As a vegetation God, Attis would have returned in the spring. In later times, he ascended to heaven to be crowned with stars.

The Creation of Aphrodite

Attis and the gallae may strike modern readers as obscure, if not disturbing. However, some of the same issues arise around a figure still considered central to Greek mythology: Aphrodite, the Goddess of Love.

The origin of Aphrodite goes back to the most basic elements of nature, the Earth and the Sky. Something has gone wrong, the myth tells us. Ouranos, the first creation of Gaia, has become arrogant, separating Himself from the Earth. He will lie with Her, but He hates the children brought forth

187

from their union, as if He cannot stand the reminders of Her power to create out of Her body. And so He hides them, taking them from their Mother as soon as they appear.

Gaia creates a stone sickle, an instrument whose shape evokes the Moon, as well as the drawn bow of Artemis and the horn held by the carved Paleolithic Goddess found in Laussel, France. (Archaeological finds suggest that women may have invented the sickle as a tool for harvesting plants. In one of the oldest cave excavations archaeologists found a curved blade which they took as the war weapon of some chieftain – until someone thought to examine it with a microscope and found traces of plants rather than blood.)

Gaia gives the sickle to Her son, Kronos, identified with the planet Saturn. Kronos severs Ouranos's genitals and throws them into the sea, thereby surrendering them to the primeval female body. We do not learn what happens to the organ itself. Instead, the myth tells us how the action stirs up a foam upon the water, from which arises the perfect female, Aphrodite.

Some feminists interpret Hesiod's story of Aphrodite's birth as an attempt to claim the Goddess of love as a male creation, comparing this story to that of Athena bursting out of Zeus's head. However, Ouranos's fate seems so weighted with anxiety for men, so terrifying for most men, that it would hardly armor them against the power of women. And Aphrodite does not retain male characteristics, as does Athena, or align Herself with males on political issues, as Aeschylus describes Athena doing in his play *The Eumenides*. Aphrodite is not so much Ouranos's daughter as His *replacement*. After He is "unsexed" He withdraws into darkness.

Did Aphrodite originate in the Stone Age? The myth reveals Her as a generation older than Zeus and the other primary Olympians. Did Her worship originally include figures like the gallae who worshipped Cybele? In the Homeric hymn to Aphrodite, the Goddess describes Herself as a daughter of Phrygia, which was the home of Cybele. Cybele first came to Rome because of a prophecy from the Delphic oracle saying that the Mother of Ida would save the city from invasion. The myth tells us that Aphrodite lay with Anchises on the slope of Mt. Ida in Anatolia, and that when Anchises discovered his lover's identity he begged the Goddess not to make him impotent. By comparison, men in India believe that the hijras possess the power to curse a man with impotence.

In the region of Amarthus, devotees of the local Goddess assimilated to Aphrodite described their deity as "double-sexed." They called Her/Him Aphroditos. Our very term "hermaphrodite" comes from Hermaphroditos, a son of Hermes and Aphrodite who merges bodies with a river nymph named Salmacis. And Robert Graves, in *The Greek Myths*, tells of a Hittite Goddess who bites off the genitals of the Sky God, Anu, and spits out their seed onto a mountain to create a Goddess of Love. The Goddess who performs this act is Kubaba, the Hittite name for Cybele.

Shamanism and Gender Changing

The world-wide religious structure known as shamanism, sometimes thought of as the world's oldest religion, often includes a change of gender. The shaman, whether male or female, wears the clothes and takes on the social role of the "opposite" sex. In some cultures, notably a number of indigenous North American peoples, women or men change gender as an expression of personal choice. Such action breaks down the artificial barriers of opposition between male and female. The people concerned, however, do not cross over to make a philosophical point. Rather, like the gallae or modern transsexuals, they follow an inner drive or compulsion. Writing about the rituals of Dionysos (yet another cross-gendered figure), Nor Hall tells us "Abandonment to the body's desire is in itself a source of revelation."

Of the many strands giving rise to Greek religion, one may have derived from the shamans who leapt the barriers of gender, males through the sacrifice of their genitals, females through the wearing of masculine clothing and artificial phalluses. Sex-changing deities and heroes appear time and again in Greek myth. Niobe sneers at Leto, the mother of Apollo and Artemis, for having a mannish daughter and a womanish son. Both Heracles and Achilles wear female clothes for a time. Teiresias, the Greek seer, begins his journey to prophecy by changing sex. Coming across two snakes copulating, he kills the female and discovers himself transformed into a woman. After seven years, during which she becomes "a celebrated harlot"

(Robert Graves), Teiresias sees the same sight, and by killing the male, once more becomes a man. The story is philosophical, for it implies that whichever we try to kill, we may become. It also suggests that male and female are incomplete, and that sacred power comes through overcoming that split – within one body.

Dionysos, "The Womanly One"

Dionysos Himself bore the epithet the "womanly one" for having been raised as a girl. According to Arthur Evans, in *The God of Ecstasy*, Dionysos's followers sometimes embodied Him as a stick decorated with a dress and a beard. Evans describes how women worshippers of the God dressed as men, with long phalluses, while men took on the clothes and roles of women. Evans cites this description of Dionysos by Diodoros of Sicily: "... quite soft and delicate of body, by far excelling others in his beauty and devoted to sexual pleasure." The description brings Dionysos closer to Aphrodite, reminding us that "ecstasy" takes us out of ourselves, but not out of our bodies.

It is said that the disguised Achilles reveals himself when he chooses a sword over more feminine gifts. Dionysos, however, when offered several toys as a child, chooses a mirror, a feminine article, not just for its concern with beauty, but also for its Moon-like reflecting powers. The mirror traps Him, and demonic forces dismember Him and throw Him into a boiling cauldron. Now, this story exactly mirrors the trance terrors of many shamans, who are cut to pieces, boiled alive, and otherwise broken down to allow for a rebirth as a new being, often in a new gender. The maenads, Dionysos's followers, were described as standing rigidly erect, like phalluses. They also acquired shamanic powers. They ran barefoot through snow for miles and wound snakes through their hair without being bitten. The maenads did not alter the body through surgery, but through trance. They became, in a sense, trance-sexuals.

Artemis and Aphrodite

At first glance, no two Goddesses seem further apart than Artemis and Aphrodite. Artemis is tough, wild, erect and strong, living hidden in the forest, merciless, mysterious as the silver Moon. Aphrodite is sensual, golden and soft as dawn, passionate, dangerous, wilful, forever falling in love, and leading others from reason and sense. Artemis is the body of strength, Aphrodite is the body of desire.

And yet, the deeper we look the more we find that these two Goddesses belong together. Both of them stem from ancient roots, clear remnants of the Great Goddess. Both may have originated outside Greece, for their names are of uncertain origin and meaning. But these are surface comparisons. A deeper power links the two. Both Goddesses embody a wildness, a body urge that takes us, as Vincent Scully says, "beyond the reach of reason or control." They remain, at all times, true to themselves.

We find some explicit connections as well. When Aphrodite makes love to Anchises on Mt. Ida she does so on a couch "spread with the skins of bears and lions, while bees buzzed drowsily about them" (Robert Graves). All three of these animals belong to Artemis.

Aphrodite and Sexuality

Unlike some deities, Aphrodite does not keep a distance between Herself and those who fall under Her power. She gives Herself to love as wildly and senselessly as any of Her subjects, lying with mortals as well as Gods. "Then love shook my heart like the wind that falls on oaks in the mountains" writes Sappho, perhaps the Goddess's greatest devotee (trans. Jim Powell). Aphrodite allows the wind to shake Her own heart as well, for how can She understand and unleash the power of desire without Her own surrender?

Despite all the attempts to reassert our sexuality over the past hundred years, we still distrust this primal aspect of our lives. We try to keep sex as an aspect of emotional relationships. If we hear of someone contracting Aids through casual sex, we speak of this terrible illness as the person's own fault. We feel guilty if we desire people we don't respect, or fantasize about actions we don't approve of. We try to control our fantasies, even in our minds, so they will not betray any unpleasant or frightening aspects of ourselves. We happily take up images of the Goddess as nurturing,

191

protective, strong, life-giving, unafraid – but we avoid portraits of Her as wanton, out of control, insatiable.

The Goddess Inanna, often seen as a Sumerian counterpart of Aphrodite/Venus, has become a favorite of modern Goddess worshippers, not least because Her praise-singer (to borrow an African term), Enheduanna, daughter of King Sargon, may be the oldest known poet in the world. We applaud Inanna's story of going from the "Great Above to the Great Below," that is, from the Sky to the Land of the Dead, where She confronts Her all-powerful sister, Ereshkigal, Goddess of Death. We see this as wholeness, as facing the dark Goddess within ourselves. But we ignore descriptions of Inanna as violent, unfaithful, patron of prostitutes who Herself visits "taverns," a Goddess who copulates with horses as well as men. We find ourselves uncomfortable with Sumerian descriptions of Her vulva as the boat of heaven, or a fallow field waiting for the plow. And we do not mention Her as Goddess of the kiss, for such things seem trivial, and worse, they might lead to recognition of Her function as Goddess of Masturbation.

We no longer tie down little girls' hands to prevent them from touching themselves "down there," but we still find it difficult to see masturbation as anything more than a joke, or a relief from annoyance, like taking a pill. We see it at best as a substitution for "the real thing," not as an expression of self love, or the power of the body to lead us to truth. Masturbation belongs to a whole range of unacceptable sexual expressions, from casual sex to fetishism to sado-masochism to orgiastic dancing. When Nor Hall writes of abandonment to the body's desire she does not mean only in the safety of a loving marriage.

Shrines to Aphrodite

As the sites of Artemis invoke the female force of mountains, the sites and temples of Aphrodite sometimes express the beauty of the female body. According to archaeologist Donald White, Her temples often took on rounded forms, like breasts. Scully writes of a temple in Segesta, Sicily, a Carthaginian temple, not Greek, but one that still recalls Aphrodite, for the temple sits on top of a rounded hill, "like a nipple on a breast." But She is not gentle. Her shrines often appear on mountain-tops. Like the passion that She rules, Her sacred places may invoke "explosive apparitions" (Scully). They take form on land masses rising from the sea, just as She Herself rose out of the foam, just as desire wells up in us out of the deep and secret waters of our own bodies.

Shrines to Asklepios, the God of Healing, contained temples to Aphrodite. Asklepios healed with the snake, the ancient Goddess energy linked so powerfully to sexuality. At His major center, Epidauros, mounded hills surround the site. Looking across the temple area from the east, and especially along the axis of the stadium, one sees an elegant rounded mountain, while the view northward, looking out from the top of the famous stadium, shows a row of low hills. Epidauros lies not far from Mycenae, but the land changes dramatically between the two sites.

Aphrodite belongs in the place of healing, for while love stabs the heart, passion heals. Sex drives away pain, liberates the body.

Aphrodite and Nature

Aphrodite belongs to the Earth, the mountains, and to the sea, where She first rose naked from the water. We see Her with goats and with dolphins. We find Her with fruits, with flowers, with roses and hyacinths, with poppies and pomegranates. Her lover Adonis, born out of a myrrh tree, dies in a field of lettuce, a plant whose fast-growing, leafy fecundity causes it to appear often in Goddess myths. Lettuce is said to form the pubic hair of Inanna. At least one kind of lettuce, rampion, bears a five-fold flower, a link to the planet Venus (Aphrodite's Roman name), with its five-petaled path through the sky. (Readers of fairy tales may know that the German name for "rampion" is *rapunzel*.) Most often we see Aphrodite holding an apple, connecting Her to Eve and those Goddesses shown offering their apples of immortality to initiates. The apple too connects us to Venus, for if we cut an apple in half horizontally we find a perfect five-pointed star.

The sky is Her place, Her home, Her origin. The God of the Sky, Ouranos, sacrificed His very sex to create Her. Aphrodite reaches back to the ancient Bird Goddesses, for doves attend Her and She rides through the

193

air on chariots of swans and geese, birds known for their fierceness as well
as their beauty. When She comes to rest She sits on a throne of swans.

Sexuality and Motherhood

Greek myth speaks of the four Queens of Heaven: Artemis, Athena, Hera,
and Aphrodite. In sexual terms, we might characterize them as a lesbian, a
chaste virgin, a wife, and a lover. Though Homer describes Aphrodite as
married to Hephaestus, the marriage does not figure much in Her stories.
We never see Her as a virgin, for while a post-Homeric myth describes Hera
regaining Her hymen every year, no myth ever tells of Aphrodite "losing"
Her maidenhead. Nor does any God or mortal ever rape, abduct, or take
Her against Her will. She surrenders to Her own passion, Her own power to
inflame the body, not to force or commandment.

The Queens do not call forth images of motherhood, despite the
assumptions of many people that "Goddess" always means "Great Mother."
Both Hera and Aphrodite bear children, but we hardly see these Goddesses
in this capacity. Artemis watches over women in labor but does not become
pregnant Herself. For the image of motherhood we need to turn to the Earth
Goddesses, and primarily Demeter, through Her relationship with
Persephone, Her daughter.

The Greek split between sexual passion and motherliness resonates with
our current society, where many people find it almost painful to imagine
their mothers as sexual beings at all, and where women with families believe
they need to act as two different people in their roles as mother and lover.

We try to forget that childbearing and desire involve the same areas of
the body, or that many women find breastfeeding their babies sensual and
erotic. Women who experience "birth orgasm" as they release the baby from
their vaginas may feel guilty, or disturbed, by an experience no one ever told
them was "normal."

Paul and Deborah Friedrich, in their book *The Meaning of Aphrodite*, call
attention to the powerful correspondences between sexual arousal and
childbearing. These include: 1 – deep breathing followed by short breaths;
2 – vocalization and gasps; 3 – strained facial expression; 4 – rhythmic
contractions; 5 – loosening of the mucous plug from the cervix; 6 –

periodic abdominal contractions; 7 – loss of inhibitions and conventional behavior; 8 – great exertion of strength; 9 – natural anesthesia of the vulva; 10 – insensitivity to surroundings; and 11 – flood of joyful emotion. The obvious difference is the great pain of childbearing compared to the pleasure of sex.

The Friedrichs see Aphrodite and Demeter as derived from a single earlier Goddess (we have seen links with Cybele and Artemis for both of them). In the patriarchal period the unity of sexuality and motherhood becomes a threat, for it gives women tremendous power. What would seem the most obvious connection becomes separated, as in the Christian myth of the two Marys, the one a sexless virgin mother, the other a whore, with the assumpion that a whore is someone to despise.

Aphrodite, Adonis, and Persephone

If Greek myth does not show an explicit link between Aphrodite and Demeter, it does establish one between Aphrodite and Demeter's daughter, Persephone. The link comes in the myth of Aphrodite's mortal lover, Adonis (whose name means "lord," and is related to "Adonai," a Hebrew title for God). Partly because of Adonis, some mythographers consider Aphrodite Asian, for her story parallels such tales as Inanna and Dumuzi in Sumer, Ishtar and Tammuz in Babylon ("Adonis" was originally a title given to Tammuz), and Cybele and Attis in Anatolia.

The story of Aphrodite does include an oblique reference to Demeter. It begins with a queen who has scorned Aphrodite. As punishment, the Goddess of Love inflames Smyrna, the queen's daughter, with passion for her own father. Smyrna seduces him in the dark, during the festival of Thesmophoria. Thesmophoria was a women's ritual performed in the name of Demeter (*see* Chapter 8). It included the sacrifice of a pig in a pit filled with snakes, and it demanded that women abstain from contact with men. By making love to her *father* during this time, Smyrna draws him, a symbol of patriarchy, into the prehistoric world of women's bodies.

Smyrna's father reasserts his control when he discovers his daughter pregnant by himself. He takes a sword (that sharp phallus) and chases her from the palace. Just before the sword would strike Smryna, Aphrodite changes her into a myrrh tree. The sword splits the tree in half and Adonis tumbles out. Some versions say he emerges nine months later.

Aphrodite hides Adonis in a chest (like a box, a symbol of the womb) and gives him to Persephone, to hide in the dark Land of the Dead just as plants hide underground in the Earth-womb until the spring. Persephone, however, opens the chest. Struck by Adonis's beauty, She claims him for Her own. When Aphrodite complains, Zeus decides that Adonis must spend one third of the year with each Goddess, with one third left to his own choice. Robert Graves tells us that in Syria, Asia Minor, and Greece, people divided "the goddess's sacred year" into three parts, ruled by the lion, goat, and serpent. The first part was sacred to the Birth Goddess (a version of Artemis) "who had no claim on Adonis," the middle part sacred to Aphrodite (the goat continued to symbolize sexuality into the Christian era), and the last part, the serpent, belonging to Persephone.

According to the myth, the Goddess of Death becomes angry when Aphrodite uses her magic to claim Adonis's love for the third of the year left vacant by the Birth Goddess. Persephone incites Ares (some versions say Apollo, and some Artemis) to send a wild boar to gore Adonis to death. The myth may have enshrined the practice in Syria, Egypt, and Greece of using pigs to thresh grain. Adonis dies in spring, the time of plant renewal and of estrus, female sexual arousal. Anemones spring from Adonis's blood.

With Adonis's death caused by a pig the story comes full circle, back to the sacrificial pig of the Thesmophoria. Though the ancient people saw Adonis as a dying and resurrected God, and celebrated his rites each year, the story does not actually tell of Aphrodite restoring him to life. This contrasts with such tales as that of the Egyptian Isis and Osiris, where the Goddess resurrects Her lover. For the most complete expression of the sacred being who dies and returns, who, in fact, achieves a full sense of life through intimate knowledge of death, we must turn, not to the Son, but the Daughter, the Queen of the Dead Herself, Persephone.

The Body With the Dead

The mystery is always of a body
The mystery is always of a body of a woman
... The mystery of the mystery is being woman
... the mystery is
always of the body in the body of a woman.

Helene Cixous

They came literally by the thousands, traveling in procession along the edge of the sea to the most famous religious shrine of the ancient world. They were the mystae, the celebrants of a nine-day ritual in honor of the Grain Mother and Her Daughter, the helpless girl who became Queen of the Dead, and in the process changed the meaning of death itself.

To this day no one knows the final secrets revealed at the end of the nine days of the Eleusinian Mysteries. We know many of the details: what they wore, what they did on each of the days, special words they said, food they ate. But the ultimate revelation remains hidden.

And yet, we do know something just as vital. We know the story. We know it as a tale of incest and rape, of terror and transformation. And we know it as a tale of a mother's love and determination, of a Goddess, a *woman*, who insisted on truth and rejected accommodation, who stopped the entire world until the Gods gave back Her daughter.

This is the literal story, the movement of characters and plot. The deeper we look, however, the more we discover. We discover the creation of agriculture and the beginnings of human law and society, the survival and subtle return of the Goddess religion in the patriarchal world, and, finally, the very origin of sexuality and death.

Eleusis – Then and Now

The small town of Eleusis stood just outside Athens, a day's walk for the *mystae*, the initiates who would start out from Athens in the morning and arrive at night at the Sacred Precinct. Today, the modern industrial suburb of Elefsis surrounds the Precinct, which has lain in ruins since 400 C.E., when Alaric and his Goths sacked the temples, apparently to please the Christian bishop. Many archaeological and tourist guidebooks describe Eleusis as destroyed, a mass of stones overpowered by the nearby shipyards and factories. As a result, few visitors make the short trip from the capital. This is both unfortunate and a minor blessing – unfortunate for the many people missing an intense connection with the past, and a blessing for those who wish to avoid the chattering crowds filling the Parthenon. For even though the architecture lies shattered, the very size of the Precinct, almost a small village in itself, and the wall which separates it from the modern town, endow it with a power all its own. At first glance, sacred Eleusis may appear as something that has died and will not return. But if one knows something of what happened there, of the 2,000 years of celebration of the Mother and the Daughter, with all the mystery of the Mysteries (for the culminating revelation remains a secret), then the broken pieces of Eleusis become a place of hope and connection.

When Maria Fernandez and I visited the site we encountered only four other people, a tourist couple who did not stay long and a mother and daughter from England, the daughter a student living in Greece. Though I did not speak with the daughter, I suspect she came in pilgrimage, for she did what so many Goddess worshippers do in such places, she simply sat, and looked, and listened to the Earth. I did speak with her mother, who told me of her fascination with the idea of past lives (as did a group of tourists at Ggantija, in Malta) – that is, of dying and living again.

In the Hellenistic and Roman periods mystery religions and cults spread through the ancient world. Eleusis, however, retained its status as unique, the actual place where the Mother gave Her two great gifts to the world: the cultivation of grain, and the secret rites of the Mysteries themselves. Some ancient writings hint that the Goddess Herself appears at the end of the rite. And in the Homeric hymn to Demeter (perhaps we should call a poem to a Goddess a hyrrh) Demeter waits for Her Daughter in the temple built for Her by the Eleusinians.

Myths and Rituals Expressing Human Development

The Eleusinian Mysteries may have evolved from another ritual, one primarily in honor of Demeter, the Thesmophoria. *Thesmoi* means "laws," after *thesmos* – "what is laid down," and concerns Demeter as law-giver, not just of civil or human laws, but the laws of nature, of life rotting and growing.

Because of Demeter's power of natural law the Greeks did indeed associate Her with civil law as well. The Athenians kept the written records of their laws in a temple of Demeter called the Metroön. We find a similar connection – a life-giving Goddess and the law – with the Sumerian Inanna, the Egyptian Isis, and the Phrygian Cybele. Cybele's gallae in Athens performed their self-sacrifice before the Metroön. Laws and agriculture go together, for both are "unnatural." They represent a movement of human culture away from the direct cycles of nature and towards human institutions.

The name Demeter means either Earth Mother, after *De*, a variation of *Ge* or Gaia, or else Grain Mother, from the Cretan word for barley grains, *dyai*. Gaia embodies the archaic Earth, from its earliest moments, through the times of the hunter-gatherers. Demeter, Goddess of Agriculture, takes over in a sense, spreading a more complex human civilization that actually refers back to the Neolithic times. The change from Gaia to Demeter traces the path from the Old Stone Age to the New. Nevertheless, the laws of death, rot, and rebirth continue. These are the laws of the Mother. Through the intervention of the Daughter, Persephone, the human spirit will reach beyond those laws of disintegration and new life. In this way, Demeter gives to the world the laws of nature, seemingly implacable, but she and Persephone together give the transformative laws of human culture and spirituality. We will see as well that the myth of the Daughter separated from the Mother by an intruding male describes the change from unisexual to bisexual reproduction, while the reunion of the two tells us that the body of life remains whole and unified despite the seeming separation into isolated sexes. While the Thesmophoria belonged solely to women, and Apollo restricted the Delphic oracle solely to men, at Eleusis, both men and women took part together. But they also merged, for all the celebrants, men as well as women, took on the role of the Goddess, not the Daughter but the primal Mother, who suffers loss and return.

The Thesmophoria

The Thesmophoria took three days and involved preparing the Earth for the sowing of grain for the winter growth (as did the Mysteries). In the religion of the body human beings do not watch passively while nature takes its own course, or God acts without concern for human will. Rather, human actions, human bodies join with the world. The first day bore the title "Kathodos and Anodos," that is, "the way down and the way up." The women brought pigs and dropped them into a chasm filled with snakes (remember the prophetic python in the chasm at Delphi). They then brought up the rotted remains of pigs sacrificed the previous year.

The second day called for fasting, "Nestia," as the women both imitated the barren time for the land, when the seed lay hidden underground, and Demeter's grief at Her Daughter vanishing from the living. The seed and the Daughter were one, for the name of the Daughter at the beginning of the Homeric hymn, *Kore*, or "maiden," also means "sprout."

The third day brought a banquet of meat as the women invoked Kalligeneia, "the goddess of beautiful birth" (Baring and Cashford) and scattered the remains of the disintegrated pigs over the fields, where they would re-integrate with the grain.

During the Thesmophoria the women abstained from sex. In our culture, we think of abstinence as a way to remain "pure," or perhaps to hold the energy of the body within the self. I suspect, however, that in such rituals as the Thesmophoria, abstinence might have carried another meaning, that of a separation from the male and a return to the primacy of the Earth as female. It may have had a political purpose as well, for in a male-dominated culture such as Greece, women would have to separate from men to know and express their power.

The Mysteries and their Seasons

Two sets of Mysteries took place at Eleusis, the Lesser and the Greater. The Lesser Mysteries, celebrated in winter, prepared the initiate for taking part in the Greater Mysteries the following autumn. The Lesser focused primarily on the *anodos*, or "the way up," of Persephone. As with the Thesmophoria and the Greater Mysteries, the Lesser involved sacrificing a pig, a surrogate perhaps for the initiate's own death.

Many modern discussions of the myth of Persephone assume that She goes down into the ground in winter and emerges in the spring. This would be the case in a northern climate. In Greece, however, much of the land lies barren in summer, the time of drought. Thus, the Greater Mysteries take place around the time of the autumnal, not the vernal, equinox, and they end with water being poured into cracks in the Earth, and the celebrants crying out "*Hye! Kye!*" that is, "Rain! Conceive!" During the summer the people stored grain in underground silos.

According to information from archaeologist Donald White, it is not clear at what time of the year and for how long Persephone remains underground. Some sources do indeed say winter, which would hint at a connection to solar as well as agricultural events. The times given range from three months (the summer season) to one third of the year, to six months. We saw with the story of Adonis that the Greeks divided the year into three parts, with one of the three as Persephone's time with the dead. Carl Kerenyi points out that this breaks the strict connection to grain, since no seed remains four months underground. Persephone's third of the year bore the title "Serpent," a creature who slithers into dark areas but also sheds its skin in a kind of rebirth.

Persephone means "She who shines in the dark." According to Klein's *Comprehensive Etymological Dictionary of the English Language, persona* derives from Persephone, in Her role as guide to dead souls (psyches). Though the English word *person*, our sense of an individual self, comes out of persona, we tend to think of persona as a fake, a mask. In fact, the word meant a mask worn by the players in Roman drama, but not as a way of hiding their identities. Rather, the personae amplified their voices, while giving them the identities of the Gods or heroes they were portraying.

The Procession

A modern highway lined with industrial sites now runs along much of the processional road from Athens to Eleusis (called Elefsis in modern Greek). Nevertheless, it remains possible to trace the way, and to observe the same landscape forms the celebrants would have seen on their sacred journey. Goddess forms appear and disappear along the whole route.

The walk begins with a climb up to the Pass of Daphni. A conical hill guards the pass on the Athens side. Through the pass, the horned peak of Mt. Kerata comes into view. The name *Kerata* itself means "horned." Vincent Scully describes Mt. Kerata as "strikingly female." These two forms, the cone and the horned peak, take us back to Crete, and the landscapes along the processional ways by Knossos and Phaestos. The ancient myths of Demeter all agree·that She came to Greece from Crete, as did so many of the other figures, including Zeus Himself. In Homer's time women participating in the Lesser Mysteries carried double axes, that great symbol of Cretan religion. The inner quality of the Mysteries, as much as the mountain shapes, suggest a direct line from the Cretan Goddess, but they have acquired their own character from having passed through the violence of patriarchal culture symbolized by the abduction and rape of the Goddess's daughter, who nevertheless gains a special power for having made that passage to death.

Further along the route Mt. Kerata vanishes from sight and the way becomes barren and hard – an embodiment for the walkers of Persephone's journey in the Underworld, out of sight of Her mother. As Scully puts it, "No opening is seen, nor does any objective beckon to the view." But then "the hills to the left are burst apart," revealing a mass of rock, the sort of abrupt form that signals Aphrodite, and indeed, a sanctuary to the Goddess of Love appears directly opposite. Though the Greek myths appear to isolate mother love and physical passion, the actual journey to Eleusis brings the two Goddesses, Demeter and Aphrodite, back together. From Aphrodite's sanctuary one glimpses the island of Salamis, off the coast from Eleusis. (The Greek ships scored an important victory against the Persians in the waters by Salamis.) A distinct cleft appears in the island hills, reminiscent of the vulva images carved into the cave walls as humanity's oldest expression of the Goddess power of life.

The sacred way moves towards the cleft hill and a pass which opens to Eleusis itself. When Salamis emerges more fully into view it takes on the quality of a body lying on its back, a form also found in the mountains near Aphrodite's shrine at Troezen. Eleusis first appears as a mounded hill under Mt. Kerata, exactly the arrangement at Knossos and Phaestos. At the Sacred Precinct itself, Mt. Kerata's double peak appears very strikingly, with a sense of lips almost as much as horns (see *Plate 22*).

The name Eleusis means either "gate" or "place of happy arrival." Gertrude Rachel Levy identified Eleusis as the Gate of Horn, Virgil's gate of true dreams in the *Aeneid*.

The Narcissus and the Pomegranate

We know the story of Demeter and Persephone primarily from the Homeric hymn to Demeter. Other myths give us important hints to implications of the central tale, but tradition connects the Mysteries themselves to the Homeric version. (Though tradition ascribes the poem to "Homer" it acutally comes from a period about 700 years after the composition of the *Iliad* and the *Odyssey*.)

At the start of the story, Persephone bears no name other than Kore, "maiden" or "girl." The poem begins with Her as an innocent, gathering flowers with the daughters of Ocean. Other versions describe Kore as accompanied by Artemis and Athena, virgin Goddesses like Kore Herself. A temple to Artemis and Poseidon stood outside the inner Precinct of Demeter (Poseidon may have been Demeter's consort, for the name means "husband of De [Earth]").

While Kore gathers flowers She does not realize that a trap awaits Her. The God Hades has decided He will take Her as His bride, and has persuaded His brother, Zeus, to help arrange this "marriage." Zeus in turn gets the help of Gaia, the Earth, who causes a magnificent narcissus to grow as bait to lure the girl away from Her friends, and from Her mother and anyone who might hear Her.

According to the *Cambridge Illustrated Dictionary of Natural History* the narcissus is a kind of lily, a flower sacred to the Goddess in many lands, partly from its resemblance to the vulva. Barbara Walker associates the lily with Lilith and Astarte, and through Astarte, Eostre. She also tells us that Mary was said to have conceived Jesus with the help of a lily. From the *Cambridge Dictionary* we learn that lilies possess the characteristic of "dying back to the ground each year," and contain "a superior ovary of many seeds," qualities that relate to Persephone and Her sexual initiation in the Land of the Dead.

The narcissus is one of two plants around which the story revolves. The bright narcissus, with its flower exposed to the air, forms a focus for the world above. And yet, its beauty is illusory, or rather a trick, for it leads to the dark Underworld. In the Underworld Persephone will eat two seeds from a pomegranate, a plant which conceals its abundance in a dark red shell. Because She has eaten there, She cannot leave for good. Thus, both plants belong to death. A plant cannot give life unless it dies. Just as the lily contains a "superior ovary," so the pomegranate contains a chemical very similar in molecular structure to the mammalian female sex hormone, estrogen (a word itself derived from the Goddess Eostre).

The Abduction

The narcissus brings delight to all who behold it, even heaven and the ground and the seas. But when Kore reaches down to pluck it the land opens up and Hades springs forth in His golden chariot. The God siezes Her and drags Her, screaming, down into the Underworld. Kore cries out for Her father, Zeus, to help Her, "But nobody, no one of the immortal gods, no one of mortal men, heard her voice" (trans. Charles Boer). Since Zeus has arranged the abduction, we can say that He *refuses* to hear His daughter, that the whole world refuses to hear the pain and terror of Her rape. Only Hecate, Goddess of the dark Moon, and Helios, the Sun, "hear" Kore (the Athenians considered Hecate a daughter of Demeter, and thus an alter ego of Persephone). Both of them stand apart from the Gods. As the light of the Sun and the dark of the Moon they form a duality complete in itself.

Demeter also hears. She hears the anguish of Her daughter, discovers Her gone, and though She streaks across land and sea, no one will tell Her anything. For nine days Demeter wanders, wild with grief, holding torches in both hands. Because of this search, the Mysteries last nine days, with a torchlit procession during the middle night. Nine, as we know, is not arbitrary. Three times three, it raises up the Goddess power of the Moon. And of course, nine is the number of months in a pregnancy (originally a month was not an arbitrary category, but the length of the lunar cycle, twenty-nine and a half days). The Mysteries took place in the second half of the lunar month, when the Moon loses itself to darkness, just as Demeter (sometimes identified with the full Moon) loses Persephone.

Finally, on the tenth morning, Hecate, holding Her own torch, appears before Demeter, to tell Her that She heard, but did not see, Persephone's abduction (the name of the Goddess appears here for the first time in the poem). Together, they go to Helios, who puts the blame where it belongs, on Zeus, who "gave her to Hades, his own brother, to be called his wife." Helios advises Demeter not to protest, for Hades will make a good husband, "not unworthy as a son-in-law."

Demeter, however, refuses to reconcile Herself. Nor does She try, at this point, to oppose Her all-powerful brother. We might think She would blight the world because of losing Her daughter, but this does not happen. Instead, She withdraws into Her grief, wandering the world disguised as an old woman. And so She comes to Eleusis.

Demeter Disguised

The royal family takes Demeter in, accepting Her as a nurse. They offer Her wine, but She refuses, drinking instead a barley drink of Her own creation. A similar drink, called *kykeon*, featured in the Mysteries. R. Gordon Wasson and others have argued that kykeon contained a grain-derived hallucinogen, ergot, which enhanced the revelations at the climax of the rite. Carl Kerenyi looks at the refusal of wine differently. He considers it hints at a secret – that Persephone's husband was Dionysos, the Wine God.

For whatever reason, the Goddess refuses the wine. A lightness enters the story at this point, as a woman comes to cheer the old nurse. Some versions call her Iambe, the king's daughter, others Baubo, the wife of a swineherd who, according to one version, lost his pigs when Hades took them down with Persephone. Whether Iambe or Baubo, she dances and tells lewd jokes. In the procession from Athens, as the mystae came over a bridge, people impersonating Baubo performed lewd dances before them. Some accounts describe them as women, others as men in women's clothes. (They could possibly have been both, since both women and men in the rite dressed in simple robes signifying their identification with Demeter.) Except for the possible mystical marriage of Persephone and Dionysos, the dance represents the only directly sexual element in the myth. It suggests the power of sexuality, and life, to assert itself in the face of grief.

G. R. Levy tells us that the Greeks sometimes equated the *anodos* of Persephone with the rising from the sea of Aphrodite. Pictures of both show women helping the Goddess to rise up out of the depths – in psychological terms, to separate Herself from the formless source of being, either of the sea or the Underworld. Nor Hall writes, "Motherhood is a preparation for maidenhood. Pregnancy is a preparation for virginity." We might add, "Death is a preparation for birth." The name Baubo means "belly," suggesting a connection not only to pregnancy but also to the ancient magical movements which have come down to us as belly dancing.

As a boon to the family, Demeter decides to make the queen's son, Demophoön, immortal, a God. Each night She lays the child in the fire that Her power has charged as an agent against death. In a sense, she defies Zeus, both literally and figuratively. Literally, because we know from other myths that Zeus, like the Hebrew God, did not like mortals being raised to godhead. And figuratively, because Zeus has taken away one immortal child, and now Demeter will replace Her with another. The effort is little more than a gesture, almost of despair, for even if it had succeeded it would not have changed the relations between life and death. Demeter has not yet reached the stage where She will dare to do that.

The god-making fails, for Demophoön's mother spies on the nurse one night. Seeing her son in the fire, she screams and rushes forward to rescue him. Finally, Demeter's anger explodes – not at the Gods, against whom She still feels powerless, but at wretched humanity. The Goddess reveals Herself and denounces human ignorance, which does not allow us to judge the difference between good and evil. "Knowing ignorance is strength" wrote Lao Tzu, the ancient Chinese sage. "Ignoring knowledge is sickness" (trans. Gia-Fu Feng and Jane English).

The Lifeless Earth

Demeter demands that the Eleusinians build Her a temple above the Well of Beautiful Dances, the place where the maidens first found Her and took Her in. There She withdraws, and in so doing blights the world, for without the Mother no plants can grow. There are some subtle ironies in Demeter's action. She too had to recognize Her own ignorance, for until Hecate and Helios came forward, Demeter knew nothing of the fate of Her daughter. And while Her anger stems from the loss of Kore to Death, Demeter responds by threatening death to the whole world. Or perhaps life does not rest entirely in Demeter's hands. For if *kore* means "sprout," and the sprouting plants remain trapped under the ground, what can even the Grain Mother accomplish on Her own?

According to Kerenyi, some versions of the myth describe Demeter Herself going down to the Underworld to bring back Her child, to restore life to the world. In Homer She remains concealed in Her temple. Though She acts against humanity, She strikes the Gods as well. She has upset the natural balance of the world, including the ecology of Earth and Heaven. Just as humans depend on plants to live, so the Gods depend on human sacrifices for a kind of sustenance. Mortal bodies act as a bridge between the raw body of nature and the ethereal body of Spirit.

Demeter's anguish and rage did nothing to alter the decree of Zeus. Her stubbornness, however, and Her simple refusal to give in and accept death, finally break the will of Heaven. The Gods cannot exist without the sacrifices of humanity. Zeus sends Hermes to the Underworld to retrieve Persephone. Death, however, is not so easily defeated. Pretending to obey, Hades gives Persephone two seeds from a pomegranate which She eats before returning to the light. Because of this act, because She has eaten the fruit of the Land of the Dead, Persephone cannot remain in the light permanently, but must return for a time every year to Her place alongside Hades, as Queen of the Underworld.

The Pomegranate

The pomegranate figures in other stories besides Persephone's. By the abundance of its seeds, its redness, and its natural estrogen it symbolizes rebirth. And yet, Persephone must stay with Death because She has eaten it, as if She has allowed Herself to be born in death. During the fast day of the Thesmophoria, the women do eat one food, pomegranate seeds, but only those which have not touched the ground. When Maria Fernandez and I came to Eleusis an earlier visitor had strewn broken pomegranates about the floor of a shallow cave sometimes identified as the place where Hades took Persephone down into the dark. Deliberately taking on the identity of Hades, Maria squeezed one, pushing out the seeds. The cut, and the white seeds oozing out, resembled the mouth of a corpse, filled with worms.

Myth also links the pomegranate to Dionysos. When the spirits leaped from the mirror to dismember the young God, the pomegranate sprang from His heart. When Persephone eats the seed She is eating *Dionysos's* seed, that is, His sperm. In this version of the myth, She becomes pregnant and bears Iacchos, whose name the mystae shout in their torchlit procession during the Mysteries.

Some versions describe Iacchos as the Son of Demeter, a sign that Demeter and Persephone are the same. At the end of the Mysteries the shout goes up that the Goddess has given birth to a son, that "Brimo has borne Brimos." *Brimo*, and its male equivalent, *Brimos*, mean "strong one." Identities have fused here, the Mother and the Daughter (since the cry does not distinguish which Goddess is Brimo), and the Mother and the Son, by the same name for both. We can describe the Mysteries as just such a fusing of selves, Goddess and mortal, mother and child, female and male, life and death.

At the same time, the eating of the seed of death leads away from fusion to individuality. Persephone never quite returns to her unknowing state as the unnamed Maiden/Daughter of Her Mother. Instead, She comes into Her own power as Queen of the Underworld.

The Gifts of Demeter

Having become queen in Her own right, Persephone rides Hades's golden chariot back to the light and Her Mother. When She arrives Her Mother demands that Persephone tell the truth, everything that happened to Her. Hearing of the pomegranate seeds, Demeter instantly recognizes Her daughter's tie to the Underworld. Nevertheless, She rejoices at Her child's return.

Now She rewards Eleusis, and all humanity. She does not simply restore plant life, but teaches the secrets of agriculture, giving humans control over their food supply. She gives this information to Triptolemos, and instructs him to take the message around the world. Some historians identify Triptolemos with an actual king of Eleusis. The name means either "three times warrior" or "three times plowman," implying a transformation from one to the other. (Christians and Jews may remember the biblical prediction that men will beat their swords into plowshares.) Along with knowledge, Triptolemos gave three commandments: Honor your parents, honor the Gods with fruits, and spare the animals.

Demeter gives agriculture as a gift to all the world. She gives another gift, just as special, to Eleusis itself – the Mysteries. In the ancient world, anyone might attend the Mysteries, so long as they spoke Greek and had not shed blood. Anyone might attend, but they had to come to Eleusis to do so.

Rape and Incest

A myth that touches so many levels of our lives – our spiritual yearnings, our sense of ourselves, the very food which keeps us alive – may lead us only to subtle interpretations. Just for a moment, let us look at the story in a different way, as a tale of rape, incest, and resistance.

Judging the meaning of incest in myths becomes difficult when we remember that the Gods and Goddesses in most mythologies form a family. Divine energy is One, and only becomes differentiated through the various personalities (personae) of the Gods. Thus, the tales describe them as related to each other. When a brother and sister marry or copulate, like Isis and Osiris, or Izanami and Izanagi, or Adam and Eve (originally from the same body, they form a "brother" and "sister"), we can see this as the re-union of the split aspects of the divine. However, when a story tells us that a father, or brother, or uncle *rapes* a Goddess, then we might look at the event more in the way we would look at incest in human society.

The significance of rape in the story grows when we find the persistence of assault in the different versions. Demeter, too, is raped. In the Arcadian version of the story, Poseidon rapes His sister, after She has changed into a mare, and He into a stallion. The Goddess becomes Demeter Erinys, Demeter the Wrathful, until, reconciled, She bathes in a river and becomes Demeter Louisa. She bears a daughter, the main figure in the Arcadian myth, but unnamed, called only *Despoina*, Mistress.

In other versions, Zeus rapes Demeter and fathers Persephone. The God comes to Her as a bull, implying the same turnaround of the Neolithic Cow Goddess and Her bull consort that we saw with Zeus and Europa. In the religion of the Goddess's body, the bull serves the cow by impregnating Her, so that She may give forth life. In the violent separation of male power from nature, rape becomes a political tool. Zeus asserts His ability to take whatever He wants, in service to nothing but His own violent will.

Having raped Demeter, His sister, as a bull, Zeus then turns on His daughter/niece, for an Orphic story tells how Zeus comes to Persephone in the form of a snake. Remember Psyche, whose sisters tell her that her husband is really a snake, and who visits Persephone under command from Aphrodite; and remember as well that Persephone's third of the year bore the title "serpent."

Out of this union Persephone bears none other than Dionysos. As already mentioned, Kerenyi and others describe Dionysos as Persephone's secret lover. Dionysos too appears as both a bull and a snake, the two prime animals of the Goddess from Crete. (To complicate the relations even further, Ovid identifies Demeter's lover, and Persephone's father, as Zagreus, a Hunter God from Crete. Zagreus became identified both with Dionysos and Hades.)

Roberto Calasso tells us that Demeter was sometimes considered the same as Rhea – Zeus's mother. If we combine the stories, Zeus rapes His own mother, then gives their daughter to His brother Hades. We begin to slide towards the ludicrous here, with Persephone simultaneously Zeus's sister, sister-in-law, daughter and niece. We cannot really push all the stories into one. What is important, however, is the kaleidoscope of images of rape. Zeus extends the rule of assault both backwards and forwards in time, to His own mother and His own daughter.

Poseidon or Zeus rapes Demeter. Zeus or Hades rapes Persephone. But many mythographers consider Poseidon and Hades other versions of Zeus. And the Homeric hymn implies that Zeus and Hades are the same, for it describes both of them as "that son of Kronos with so many names." Thus, Zeus rapes His own sister, and then kidnaps and rapes His daughter/niece. If we think of Demeter for a moment as we would a human woman, we can well imagine Her wild rage and agony.

If we take the Homeric version at face value the pain in the story hardly lessens. For then one of Her brothers, Zeus, rapes Demeter, and another one, Hades, rapes Demeter's daughter. And further, Hades does not act alone. The entire patriarchy rapes Persephone, for Hades first arranges this with Zeus, the Great Father who rules the world. In the story, Hades comes to Zeus and tells of His desire for Persephone. Zeus then sets up the kidnapping. The two male Gods decide who will *own* Persephone. Again, translate this into a family. The head of the family rapes his sister. When the child becomes a maiden, a younger brother goes to the head and says he wants the child. The two of them then sit down and find a way to arrange this second rape, in secret, so that neither of them will get caught.

The Collusion of Women

The method the Gods use to entrap Kore involves the help of Gaia. The Earth causes the glorious narcissus to spring up, luring Kore into the place where Hades will ride forth from the ground. This may seem strange to us until we remember the ways mothers and grandmothers have betrayed their daughters over and over again, in the name of tradition. Some years ago, I read an interview with an Egyptian feminist. She described the horror she experienced as a child when the women came to her, with no warning (and certainly no consent), and surgically excised her clitoris. The woman described how she called out for her mother to save her, only to look up and discover her mother on the side of the knife. This is an extreme example, as are the situations of women sold into forced marriages, prostitution, or slavery. But in our "modern" society as well, women re-enact Gaia's betrayal whenever they push their daughters to take on roles for which the daughters feel nothing, or to stay with a husband who abuses them, or to keep silent about incest or marital rape, or in the case of lesbians, to suppress their natural desires in order to act "normal."

But if Gaia betrays Her great-grandchild, Demeter does not betray Her Daughter. She rushes through the world, searching for news of Her Daughter. In an article on the Mysteries, Pam Wright points out that Hecate alone refuses to take part in the conspiracy. Hecate, the dark aspect of the Goddess, dares both the threat of Zeus, and the terrible rage and grief of Demeter. She alone will tell the Mother what has happened to Her Daughter. Only when Hecate has "broken the silence" (to use a current expression) can Demeter go to Helios and learn the details.

Wright, an educator on issues of child abuse and neglect, points out the significance of truth in the story. When Persephone returns, Demeter tells Her, before anything else, to speak the truth, to tell everything that has happened to Her. Demeter's absolute commitment to Her Daughter, and to the truth told openly, gives Her the power to overturn the decrees of Zeus, enacted in secret. Like women in patriarchal societies, Demeter is powerless to wage war against Olympus. In the end, however, Her will, Her simple refusal to abandon Her child, proves stronger than Zeus's thunderbolts.

The Power of Knowledge

Because the story of Demeter and Persephone is a myth, it reaches beyond the moral lessons of the family drama. Myth embodies both historical and psychological truth. The refusal of Demeter to accept the loss of Her Daughter symbolizes the refusal of the matrifocal culture to disappear, or give up its wisdom. The survival and return of Persephone speaks to so many women and men today partly because it describes the dramatic return of the Goddess religion. In our ignorance of the past, we have enacted the myth of the Ona people, whose men killed all the women with knowledge (as the European witch burnings killed hundreds of thousands, perhaps millions, of women) and kept the girls from learning of their power. And we have enacted the myth of Genesis, allowing a "jealous" God (His term for Himself) to put enmity between us and the serpent, the bringer of knowledge. The patriarchies did not just attack the Goddess religion, they *abducted* it, stole it away and buried it underground through their insistence that human history and civilization began 5,000 years ago in Mesopotamia.

Like Demeter, however, we have finally turned away from acceptance. We have insisted on the truth. And like Persephone, we will return, to ourselves, and to our ancestral beginnings. We will return no longer innocent, or naïve, but with knowledge of death, and the terrible effects of wanton power, especially as demonstrated in so many ways in the last century. But the knowledge itself – knowledge of the dangers we face as well as knowledge of other cultures and other times – helps us to face our own danger of extinction and a lifeless planet.

The Mother and the Daughter

The body of the Goddess cannot be destroyed. Paul Friedrich charts the many instances in which the rape of a Goddess produces a daughter, as if, when the patriarchal God seeks to break the Goddess, She instead transfers Her power to the next generation. Zeus rapes Leto, who gives birth to Artemis (to Apollo as well, but to Artemis first). Zeus rapes Demeter, who bears Persephone. Poseidon (Zeus of the sea) rapes Demeter Erinys, who gives birth to "the Mistress." Another version has Poseidon raping the Gorgon, Medousa, who gives birth to Persephone.

But when Hades rapes Persephone something different happens. No child is born. The mystae call out the name "Iacchos" during the Mysteries; but the myth describes no birth in the Underworld. Only at the end, when the Goddess has returned, does Brimo bear Brimos.

It makes sense that no new life should appear in the Land of the Dead. But we also can say that the transference has stopped. Persephone does not surrender Her power and give it over to a daughter. Instead, She finds Her own strength and becomes ruler in Her own right, for while Hades simply presides over the dead souls, He gives them nothing. Persephone gives them comfort, and something more, for participation in the Mysteries promised joy and salvation.

When Zeus rapes Demeter, the Goddess finds Herself powerless. Instead, She takes comfort in Her daughter. But when Hades, with help from Zeus, comes for Kore, then at last Demeter resists. Thus, by not accepting this further rape, both the Mother and the Daughter find their power. And the rest of the world benefits. While Persephone brings us life after death, Demeter brings us life in the form of knowledge, and a deeper involvement in the production of the grain that feeds our bodies.

In her book *The Laughter of Aphrodite* Carol Christ describes how she and a group of women performed what may have been the first organized rituals done at Eleusis since 400 C.E. Instead of trying to duplicate what may have happened in ancient Greece, the women created their own ritual, which celebrated the bond between mothers and daughters, and included time for each of the women to tell their own stories of separations, and healing. As part of this healing they rejected the patriarchal myths that have come down to us, and instead used a version created by Charlene Spretnak. In this story, no one abducts Persephone. Instead, as Persephone grows and becomes a woman, she knows that she must "find her own way." She begins to wander farther and farther, learning about joy, and pain, until one day She "came to a chasm and heard the cries of the dead. Taking a torch she climbed slowly down. The cries of the dead ceased when they saw the light she had brought them" (Carol Christ). But Demeter is desolate, and so Persephone agrees to spend part of the year above ground, and part below.

This version of the myth helps women to see themselves as powerful in their own right, and to define relations between women in their own terms, without men as intermediaries. And yet, the Classical versions also can teach us powerful lessons. On a sociological level, they can help us confront, like Demeter demanding the truth about Persephone's experience, the reality of rape in our society. In the United States especially, the incidence of rape is astonishingly high – as is incest and child abuse.

Persephone's Power: Consciousness Shining in Darkness

So far, we have looked at Persephone's encounters solely as terror and destruction, and Her return as a triumph over violence. In a way, this approach assumes Demeter's point of view, as do the Mysteries themselves. But the God who abducts Persephone is Death Himself, and She does not simply escape Him. She becomes intimate with Death, Death's lover, literally taking Death into Her immortal body. In a way, Death abducts all of us, for no one really expects to die, despite our conscious awareness that we can never escape it. And because of this stubborn belief in our own immunity, Death violates each of us, entering our bodies one by one.

And yet, Persephone does not simply fall to Death. Nor does She defeat Him, in the manner of the patriarchal hero killing the dragon. Instead, She joins with Death, and in so doing becomes Queen of the Underworld. Her way of comfort, and promise of new life displace Hades, though officially She rules alongside Him.

We have seen how the Greek idea of the afterlife became dismal and pessimistic as the Olympian religion separated itself from the self-renewing cycles of nature. The Mysteries overcame the terror of death when they restored the identification of human beings with the seed that falls from the dying plant to lie underground, hidden from life, only to spring up, miraculously alive. At the end of the final ritual, the Hierophantos showed an ear of grain to the celebrants. Some say that the grain grew miraculously before their eyes, or simply that fresh grain should not have existed after the summer drought. The vision promised two things, the rebirth of the plants, but also life after death.

Usually, the story describes Persephone's eating of the pomegranate seeds as a mistake, even a tragedy, because it gives Death power over Her. We might recast the myth to say that She *chooses* to embrace the reality of Death, to make Death Her lover so that She will not abandon the dead souls who depend on Her.

If we think of Kore/Persephone as a character in a story, and not just a manipulated symbol, then a certain question pushes itself at us. How does Persephone come into Her power? We know what gives Demeter Her power. We know that Her rage, and Her love for Her daughter transform Her from a grieving victim to Brimo, the strong one. But what gives Persephone *Her* power? What transforms Her from a nameless "maiden" to the Queen of the Dead?

Calasso tells us that *kore* means "pupil of the eye" as well as "girl," and he suggests that Kore becomes conscious when She sees Herself reflected in the eye of Hades. Let us think for a moment about sight, and consciousness. The mythical character Narcissus dies when his own image in water captivates him. Kore separates from Her friends when the sight of the narcissus flower lures Her away. Thus, sight moves both characters away from consciousness and into death.

And then it changes. In death, Kore becomes conscious because She does *not* turn away. Death and seeing are enemies. When someone dies, we close the eyelids. But Persephone looks. Awareness is not something that just happens to us. It is a decision we must make. Kore comes into Her power, She becomes Persephone, the one who shines in the dark, when She chooses awareness in the Land of the Dead. Death takes Her, as it takes all mortals, but unlike mortals the Goddess does not allow it to obliterate Her. Through Her move into self-awareness She changes the terms of death for all of us – but only if we too will become conscious.

Sophocles wrote "Thrice blessed are those mortals who have seen these rites and thus enter into Hades; for them alone there is life, for the others all is misery." (Fragment quoted in Burkert, *Greek Religion*.) Those who did not pass through the Mysteries continued to experience death in the old way, as empty shadows. The initiated perceived death in a wholly different way, and so they were saved. Not in the manner of Christ, who saves us all, as long as we give Him permission by "accepting" Him. Persephone asked something more of Her worshippers, that they become fully aware of Her through the nine days of Her Mysteries.

In our time, with the Greater Mysteries long gone from the world, Persephone can become an image of our own awareness. We might think especially of rape and incest. Persephone is the Goddess of those who have suffered violations. The message She gives them is simple: do not become unconscious, do not become mindless. Enter into this death and you will transform it. You will make of yourself something greater than the destruction of your innocence.

Persephone returns through the loyalty and anger of Her mother. But She does not simply return for good, putting Her experience behind Her. Here, too, She comes into Her power, Her name. For how can She shine in the dark if She turns only to the light? She goes down to Hades for part of every year – the time of the Serpent.

Persephone and Dionysos: Consciousness Married to Ecstasy

I do not wish to suggest that we take so subtle a view of this story that we end up justifying rape. Some modern writers seem to imply that Persephone needs Hades to rape Her so that She might separate from Her mother and become Her own person. Is there another way to look at this story, another version? We already have tried recasting the crucial moment of the pomegranate seeds, suggesting that Persephone chooses to eat the seeds, thereby changing Death from Her captor to Her consort. Can we carry this change further?

Here Carl Kerenyi's idea (developed from Friedrich Schelling, Jane Ellen Harrison, and others) that Persephone does not actually join with the shadowy figure of Hades, but the much more vital being of Dionysos becomes truly significant. For Dionysos is the God of Ecstasy, and to be ravished by ecstasy is very different from being raped by violence. The word *ecstasy* means "standing beside," that is, outside ourselves, lifted out of the narrow box of ordinary perception. But if ecstasy takes us out of our selves, it takes us *into* our bodies, to the revelations that come when we abandon our selves to the body's desire.

The Homeric hymn tells us that the Earth gapes open on the Nysan Plain, "named after the Dionysian mountain of Nysa" (Kerenyi). The poem also says that Hades rides Kore across the world in His chariot, before taking Her back down into the Underworld by the river Kephisos, near Eleusis. The name for the place where this happens is Erineos, the word for a wild fig tree which stood alongside. The wild fig tree was sacred to Dionysos. A mask of the God was cut from its wood in Naxos. And yet, in Greece, wild fig trees often signified an entrance to the Underworld. Even today, some Greeks fear sleeping under a fig tree may bring bad luck – or death.

The philosopher Herakleitos wrote, "Hades is the same as Dionysos." Both death and ecstasy take us beyond the limitations of ego. Kerenyi argues that Demeter's refusal to drink wine comes from Her anger at the Wine God who has taken Her Daughter. More significantly, an archaic vase painting shows Persephone with Dionysos in a pose which suggests marriage (Dionysos holds out a cup to Her), while Demeter and Hermes look on from the side. Similarly, vases showing Triptolemos often depicted Dionysos on the other side.

We have seen how the Arcadian version of the myth describes Dionysos as Persephone's *son*. There is a profound difference between a Father God who rapes His Daughter and a Mother Goddess who takes Her Son as a willing lover. The first establishes the rule of force. The second re-enacts the prehistoric drama of unity between the Mother and Child who grew in Her body, between the eternal Earth and the plants that grow and die and return.

Demeter's consort in Crete, Zagreus, also was identified with Dionysos. Thus, Demeter and Persephone become one, while Zagreus/Hades/Dionysos becomes the lover who dies, goes into the ground, and replaces Himself. Once more we recall Dionysos's dismemberment. The cutting down of the consort identified the God with the harvested wheat, and the return of the seed to the Earth. We can identify Brimos, the Goddess's son, as Dionysos reborn, with Persephone as Brimo, His mother, so that at the end of the Mysteries the circle closes, unbroken. Remember the miraculously grown wheat or barley in the final ritual.

Was the true identity of Persephone's "ravisher" part of the secret at the end of the Mysteries? That which cannot be spoken may have included a manifestation of Persephone Herself, either portrayed by a priestess, or as a vision brought about through prayer and the intensity of nine days of mystical celebration. (A vision is not the same as an hallucination, one difference being that with a genuine vision everyone sees the same thing.) Could this revelation have included the knowledge of a sacred marriage, in the Land of the Dead, between the Goddess of Life and the God of Ecstasy?

The Gift of Agriculture

Politically, the myth of Demeter and Persephone symbolizes the invasion of patriarchal tribes into the old matrifocal order. Where the sacred world previously moved between the Mother and Her daughter and Son/consort, now the ruling male, Zeus/Poseidon/Hades, seizes control. Demeter resists this change, saying that if Her daughter must die, so will the world. When Persephone returns, She does not restore the status quo; the matrifocal world has vanished. Instead, She brings a triumph over the simple violence of the invaders. Life – the life of the seed willing to return to the ground – becomes stronger than death. Violence cannot destroy the body of the Goddess, for Her body is the world itself. Humans who understand the power of life, and embrace its twin, death, overcome their fear, and their own terror and rage. They become "thrice-blessed," free of fear, free of anger, free to join with the Earth.

Demeter recognizes that She cannot restore the old ways. Instead, She gives the world Her two great gifts, the Mysteries and agriculture. Together, they establish human culture on a new level. Kore and Her companions picking wild flowers embody the old way of the hunter-gatherers. Demeter's consort, Zagreus, was called a hunter as well as lord of the Underworld. But now humanity moves into agriculture. The circle does not actually close, but opens into a spiral.

Demeter goes beyond resistance, to creation of new knowledge. At the beginning of the story, Hades roars forth in His chariot to steal Kore. Persephone rides back in the chariot without Him. Vase paintings showed Triptolemos riding in his chariot around the world to teach agriculture to humanity. When the "three times warrior" changes to the "three times plowman" the eternal truth of the Mother has transformed the aggression of the original male invaders.

The myth, and the Mysteries, give us a way to overcome the guilt of violating the Earth through agriculture. For the plow, as well as the sword, forms an aggression, now directed against the Mother's body. We have seen how indigenous Americans and others consider plowing a sin, a cutting open of their Mother's breast. Because Persephone confronts death, Demeter can give agriculture as a gift, removing all guilt from humanity.

Sexuality, Loss, and Reconciliation

In a narrow cultural sense, the tale tells of the Indo-European tribes with their warrior Gods overthrowing the thousands of years of Goddess rule in Old Europe. However, the myth also recounts the much wider story of the development of sexuality. For most of the history of life on Earth, reproduction occurred through the "splitting" of cells. The "mother" separated into two "daughters" who formed exact copies of the original. Greek and Roman art depicted Demeter and Persephone as identical. At a certain point, a mutation occurred, bringing something new into existence, the male. The male intruded into the perfect unity of mother and daughter. From that moment, children would no longer be copies of their mother.

The development of sexuality brings death. One-celled organisms never actually die, they split, with the two daughters a direct continuation of the life of the mother. When both daughters and sons result from combining a male and female parent, they become something new, a unique child that is not the same as either parent and is more than a combination of the two. But now, the parent dies instead of reproducing copies of itself. Persephone's abduction symbolizes this loss of cellular immortality. Her return signifies the possibility of reconciliation, though not the restoration of the previous condition. For She does not return to Her innocence. She has eaten the seeds of death and of knowledge. She has become something more than She was, with an awareness, and existence, in both the world of the living and the world of the dead.

"The myth of mother and daughter," writes the poet Diane di Prima, "is not a myth of overthrowing (as in myths of the son and the father) ... but one of loss and recovery." As such, it speaks to all of us, men as well as women, for we all have lost the unity we knew as fetuses, when we lived within the universe of our mothers' bellies.

At Eleusis, all the celebrants became identified with Demeter. Men who took part were given names with feminine endings. All the mystae wore the same clothes, simple robes, which later became used as swaddling clothes for babies. A Roman emperor who had been initiated at Eleusis bore the title "Goddess" on coins showing his face. In the early stages of the Mysteries, the initiates all sat on stools, mourning the loss of Kore, just as

Demeter had sat by the well at Eleusis. Becoming Demeter allows all people to suffer the loss of the child, and the joy of Her return.

It is common in our society for women to act out the male myth of overthrowing the father, particularly in the workplace, or other areas where women confront tasks and problems in the outer world. It is less common for men, and even, to some extent, women to act out the myth of loss and recovery inherent in the Mysteries. For men and women both, the identification with Demeter would have allowed them to experience the pain of whatever they themselves had lost. Women need this as much as men, for the "femaleness" of a myth does not mean that all women automatically experience it. Rather, we all need ways to take the myths into our lives. The fact that as many as several thousand people celebrated the Mysteries, living as a community for nine days, all doing the same things, must have given the final moments an overwhelming intensity.

All people became the Mother in the Mysteries. They also may have identified powerfully with Persephone as She returns at the end, especially if She appeared to them in a vision. And they may have seen themselves in the Son proclaimed at the end, the Brimos who is born to Brimo.

The miracle of reproduction can be described as the one becoming two becoming many. The one-celled organism splits and becomes two, but actually remains one, for they are the same. With the introduction of the male, a different kind of two becomes possible. From their union, the many emerge, all the diversity of life. And yet, we carry within us a sense of something lost. Death returns us to the one, for our bodies decay back into the body of the Earth. The Mysteries gave the celebrants the possibility to return through a truth other than death. Through the collective ritual the many (up to 5,000) joined together, passing through the experience of two, the Mother and the Daughter, to return finally to the knowledge of one, the unity and continuous life found within the body of the Goddess.

Hye! Kye!
Rain. Conceive.

The Body Alive

All lives, all dances, and all is loud.

Gabon Pygmy song

*I*n Ancient Greece the Goddess came alive through storytelling, ritual, processions, temple building, and sacrifice. Today She returns to us through archaeology, intuitive revelations, storytelling, ritual, art, and a way of knowledge many people think of as the opposite of religion – science. The Gaia Theory of James Lovelock, Lynn Margolis, and their co-workers describes the Earth as a living organism, a single being made up in part of the many smaller organisms living on its surface. They do not suggest this as a metaphor, but as an actual description of the world. We have become so used to thinking of myths and Gods and Goddesses as *symbolic* it may take us a moment to realize the radicalness of describing the planet as an actual living creature. The concept allows us to regain the full power of myth as a story that is genuinely true, both physically *and* metaphorically. The Gaia Theory restores myth to science and science to myth.

As we consider the Gaia Theory we may find that it accomplishes even more than giving us back a literal image of a living Goddess. Once we learn to contemplate the planet as a creature, we can extend that awareness in different directions. Is the solar system alive? Are the galaxies? And if we and the other creatures who live on the Earth are both independent creatures and parts of a greater being, what of the vast number of invisible micro-organisms who live on and within our own bodies? What part do they play in the very construction of our bodies? And if we can learn from the massive organism Gaia, what might we learn from bacteria?

The Gaia Theory

By now, most people have seen the photos of the Earth taken from space by the astronauts. The elegant ball of blue and swirling white has touched many with a sense of the planet's oneness, and sometimes with a sense of its fragility. For a group of scientists led by James Lovelock and Lynn Margolis the pictures inspired a more revolutionary idea – that the Earth may be a single living organism. In Lovelock's book *Gaia: A New Look at Life on Earth* he calls this concept the "Gaia Hypothesis," a term suggested by the novelist William Golding (whose books often have explored the psychological truth of myth). In recent writings Lovelock has declared that he and his colleagues have gathered enough evidence to change the "Gaia Hypothesis" to the "Gaia Theory."

At first glance the Gaia Theory sounds like an extension of ecology. Elisabet Sahtouris, in her book *Gaia: The Human Journey from Chaos to Cosmos* (virtually all the recent books on this subject begin with "Gaia:"), points out the essential difference. Ecology studies the unity of life *on* Earth. The Gaia Theory describes the Earth itself as alive. The difference is something like that between describing all the micro-organisms that live on the skin and shell of a turtle – and recognizing the turtle itself as a distinct creature.

The origins of the Gaia idea actually go back several years before the famous astronaut photographs. In 1965 NASA asked Lovelock and Dian Hitchcock to examine planned experiments to determine if life existed on Mars. In their attempt to get away from assumptions that life on Mars would have to look the same as it looked on Earth, the two scientists decided to examine the Martian atmosphere for processes which they could not justify by inorganic chemistry alone. They found, in fact, that the atmosphere of Mars remains always chemically stable.

When they examined Earth, however, they found the presence of methane, an unstable gas, as "proof" of life (that is, a proof independent of observing the actual creatures close at hand). Methane is a by-product of living organisms. This led them to wonder how the Earth managed to keep a constant atmospheric composition despite the presence of highly unstable gases. It occurred to them that the air might form a basic part of life, rather than being just a lifeless environment. Lovelock compares the air to the fur on a cat, or the paper of a hornet's nest – not actually alive in itself, but "made by living things to sustain an environment."

Lovelock and his colleagues have insisted that they are not claiming consciousness for the Earth, let alone a divine consciousness. They are not suggesting that the planet is the same as the Greek Goddess. For many, however, it is precisely this possibility that makes the idea such an opening to new ways of thinking. William Irwin Thompson, in his book *Imaginary Landscapes* (lest we consider Thompson an exception in that he does not title his book "Gaia: ...", he titles his chapter on this subject "Gaia: Cosmology Regained"), suggests that Lovelock and his associates chose the name partly for its dramatic impact. If they had called the hypothesis "Homeorrhetic Mechanisms of Planetary Dynamics" Thompson says, it would never have received the same public attention.

Thompson implies that the name has inspired the public's leap to assume that "Gaia" is conscious as well as alive. But Thompson does not see this as a mistake. A student of the unity of myth and science found in the Stone Age, he writes of the "ancient cosmology lurking behind the rocks and streams of the Gaia hypothesis."

Body Heat

If scientists do *not* see the Earth as a conscious being, what does it mean to call the Earth alive? One primary point of the Gaia Theory involves the idea of self-regulation. Living organisms change such things as body temperature in response to changes in the environment. According to Lovelock, the Earth does exactly this, keeping the environmental temperature roughly constant over millions of years, despite the fact that the sun has steadily grown hotter over this long period of time. Lovelock calculates that the Sun's output has risen between 30 and 50 percent during the period since the origin of life. And yet, by all the evidence, the Earth's temperature has remained constant.

One way this could have happened would have been if a blanket of some gas, ammonia or carbon dioxide, kept the Earth warm during the early period, when the Sun did not generate that much heat. As the Sun became hotter, the blanket would have been steadily stripped away, keeping the temperature on the planet constant. Now, this sounds simple but in fact would be a remarkable process. It supposes that the Earth somehow could remove its excess warming gases at precisely the correct pace over billions of years, never too fast or too slow, to keep the temperature constant.

We might assume that the increase in heat itself determined how much gas disappeared. According to Lovelock, it is not that simple. He points out that the Earth's temperature is not uniform across the planet; it changes from the frozen poles to the heat of the equator. This occurs because the same intensity of light does not fall everywhere on the planet. Such complexity makes it hard to assume a rigid chemical process which might account for the Earth's constant average temperature in the face of the Sun's ever-increasing warmth. Instead, the Gaia Theory argues, the planet regulates its own heat.

Cultural Assumptions

It is hard for us to recognize the Earth as a living being, partly because we ourselves live on it, and partly because the Earth is so much bigger than us – and partly because we have learned to think of the planet as lifeless rock containing the plants and animals we think of as alive. Other cultures would find the idea less strange, for most people have envisioned the planet as organic, as the ancient Mother, the Goddess. Amadou Hampote Ba writes that in the Sudan "Earth is thought of as a living being. She grows, she diminishes, she dies."

Our bodies too contain vast numbers of living beings. We can imagine bacteria not recognizing us as alive because of our huge size. A living being is composed of other living beings, each one an independent organism. At the same time, it acts as a whole, with a boundary that gives it form and distinguishes it from its surroundings. A cat's fur, human skin, and the Earth's atmosphere all perform similar functions. And yet, the boundary is never absolute, never a barrier, for us or the Earth. Living creatures cannot remain wholly separate from the environment. Life demands that we exchange energy with the world outside us. Human beings eat other creatures, whether plants or animals. We transform their substance and energy into parts of our own bodies. We excrete wastes back into the environment where they then act as a fertilizer, which is to say nutrients for creatures outside ourselves. With every breath we take we receive the gift of oxygen from the plants around us, and give back carbon dioxide. The Earth as a whole receives light from the Sun and the other stars and gives off heat and gases into space.

Our education has taught us that we and the plants and animals are alive, but other aspects of our world are not. Many other cultures have seen all parts of the world as alive. We tend to consider this view primitive, or naïve, but maybe we are the ones with a simplistic understanding of life.

Extending the Definition of Life

The distinction between living and non-living begins to break down when we look at our own and other creatures' bodies. Bone, hair, shells, and scales can all be described as inorganic. According to Sahtouris, 95 percent of a redwood tree is actually dead wood, yet the tree lives. She also writes as well that over vast time rock transforms into living creatures which then eventually transform back into rock. Almost all the rocks on the surface of the planet are made of atoms which once belonged to living creatures. And those atoms came originally from the stones of earlier ages. Much of the dust in our homes comes from skin that has flaked off our bodies during the course of the day. And the Earth itself and everything on it comes from starlight, for the dust which originally formed the planets began as the remains of exploding stars.

When we begin to look at the planet as alive, we start to extend our definition of life further and further. Despite constant expansion and movement through space, galaxies maintain a definite shape and boundaries. Can we think of galaxies as organic? On our planet nature produces far more cells and seeds than strictly necessary. The excess allows for a large number to die off while a small percentage come alive and form organisms. Dead planets may form the excess cells of the galaxies.

The Gaia Theory begins to return us to the powerful intuition that life – and yes, consciousness – exist at all levels of being. "All lives, all dances, and all is loud." So many of the myths of the Goddess as the cow describe the Milky Way, our galaxy, as the milk from Her body. And yet, for most of us, these remain nice stories, psychological metaphors maybe, but not a description of the real world. The Gaia Theory opens the way to a new unity of science, myth, and intuition.

In this unity, the science of biology becomes vital and exciting – alive. When I was growing up, and taking science classes in school, biology did not seem very exciting. In school, it consisted mostly of taxonomy, long lists of classifications. At that time, we looked to physics for poetry, for mystery. With the sudden appearance of Gaia where we least expected Her, biology becomes a new focus of wonder. Just as the return of the Goddess means the return of history, so the return of Gaia means the return of the body, and the knowledge that the body – our bodies, Earth's body – exist simultaneously in the world of objects and the world of story.

The Dismembered Body

The many myths of the Goddess's dismembered body arise from a sense that everything is alive, and yet in pieces. This is not an intellectual construction but rather a deep intuition. And so we create stories of a Goddess who sacrifices Her body to make the world. In the Big Bang theory of modern science, all of existence began as a unit, bound together in a kind of perfect egg called the *ylem*. The ylem exploded into light and energy, some of which converted into the particles of matter.

The conversion of light energy into matter follows Einstein's formula $E=mc^2$. This involves a bonding of massive amounts of energy since the formula translates as "energy equals mass times the speed of light squared." Light speed is so great that a small amount of matter contains tremendous energy. Nuclear bombs demonstrate this fact in a horrible way, but if we look past that destructive application the relation of matter to energy gives us much to think about. We might describe our own bodies, along with all other matter, *as light slowed down*.

228

In the Kabbalah tradition of Jewish mysticism we find a strikingly similar idea to the Big Bang. There we learn that God sent out His light from a single unknowable point. God directed the light into "vessels" which turned out to be too weak to contain the power. They broke apart to form our universe. We live, therefore, in a universe of broken fragments. From this comes our pain and fear, our unrealized hopes, our cowardice and hatred, our failed loves and all the weaknesses that separate us from one another and our own true selves. And yet, the light of perfect being remains, embedded in the sherds.

So many of the myths (including the scientific ones) see the universe as fragmented, endless pieces which no longer fit together, no longer form a whole and living being. The Gaia Theory takes us to a possibility that the body of the Goddess remains whole while at the same time containing the endless parts of creation.

The theory answers something deep in ourselves, an awareness that insists, if I am alive, so is everything else. Bacteria live their own existences, yet form part of our bodies. Our bodies take part in the life of the planet, which in turn fills its place in the body of the solar system. A unit in itself, the solar system nevertheless helps to make up the galaxy. The galaxies take part in a complex dance of "clusters," and "super clusters" which eventually make up the universe, whose very name describes its wholeness. Can we trust that inner sense of the universe as a vast organism, physically and spiritually alive?

The name Gaia for the planetary being fits very well, despite its limited origin from a particular, European, culture. For Gaia embodied the Earth in the planet's most basic form. Gaia was the first being, self-created, before all the later stages of evolution and human development. We also might think of the Native American term "Grandmother" for the earliest creation. (Imagine if Lovelock and the others had named their idea "the Grandmother Hypothesis.") We know from science that our planet did not arise from nothing but formed out of dust in a universe already billions of years old. Mythologically, however, we can think of Gaia as the cosmos, even the ylem, as well as using the name for the planetary organism.

A Self-created Universe

Followers of transcendent religion often object to the idea of the universe as self-created. Where did the universe come from, they argue. Something – some One – must have created it. But we can say the same thing about God. Where did God come from? God didn't just come out of nowhere, someone must have made Him. At some point we need to leave the argument behind. Within the insistence that God must have made nature lies the assumption that nature is too imperfect, too messy, too alive, to form the "real" world. We die in nature. Our bodies desire impossible things, to fly, to live forever, to merge totally with other beings. We cannot control our desires, or our bodies. They become sick and useless. They embarrass us with their longings, and their pain. And so we long for something more perfect, something detached from the mess of bodies. And *that* we will accept as real, as self-created.

But we pay a price for this transcendence. We give up our own reality. We become dissatisfied, in the deepest way, with life as it exists. If we think of God as perfect and detached, then we will try to make ourselves perfect as well, detached from bodies, unchanging. In Ancient Greece, Pythagoras and Plato described true existence as geometry, ideal forms accessible through "pure" reason.

In much of modern science we have sought another kind of perfection, that of the machine, which always keeps the same form, and does the same thing over and over. We attempt to describe the body, and especially the brain as some sort of mechanism – a pump system, a clock, a telephone exchange, a computer – whatever current fashion dictates. But a vital difference exists between machines and organisms. Organisms do not act in the same way at all moments. Through the Gaia Theory we begin to recapture a sense of ourselves, and the universe, as dynamic, as rotting and growing, as ever-changing. Alive.

Life as Co-operation

The idea that no real boundaries exist between life and non-life leads us to a vision of the world based on co-operation rather than competition. William

Irwin Thompson points out two competing theories about the origin of human culture. In one, humanity begins with making tools and, especially, weapons. The technology of killing becomes the basic human act distinguishing us from other species. In the other, however, human culture begins with the sharing of food. Though the first theory still holds a lot of influence in our technological and military world, more and more evidence points to the second. Actually, hunting as well as gathering requires co-operation and the sharing of information. According to Thompson, Glynn Isaac has found indications that the earliest pre-humans, the proto-hominids, made group efforts to transport food away from dangerous places to places where they all could share it in safety. And remember Alexander Marshack's idea that human culture began with "stories." Stories, too, imply sharing, for a story demands an audience.

Lynn Margolis, in her work on bacteria, has developed a theory of co-operation at the very basis of life. While Lovelock has focused primarily on the very large scale of "planetary dynamics," Margolis has looked in the other direction, at the organisms living within the larger creatures we normally recognize as living beings. Margolis considers bacteria the primary life form within Gaia. From the point of view of bacteria, we might describe humans as bacteria's transport and feeding mechanisms.

In our science classes, many of us learned to think of bacteria as enemies, the carriers of disease. There is, of course, truth in this view. At the same time, the idea originates partly in the desire to see our bodies as completely separate from the world: egos encased in impervious fortresses. Margolis reminds us that we cannot live without the bacteria that help us digest our food.

More significantly, Margolis has demonstrated that bacteria are capable of sharing genetic information. In her research she has found situations where bacteria will break down their cell walls and merge genetic material from their nuclei. To those of us not trained in science, this discovery may appear obscure, or arcane. In fact, it too is revolutionary.

For one thing, it leads to a theory of evolution based on co-operation rather than competition, with all that that implies for our view of the world and our own place in it. The Darwinian concept of natural selection holds that genetic change can come about only through random mutation of the DNA. Organisms produce various mutations of themselves and the ones that best adapt to their environment survive, while the others die out. Margolis's work brings the possibility of bacteria recombining their DNA in a direct response to environmental pressures. As an example of rapid and complex change we can think of the ways bacteria adapt to antibiotics. According to Margolis, these adaptations carry an element of shared deliberation.

The Place of Mind

Can we think of "mind" as somehow involved in this bacterial sharing of information? As a scientist, Margolis presumably would shy away from such a suggestion, just as Lovelock and others deny any hint of consciousness for planetary Gaia. But maybe bacteria – and Gaia – can help us find a wider definition of mind. If the work of these biologists leads us to the "primitive" or "mystical" perception of all existence as alive, maybe we also should honor the second half of that perception, that all existence is conscious. Sahtouris writes "Those who believe that life is self-creating in a dynamically alive universe rather than a mechanical one also believe that life can create its own meaning and purpose." Since writing her book on Gaia, Dr. Sahtouris has worked to create a world-wide network championing the scientific knowledge of indigenous peoples.

Just as with the hunter-gatherers, human society today needs to co-operate to succeed. We need to communicate knowledge, requirements, skills, and information. Just as the proto-hominids did, we need to transport food. In short, we need to create a co-operative social *body*. The requirements remain the same, just on a much larger scale. A vision of the entire planet as an organism made up of smaller organisms helps us to see human society as an organism as well – not some sort of monster that swallows individuals, but one where the individuals share experience and knowledge to create the larger organism. And this creation goes on all the time, not once and for all. While organisms maintain an outer form and continuous life processes, they change constantly, taking in and giving out energy. A society based on the body also would change constantly while keeping an inner sense of its form, its boundaries, and its values. And a society based on the *divine* body would keep an awareness of the unity of science, daily life, and the sacred – for individual organisms as well as the greater organism of culture.

Our Place

Discussions of Gaia as an organism made up of smaller organisms seem to lead inevitably to a discussion of humanity's function in this greater body. Often the discussion flows from an assumption that humanity occupies some vitally important position in Gaia's existence. Some writers treat humanity as a menace, some treat us as a blessing to planetary life – but most consider us central.

One theory looks at humanity as an experiment in consciousness. With the human brain, Gaia is trying out self-awareness. Elisabet Sahtouris describes us as an experiment in free choice, and suggests, optimistically, that our qualities of egotism, anxiety, shortsightedness, fear, and aggression, are signs of adolescence. By implication, we will outgrow these limitations and become something better than our history.

Peter Russel argues that human beings form Gaia's central nervous system. Soon, Russel writes, the world will contain as many humans as an individual brain contains neurons. At that point, humans may organize into a planetary intelligence (this idea gives us a whole new look at the "population explosion" of recent decades).

Other writers take the more conventional view that humanity endangers life on the planet and adapt this to Gaia Theory. A. I. W. Summers turns the intelligence idea on its head. He compares our destruction of nature with psychosomatic illness. "Psychosomatic" does not describe sickness as imaginary or fictional. Rather, it refers to situations where the psyche makes the body truly ill. If humans indeed represent Gaia's brain, then the brain has distorted its relationship with the rest of the body, causing the body to become sick.

Another idea begins with describing humanity's behavior as seen from outside. Unlike most other creatures, humans spread all over the planet. Wherever we go we multiply out of control. Because of our uncontrollable population growth we eat up all the resources of whatever place we inhabit. As a result, the creatures belonging to those places all die off and the places themselves suffer great damage, sometimes turning into deserts or dead waters. Now, if we take the same sort of description and apply it to cells within an animal we discover that we are talking about cancer. Thus, human beings form a kind of cancer in the planetary body, threatening to choke off all life.

Do human beings really occupy such a central role in Gaia's life and destiny? For one thing, are we the only creatures with awareness? Experiments in inter-species communication demonstrate the strong possibility of self-awareness in such creatures as chimpanzees and dolphins. And anyone who has lived with a dog and watched it sleep will know the possibility that animals other than humans dream.

For many people working with the Gaia Theory, the idea that humanity can destroy all life on the planet forms yet another example of human arrogance. Lovelock looks at that common description of Gaia as "fragile" (as in the expression "our fragile ecosphere") and compares it to the same term used for his grandmother and other women in the Victorian era. He points out that Victorian men described women as fragile so that the men could justify their total control of society and even women's bodies. Similarly, when we describe the Earth as fragile, we justify our own control and management of the environment.

In fact, Lovelock comments, his grandmother was very tough. And so is Gaia. If indeed the Earth forms an organism with the ability to regulate its conditions in order to keep alive, then perhaps it will make whatever adjustments it needs to deal with the current threats to its outer environment.

Some people see this as a dangerous invitation to complacency. To them it sounds as if the Gaia people are saying we can pollute the Earth as much as we like because Gaia will take care of it. In fact, the idea of Gaia adjusting Herself should not make us complacent at all. Gaia, so the theory goes, does not act with any particular benevolence to any single species. She takes care of Her own interests, not ours. When we get sick we do whatever we need to do to get better, even if that involves the death of vast numbers of microbes living inside our bodies. If we keep pushing Gaia, She may indeed adjust – and make life very difficult for us.

An Earlier Crisis

Gaia has faced environmental crises in the past. The early organisms produced energy through fermentation. As their population exploded the energy began to run out and so they developed the ability to use sunlight to split molecules into atoms and use these to build up other molecules. Thus they developed photosynthesis. However, photosynthesis produced a deadly poison: oxygen.

The appearance of oxygen in the Earth's atmosphere created a far greater threat to the environment than our contemporary pollution. Without anything to consume the oxygen it built up in the atmosphere to a level capable of spontaneous combustion – setting itself on fire. The bacteria which created it began to burn up. As a result, however, they learned to form colonies. The outer levels would burn, but then the dead matter of their "corpses" protected the inner layers. Life became more complex. Over a period of two billion years Gaia developed creatures, such as ourselves, who could burn oxygen for energy. Since then, the atmosphere has remained stable. If we indeed manage to threaten that stability we cannot know what adjustments Gaia will make to take care of the problem. Rather than trying to manage the Earth, we might study Her processes in the hope that we can learn how to manage ourselves.

A Different View

Feminist and Native American scholar Paula Gunn Allen has put forward a visionary, mythic interpretation of the planetary crisis. She describes it as Grandmother Earth giving birth to Herself (the Grandmother Theory). The Earth is passing through an initiation into a new state of consciousness. This great change brings with it the pain of labor, just as a woman's pain and turmoil increase the closer she comes to delivering her baby. Allen's sense of the Earth's emergence exemplifies several qualities of the Goddess-based interpretation of the world. First, it allows both intuition and sacred traditions to reveal ideas. These ideas and visions may or may not match the current scientific analysis, but they will not contradict the actual information we get from science. They add a different kind of knowledge. Very often, this knowledge comes from women's awareness of their bodies. Allen uses the experience of labor to understand the upheavals of our planet. And finally, she shows the way Goddess worshippers deliberately interpret experience optimistically, as new life rather than destruction.

Dismemberment and Unity

Above all else, the Gaia Theory gives us a vision of the Earth's wholeness. Return again to those myths of the Goddess's dismembered body. People sense that everything in the world belongs together, but has broken apart. We can *feel* the connections, but we *see* the fragments. And so we come to a belief that the world can only exist, *we* can only exist, because the Goddess has sacrificed Her body. Either She has given Herself freely to make the Earth and the Sky and everything in them, or else some force has broken or torn Her to pieces.

In some places, this inner perception becomes mingled with the cultural history of male takeover. In Babylon, Tiamat becomes a monster, and Marduk rips her apart as a validation of the male-centered civilization which overthrew the earlier matristic one. In Mexico, the Goddess Coyolxauhqua was torn savagely by Her two brothers, with a similar cultural message. When we read that the myth describes the brothers as snakes, we find ourselves back outside the gates of Eden, where the patriarchy has created enmity between the woman and the serpent.

The Mexican story also describes the Moon's death and return, at the end of each month, for the brothers cut Her into 14 pieces, approximately half the lunar cycle. In Egypt the God Set cuts His brother Osiris into 14 pieces. Myths always contain many things simultaneously – political messages, scientific descriptions, spiritual perceptions.

We can find something deeper here than sexual politics, or even explanations of nature. These myths of dismemberment carry a sense of anxiety about our very existence. We live only by eating other creatures, whether animals or plants (and by preventing them from eating us). We live because our Mother sacrificed Her perfect Oneness.

The dismembered Goddess becomes diffused, that is, spread into so many parts that She becomes everywhere and nowhere, visible in all things, and yet invisible at the same time. The necessities of creation have broken the integrity of Her form.

In the Gaia Theory, we see a possible answer to this anxiety. Here, Gaia does not begin as a unity and break into fragments. Instead, the unity emerges from the play of all the different parts. And not just the "living" parts. The mountains, the rain and the seas, the wind, the light from the Sun and stars, the gravitational waves from the Moon, the dust, and the bones of creatures dead for millions of years, all of these, and us, bring Gaia's body into existence.

A Ritual and a Dream

I will end this book with one more story, a dream of Gaia. In October of 1990 I moved into my house near the Hudson River in New York State. A short time after I moved in I discovered a remarkable stone mound in the woods just the other side of my driveway (see *Plate 23*).

Clearly, people piled these rocks together at some time, but when, and for what purpose I do not know. The opening looks east, towards the sunrise. The crystalline white rocks were lying scattered in front of it when I came across it. These rocks are common to the area, but never so many in one place.

Whatever the origin or purpose of this mound, I found it a wonderful surprise after traveling to mounds and circles and ruined temples in so many countries. As the winter solstice approached, I decided to do a ritual at my new home, focusing on the mound, as a way of thanking the Goddess for bringing me to this place.

Two friends joined me on the solstice. Together we performed a simple ceremony. I asked each of them to bring something they wanted to offer to the Earth. For my own contribution I baked a flat cake in the form of a Goddess, and brought that out, along with seeds, and rocks found on journeys to sacred sites in other countries. We then made a procession, going to different trees and other special places around my house, while singing songs, carrying Goddess statues, and playing instruments. When we came to the mound we each spoke of things in our lives we wanted to give away to the Earth. We said a prayer honoring the rising of the light at this turning point of the year, when the Sun starts gaining back its power. As we laid our offerings inside the mound, I broke off pieces of the cake – the "Goddess's" body – and gave them to each of us to eat. We lay the head down in the dirt for the animals.

The night before this ritual, the longest night of the year, Gaia came to me in a dream. She did not appear in any particular shape, but She spoke to me, and I knew Her voice without question. Gaia told me yes, She had broken Her body into millions of pieces to make the world. But Her Self remained, complete, unbroken, in every fragment. And so Her body remains as well, whole and perfect in every stone or hair, every star or kiss, every moth or elephant. She becomes at every moment what She has always been, the Body of the Goddess, in every flash of light, in every dream and whisper.

Hudson Valley, New York
Completed on the 145th birthday of
Sir Arthur Evans, excavator of Knossos

Bibliography

Adler, Margot, *Drawing Down the Moon*, Beacon, Boston, 1987

Alexiou, Stylianos, *Minoan Civilization*, trans. Cressida Ridley, Spyros Alexiou Sons, Heraklion, Crete, n.d.

Allen, Paula Gunn, *The Sacred Hoop: Recovering the Feminine in American Indian Traditions*, Beacon, Boston, 1986
— *Spider Woman's Granddaughters*, Beacon, Boston, 1989

Allman, William F., "The Dawn of Creativity", in *U.S. News and World Report*, 20 May, 1996

Austen, Hallie Inglehart, *The Heart of the Goddess*, Wingbow Press, Berkeley, 1990

Barber, Robin, *Blue Guide to Greece*, A. & C. Black, London, 1987

Baring, Anne, and Cashford, Jules, *The Myth of the Goddess*, Viking, London, 1991

Beach, Edward A., *The Ecole Initiative: The Eleusinian Mysteries*, article published on the World Wide Web, 1995

Bell, Diane, *Daughters of the Dreaming*, McPhee Gribble/George Allen and Unwin, Sydney, 1983

Biaggi, Christina, *The Goddess Mound*, pamphlet
— *Megalithic Sculptures that Symbolize the Great Goddess*, Dissertation, New York University, New York, 1982

Black Elk, *The Sacred Pipe*, ed. Joseph Epes Brown, University of Oklahoma Press, 1953

Boer, Charles, *The Homeric Hymns*, Swallow Press, Chicago, 1970

Bolin, Anne, *In Search of Eve: Transsexual Rites of Passage*, Bergin and Garvey, South Hadley, Massachusetts, 1988

Brennan, Martin, *The Boyne Valley Vision*, Dublin, 1980
— *The Stars and the Stones: Ancient Art and Astronomy in Ireland*, Thames and Hudson, London, 1983

Bridges, Marilyn, *Markings: Aerial Views of Sacred Landscapes*, Aperture Foundation, New York, 1986

Briffault, Robert, *The Mothers*, George Allen and Unwin, London, 1959

Brodsky, Anne Trueblood, Daneswich, Rose, and Johnson, Nick (eds.), *Stones, Bones, and Skin: Ritual and Shamanic Art*, Society for Art Publications, Toronto, 1977

Buckley, Thomas, and Gottlieb, Alma, *Blood Magic*, University of California, Berkeley, 1988

Budapest, Zsuzsanna E, *Grandmother Moon*, Harper SanFrancisco, San Francisco, 1991

Burkert, Walter, *Greek Religion: Archaic and Classical*, trans. John Raffan, Basil Blackwell, Oxford, 1985

Calasso, Roberto, *The Marriage of Cadmus and Harmony*, trans. Tim Parks, Knopf, New York, 1993

Cameron, Dorothy, *Symbols of Birth and Death in the Neolithic Era*, Kenyon-Deane, London, 1981

Campbell, Joseph, *The Flight of the Wild Gander*, Gateway, South Bend, Indiana, 1951
— *The Hero with a Thousand Faces*, Bollingen Foundation, New York, 1949
— *The Inner Reaches of Outer Space*, Harper and Row, New York, 1986
— *The Masks of God, Vol. 1, Primitive Mythology*, Viking, New York, 1962
— *The Masks of God, Vol. 2, Oriental Mythology*, Viking, New York, 1962
— *The Masks of God, Vol. 3, Occidental Mythology*, Viking, New York, 1964
— *The Masks of God, Vol. 4, Creative Mythology*, Viking, New York, 1968
— *Historical Atlas of World Mythology, Vol. 1, The Way of the Animal Powers*, Times Books, London, 1983
— *Historical Atlas of World Mythology, Vol. 2, The Way of the Seeded Earth*, Harper and Row, New York, 1988
— (ed.) with Charles Muses, *In All Her Names*, Harper San Francisco, San Francisco, 1991
— ed. *The Mysteries: Papers from the Eranos Yearbooks*, Vol. 30, No. 2, Bollingen, Princeton, New Jersey, 1955

Canan, Janine, *She Rises Like the Sun*, Crossing, Freedom, California, 1989

Charles-Picard, Gilbert, *Larousse Encyclopedia of Archaeology*, trans. Anne Ward, Hamlyn, London, 1972

Chatwin, Bruce, *The Songlines*, Penguin, London, 1987

Chippindale, Christopher, *Stonehenge Complete*, Thames and Hudson, London, 1983

Christ, Carol P., *Diving Deep and Surfacing*, Beacon, Boston, 1980
— *The Laughter of Aphrodite*, Harper and Row, San Francisco, 1987
—ed. with Judith Plaskow, *Womanspirit Rising*, Harper and Row, San Francisco, 1979

Colegreave, Sukie, *The Spirit of the Valley*, Virago, London, 1979

Conner, Randy P., *Blossom of Bone*, HarperCollins, San Francisco, 1993

Cook, Roger, *The Tree of Life: Image for the Cosmos*, Thames and Hudson, London, 1974

Cowan, James, *Mysteries of the Dream-Time*, Prism, Dorset, 1989

Craighead, Meinrad, *The Mother's Songs*, Paulist Press, New York, 1986

Crawford, O. G. S., *The Eye Goddess*, Phoenix House, London, 1957

Critchlow, Keith, *Time Stands Still: New Light on Megalithic Science*, St. Martin's, New York, 1980

Crumlin, Rosemary, and Knight, Anthony, *Aboriginal Art and Spirituality*, HarperCollins, Victoria, Australia, 1991

Dames, Michael, *The Avebury Cycle*, Thames and Hudson, London, 1983
— *The Silbury Treasure*, Thames and Hudson, London, 1976

Delluc, Brigitte and Gilles, *Discovering Lascaux*, Editions Sud-Ouest, Bordeaux, 1990

Denny, Dallas, "Transsexualism At Forty," in *Chrysalis Quarterly*, Vol.1, No.6, 1993

Dexter, Miriam Robbins, *Whence the Goddesses: A Source Book*, Pergamon, New York, 1990

di Prima, Diane, *Loba*, Wingbow, Berkeley, 1973

Dingus, Rick, book co-ordinator, *Marks in Place: Contemporary Responses to Rock Art*, University of New Mexico Press, Albuquerque, 1988

Doolittle, Hilda, *Hermetic Definition*, New Directions, New York, 1958

Dove, Rita, *Mother Love*, W. W. Norton, New York/London, 1995

Downing, Christine, *The Goddess: Mythical Images of the Divine*, Crossroad, New York, 1987

Durdin-Robertson, L., *The Year of the Goddess*, Thorsons, Wellingborough, Northamptonshire, 1990

Eisler, Riane, *The Chalice and the Blade: Our History, Our Future*, Harper and Row, San Francisco, 1987

Eliade, Mircea, *From Primitives to Zen*, Harper and Row, New York, 1967
— *A History of Religious Ideas*, trans. Willard R. Trask, University of Chicago, Chicago, 1978
— *Myths, Dreams, and Mysteries*, trans. Philip Mairet, Harvill Press, London, 1960
— *Rites and Symbols of Initiation*, trans. Willard R. Trask, Harper and Row, New York, 1958
— *Shamanism*, trans. Willard R. Trask, Bollingen, Princeton, 1964

Erasmus, Udo, *Fats That Heal, Fats That Kill*, Alive Books, Burnaby, British Columbia, 1986

Estrada, Alvaro, *Maria Sabina, Her Life and Chants*, trans. Henry Munn, Ross-Erikson, Santa Barbara, California, 1981

Evan, J. D., *The Prehistoric Antiquities of the Maltese Islands*, Athlone Press, London, 1971

Evans, Arthur, *The God of Ecstasy: Sex Roles and the Madness of Dionysos*, St. Martin's, New York, 1988

Fanlac, Pierre, ed., *The Font-de-Gaume Cave*, Imprimerie Reymondie, Périgueux, 1984

Francia, Luisa, *Dragontime*, trans. Sasha Daucus, Ash Tree Publishing, Woodstock, New York, 1991

Friedrich, Paul and Deborah, *The Meaning of Aphrodite*, University of Chicago Press, Chicago, 1978

Frick, Thomas, *The Sacred Theory of the Earth*, North Atlantic Books, Berkeley, 1986

Gabriel, Davina Anne, ed., TransSisters *The Journal of Transsexual Feminism*, Kansas City

Gadon, Elinor W., *The Once and Future Goddess: A Symbol for our Time*, Harper and Row, San Francisco, 1989

Gimbutas, Marija, *The Civilization of the Goddess*, Harper San Francisco, San Francisco, 1991
— *The Goddesses and Gods of Old Europe*, Thames and Hudson, London, 1974, 1982
— *The Language of the Goddess*, Harper and Row, San Francisco, 1989

Gleason, Judith, *Oya: In Praise of the Goddess* Shambala, Boston, 1987

Goldstein, David, *Jewish Mythology*, Hamlyn, London, 1980

Goodman, Felicitas D., *Where the Spirits Ride the Wind*, Indiana University Press, Bloomington, 1990

Grahn, Judith, *Blood, Bread, and Roses: How Menstruation Created the World*, Beacon, Boston, 1993
— *The Queen of Swords*, Beacon, Boston, 1987

Grant, Campbell, *The Rock Art of the North American Indians*, Cambridge University Press, Cambridge, 1983

Graves, Robert, *The Greek Myths, Vols. 1 and 2*, Penguin, London, 1955

Great Goddess Collective, *Heresies*, Vol. 2, No. 1, New York, 1982

Green, Marian, *The Path Through the Labyrinth*, Element, Shaftesbury, 1988

Griffin, Susan, *Woman and Nature*, Harper and Row, New York, 1978

Grimal, Pierre, ed., *Larousse World Mythology*, Chartwell, Secaucus, New Jersey, 1965

Haindl, Hermann, *Der Haindl Tarot* (Tarot cards), Droemer Knaur, Munich, 1988

Halevi, Z'ev ben Shimon, *Kabbalah: Tradition of Hidden Knowledge*, Thames and Hudson, London, 1979

Halifax, Joan, *Shaman: The Wounded Healer*, Thames and Hudson, London, 1982
— *Shamanic Voices*, Dutton, New York, 1979

Hall, Nor, *The Moon and the Virgin*, Harper and Row, New York, 1980
— *Those Women*, Spring, Dallas, 1988

Harding, M. Esther, *Woman's Mysteries, Ancient and Modern*, Harper and Row, New York, 1971

Harjo, Joy, *In Mad Love and War*, Wesleyan University Press, Middletown, Connecticut, 1990
— *She Had Some Horses*, Thunder's Mouth Press, New York, 1983

Harrison, Jane Ellen, *Prolegomena to the Study of Greek Religion*, (reprint) Princeton University Press, Princeton, New Jersey, 1991

Hawkins, G., *Beyond Stonehenge*, Harper and Row, New York, 1973
— *Stonehenge Decoded*, Dell, New York, 1965

Hertz, J. H. (ed.), *The Pentateuch and Haftorah*, Soncino, London, 1960

Highwater, Jamake, *Myth and Sexuality*, NHL, New York, 1990
— *The Primal Mind*, Harper and Row, New York, 1981

Homer, *The Iliad*, trans. Richmond Lattimore, University of Chicago, Chicago, 1951
— *The Odyssey*, trans. Richmond Lattimore, Harper and Row, 1965

Huet, Michel, *The Dance, Art, and Ritual of Africa*, Pantheon, New York, 1978

Inglehart Austen, Hallie, *The Heart of the Goddess*, Wingbow, Berkeley, 1990

Johnson, Buffie, *The Lady of the Beasts: Ancient Images of the Goddess and Her Sacred Animals*, Harper and Row, San Francisco, 1988

Kerenyi, Carl, *Eleusis: Archetypal Image of Mother and Daughter*, Bollingen, Princeton, New Jersey, 1967
— *The Gods of the Greeks*, Thames and Hudson, London, 1951

Klein, Dr. Ernest, *A Comprehensive Etymological Dictionary of the English Language*, Elsevier Publishing Company, Amsterdam, 1971

Koltuv, Barbara, *The Book of Lilith*, Nicholas-Hayes, York Beach, Maine, 1986

La Chapelle, Dolores, *Earth Wisdom*, Finn Hill Arts, Silverton, Colorado, 1978
— *Sacred Land, Sacred Sex*, Finn Hill Arts, Silverton, Colorado, 1988

Laming-Emperaire, Annette, *La signification de l'art rupestre paléolithique*, Paris, Presses Universitaires de France, 1964

Lao Tzu, *The Tao Te Ching*, trans. Gia-Fu Feng and Jane English, Vintage, New York, 1989

Lehrman, Frederic, *The Sacred Landscape*, Celestial Arts, Berkeley, 1988

Lerner, Gerda, *The Creation of Patriarchy*, Oxford Unversity Press, London, 1986

Leroi-Gourhan, André, *The Dawn of European Art*, Cambridge University Press, Cambridge, 1982

Lewis-Williams, J. D., *Believing and Seeing*, Academic Press, London, 1981

Levy, Gertrude Rachel, *The Gate of Horn*, Faber and Faber, London, 1946

Lhote, Henri, *The Search for the Tassili Frescoes*, E. P. Dutton, New York, 1959

Lippard, Lucy, *Overlay: Contemporary Art and the Art of Prehistory*, Pantheon, New York, 1983

Lobell, Mimi, "The Goddess Temple," *Journal of Architectural Education*, Vol. XXIX, No. 1
— "Temples of the Great Goddess," *Heresies*, Issue 5, New York, 1978
— "Spatial Archetypes," *ReVISION*, Vol. 6, No. 2, Winter, Boston, 1983-84

Lockyer, N. J., *Stonehenge and other British Stone Monuments Astronomically Considered*, London 1909

Lovelock, James E., *Gaia: A New Look at Life on Earth*, Oxford University Press, London, 1979

Lubell, Winifred Milius, *The Metamorphosis of Baubo: Myths of Woman's Sexual Energy*, Vanderbilt University Press, Nashville, Tennessee, 1994

Lubsen-Admiraal, Stella, and Crouwel, Joost, *Cyprus and Aphrodite*, SDU, 's-Gravenhage, Netherlands

Maclagen, David, *Creation Myths: Man's introduction to the world*, Thames and Hudson, London, 1979

Marshack, Alexander, *The Roots of Civilization*, McGraw-Hill, New York, 1972

Matt, Daniel Chanan (trans.), *The Zohar*, Paulist Press, Ramsey, New Jersey, 1983

Matthews, Caitlín, *The Elements of the Goddess*, Element, Shaftesbury, 1989
— *Sophia: Goddess of Wisdom*, HarperCollins, London, 1991

Mazonowicz, Douglas, *Voices From the Stone Age*, Gallery of Prehistoric Paintings, New York, 1974

Mellaart, James, *Çatal Hüyük: A Neolithic Town in Anatolia*, McGraw Hill, New York, 1967

Meltzer, David, *Birth*, North Point Press, San Francisco, 1981
— *Death*, North Point Press, San Francisco, 1984

Micallef, Paul I., *Mnajdra Prehistoric Temple: A Calendar in Stone*, Malta, 1989

Michell, John, *The Earth Spirit*, Thames and Hudson, London, 1975

Miller, Sherrill, *The Pilgrim's Guide to the Sacred Earth*, Western Producer Prairie Books, Saskatoon, Saskatchewan, 1991

Milne, Courtney, *The Sacred Earth*, Western Producer Prairie Books, Saskatoon, Saskatchewan, 1991

Monaghan, Patricia, *The Book of Goddesses and Heroines*, E. P. Dutton, New York, 1981

Neruda, Pablo, *Stones of the Sky*, trans. James Nolan, Copper Canyon Press, Port Townsend, Washington, 1970

Neumann, Erich, *The Terrible Mother*, trans. Ralph Mannheim, Princeton University Press, Princeton, 1955

New English Bible, Oxford University Press and Cambridge University Press, London, 1970

Nicholson, Shirley, *Shamanism*, Theosophical Publishing House, Wheaton, Illinois, 1987

Noble, Vicki, "Female Blood Roots of Shamanism," *Shaman's Drum*, No. 4, Spring, 1986
— *Motherpeace: A Way to the Goddess Through Myth, Art, and Tarot*, Harper and Row, San Francisco, 1983
— *Shakti Woman*, Harper San Francisco, San Francisco, 1991
— (ed.) *Snake Power: A Journal of Contemporary Female Shamanism*, Berkeley
— (ed.) *Uncoiling the Snake*, Harper San Francisco, San Francisco, 1993

Oda, Mayumi, *Goddesses*, Volcano Press, Volcano, California, 1981

O'Flaherty, Wendy, *Hindu Myths*, Penguin, London, 1975

O'Kelly, Claire, *A Concise Guide to Newgrange*, C. O'Kelly, Cork, 1989
— *Guide to Newgrange*, John English, Wexford, 1967

O'Kelly, Michael, J., *Newgrange: Archaeology, art, and legend*, Thames and Hudson, London, 1982

Orenstein, Gloria Feman, *The Reflowering of the Goddess*, Pergamon, Elmsford, New York, 1990

Ovid, *Metamorphoses*, trans. Charles Boer, Spring, Dallas, Texas, 1989

Pagels, Elaine, *Adam, Eve, and the Serpent*, Random House, New York, 1988

Parabola, "Androgyny," Vol. 3, No. 4, New York, 1978
— "The Body," Vol. 10, No. 3, New York, 1985
— "The Mountain," Vol. 13, No. 4, New York, 1988
— "The Tree of Life," Vol. 14, No. 3, New York, 1989

Paris, Ginette, *Pagan Grace*, Spring, Dallas, 1990
— *Pagan Meditations*, Spring, Dallas, 1986

Patai, Raphael, *The Hebrew Goddess*, Avon, New York, 1967

Pennick, Nigel, *Games of the Gods*, Rider, London, 1988

Perera, Sylvia Brinton, *Descent to the Goddess*, Inner City Books, Toronto, 1981

Peterson, Natasha, *Sacred Sites*, Contemporary Books, Chicago, 1988

Pfeiffer, John E., *The Creative Explosion*, Harper and Row, New York, 1982

Plaskow, Judith and Christ, Carol (eds.), *Weaving the Visions*, Harper and Row, San Francisco, 1989

Platon, Nicholas, *Zakros: The Discovery of a Lost Palace of Ancient Crete*, Charles Scribner's Sons, New York, 1971

Pollack, Rachel, *The Haindl Tarot Vols. 1 and 2*, Newcastle, North Hollywood, California, 1990
— *The New Tarot*, HarperCollins, London, 1989
— *Shining Woman Tarot* (Tarot cards and book), HarperCollins, London, 1994
— *78 Degrees of Wisdom, Part 1*, Aquarian, Wellingborough, 1980
— *78 Degrees of Wisdom, Part 2*, Aquarian, Wellingborough, 1983

Powell, Jim, (trans.), *Sappho: A Garland*, Farrar, Straus, Giroux, New York, 1993

Preziosi, Donald, *Minoan Architectural Design*, Mouton, New York, 1983

Rafferty, Andrew, and Crossley-Holland, Kevin, *The Stones Remain*, Rider, London, 1989

Renfrew, Colin, *Before Civilization*, Penguin, London, 1976
— (ed.), *The Megalithic Monuments of Western Europe*, Thames and Hudson, London, 1991

Ridley, Michael, *The Megalithic Art of the Maltese Islands*, Dolphin House, Poole, Dorset, 1971

Ritchie, Carson I. A., *Rock Art of Africa*, A. S. Barnes, Cranbury, New Jersey, 1979

Roscoe, Will, *We'what: The Zuni Man-Woman*, University of New Mexico Press, Albuquerque, 1991

Rothenberg, Diane, and Rothenberg, Jerome (eds.), *Symposium of the Whole*, University of California Press, Berkeley, 1983

Rothenberg, Jerome, ed., *Technicians of the Sacred*, University of California Press, Berkeley, 1985

Rufus, Anneli S., and Lawson, Kristan, *Goddess Sites: Europe*, Harper San Francisco, 1991

Ruspoli, Mario, *Lascaux: The Final Photographs*, Harry F. Abrams, New York, 1986

Ryan, Judith, *Mythscapes: Aboriginal Art of the Desert*, National Heart Foundation of Australia, n.d.

Sahlins, Marshall, *Stone Age Economics*, Aldine de Gruyter, Hawthorne, New York, 1972

Sahtouris, Elisabet, *Gaia: The Human Journey from Chaos to Cosmos*, Simon and Schuster, New York, 1989

Sanday, Peggy Reeves, *Female Power and Male Dominance: On the Origins of Sexual Inequality*, Cambridge University Press, New York, 1981

Scholem, Gershon, *Major Trends in Jewish Mysticism*, Schocken, New York, 1946

Scully, Vincent, *The Earth, the Temple, and the Gods*, Yale University Press, New Haven, Connecticut, 1962
— *Architecture: the Natural and the Manmade*, St. Martin's, New York, 1991

Sieveking, Ann, *The Cave Artists*, Thames and Hudson, 1979

Sjoo, Monica, and Mor, Barbara, *The Great Cosmic Mother*, Harper and Row, San Francisco, 1987

Spretnak, Charlene, *Lost Goddesses of Ancient Greece*, Beacon, Boston, 1978
— ed., *The Politics of Women's Spirituality*, Anchor Press, Garden City, New York, 1982

Sproul, Barbara C., *Primal Myths: Creating the World*, Harper and Row, San Francisco, 1979

Starhawk, *Dreaming the Dark*, Beacon, Boston, 1982
— *The Spiral Dance*, Harper and Row, San Francisco, 1979
— *Truth or Dare*, Harper and Row, San Francisco, 1979

Stein, Charles, *Horse Sacrifice*, Station Hill, Barrytown, New York, 1980

Stein, Diane, *The Goddess Book of Days*, Llewellyn, St. Paul, Minnesota, 1988

Stevens, Wallace, *Selected Poems*, Faber and Faber, London, 1953

Stone, Merlin, *Ancient Mirrors of Womanhood*, Beacon, Boston, 1979
— *When God was a Woman*, Harcourt Brace Jovanovich, 1976

Streep, Peg, *Sanctuaries of the Goddess*, Bullfinch, Boston, 1994

Stuart, Gene, *America's Ancient Cities*, National Geographic Society, Washington, 1988

Stuart, George E., "Maya Art Treasures Discovered in Cave," *National Geographic*, Vol. 160, No. 2, Washington, 1981

Sutton, Peter, *Dreamings: The Art of Aboriginal Australia*, George Braziller, New York, 1988

Thom, Alexander, *Megalithic Sites in Britain*, Oxford University Press, London, 1967

Thompson, Robert Farris, *Flash of the Spirit: Afro-American Art and Philosophy*, St. Martin's, New York, 1984
— *Face of the Gods*, The Museum for African Art, New York, 1993

Thompson, William Irwin, ed., *Gaia: A Way of Knowing*, Lindisfarne, Hudson, New York, 1987
— *Imaginary Landscapes*, St. Martin's, New York, 1989
— *The Time Falling Bodies Take To Light*, St. Martin's, New York, 1981

Trump, David H., *Malta: An Archaeological Guide*, Faber and Faber, London, 1972

Vastokas, Joan M., and Vastokas, Romas K., *Sacred Art of the Algonkins*, Mansard Press, Peterborough, Ontario, 1973

Vermaseren, Maarten J., *Cybele and Attis: The Myth and the Cult*, trans. A H Lemmers, Thames and Hudson, London, 1977

Vernant, Jean-Pierre, *Mortals and Immortals*, Princeton University Press, Princeton, 1991

von Cles-Reden, Sibylle, *The Realm of the Great Goddess: The Story of the Megalith Builders*, Prentice-Hall, Englewood Cliffs, New Jersey, 1962

Walker, Barbara, *The Woman's Encyclopedia of Myths and Secrets*, Harper and Row, San Francisco, 1988

Wasson, R. Gordon, Kramrisch, Stella, Ott, Jonathan, and Ruck, Carl A. P., *Entheogens and the Origins of Religion*, Yale University Press, New Haven and London, 1986

Weed, Susan S., *Healing Wise: The Wise Woman Herbal*, Ash Tree Publishing, Woodstock, 1989

West, K. C., ed., *The Inspired Dream*, Queensland Art Gallery, South Brisbane, 1988

Wittig, Monique, *The Lesbian Body*, trans. David Le Vay, Beacon, Boston, 1973

Wolkstein, Diane and Kramer, Samuel, *Innana: Queen of Heaven and Earth*, Harper and Row, New York, 1983

Woodward, Susan L., and McDonald, Jerry N., *Indian Mounds of the Middle Ohio Valley*, Mcdonald and Woodward, Blacksburg, Virginia, 1986

Wright, Pam, untitled article published in *Fireheart*, n.d.

Wynne, Patrice, *The Womanspirit Sourcebook*, Harper and Row, San Francisco, 1988

Young, Dudley, *Origins of the Sacred*, St. Martin's, New York, 1991

Zammit, T., *The Copper Age Temples of Hagar Qim and Mnajdra*, Malta, n.d.
— *The Copper Age Temple of Tarxien, Malta*, Malta, 1980

Zammit, Vincent, *Tarxien Prehistoric Temples*, Malta, 1986

Index